PRACTICAL SOFTWARE METRICS FOR PROJECT MANAGEMENT AND PROCESS IMPROVEMENT

Robert B. Grady

P T R Prentice Hall, Englewood Cliffs, New Jersey 07632

Library of Congress Cataloging-in-Publication Data

Grady, Robert B., 1943-
    Practical software metrics for project management and process
improvement / Robert B. Grady.
        p.   cm.
    Includes bibliographical references and index.
    ISBN 0-13-720384-5
    1. Computer software--Development--Management.   I. Title.
QA76.76.D47G72   1992
005.1'4--dc20   92-6869
                                                            CIP

Editorial/production supervision: *Brendan M. Stewart*
Prepress buyer: *Mary McCartney*
Manufacturing buyer: *Susan Brunke*
Acquisitions editor: *Greg Doench*

© 1992 by P T R Prentice Hall
Prentice-Hall, Inc.
A Paramount Communications Company
Englewood Cliffs, New Jersey 07632

The publisher offers discounts on this book when ordered in bulk quantities. For more information, write: Special Sales/Professional Marketing, Prentice Hall, Professional & Technical Reference Division, Englewood Cliffs, NJ 07632.

Printed in the United States of America
10 9 8 7 6 5 4

ISBN 0-13-720384-5

Prentice-Hall International (UK) Limited, *London*
Prentice-Hall of Australia Pty. Limited, *Sydney*
Prentice-Hall Canada Inc., *Toronto*
Prentice-Hall Hispanoamericana, S.A., *Mexico*
Prentice-Hall of India Private Limited, *New Delhi*
Prentice-Hall of Japan, Inc., *Tokyo*
Simon & Schuster Asia Pte. Ltd., *Singapore*
Editora Prentice-Hall do Brasil, Ltda., *Rio de Janeiro*

To
Jan, Sean, and Erin
(again)

Contents

13   Elements of Software Engineering   158

14   Justifying Change   177

Appendices

ACKNOWLEDGMENTS

It's a privilege to work for a company like Hewlett-Packard where people are motivated and encouraged to make improvements such as the ones I've been able to describe in this book. I am especially grateful for the management support that I have received from Chuck House, Sheryl Root, and Gail Hamilton.

It's exciting to learn new things about software development, and I've been fortunate to share data from many HP people and projects. It's difficult to name them all, but I'll try. My thanks to Ron Benton, John Burnham, Kwang Cho, Dave Classick, Sylvia Davey, Dave Decot, Dean Drake, Bob Horenstein, Henry Kohoutek, Greg Kruger, Danny Lau, Chuck Leath, Dick Levitt, Deborah Mallette, Stuart Liroff, Alvina Nishimoto, Barbara Noble, John Podkomorski, Steve Rodriguez, Brian Sakai, Len Schroath, Barbara Scott, Chuck Sieloff, Rich Simms, Masato Tada, Gary Tier, Tim Tillson, Fumiro Tsuruda, and Jack Walicki.

I've been particularly lucky to have had the continuing support and constructive criticisms of my wife, Jan Grady (who is also an outstanding software manager), and of my talented coauther of *Software Metrics: Establishing a Company-Wide Program*, Debbie Caswell. Their patience in reading my papers and the manuscript for this book (multiple times!) has significantly helped to improve its quality and clarity.

I would also like to thank all of the other reviewers for their valuable comments and suggestions, especially David Card, Tom DeMarco, Sally Dudley, Robert Dunn, Robert Glass, Bob Horenstein, Cathleen Meyer, and Stan Rifkin.

1
The Tactical and Strategic Faces of Software Metrics

Software metrics are used to measure specific attributes of a software product or software development process. We use them to derive a basis for estimates, to track project progress, to determine relative complexity, to help us understand when we have achieved a desired state of quality, to analyze our defects, and to experimentally validate best practices. In short, they help us to make better decisions.

This book is about practical applications of software metrics. This means that the emphasis is on proven practices and results. My goal is for you to directly apply what you learn from the experiences described here. These include:

- What software development "rules" are supported by measured evidence,
- How measurements should be tightly linked to organizational strategies,
- How the metrics that engineers find useful help project managers as well,
- What people feel about metrics and what approaches you can take to gain their support,
- How metrics are used to achieve continuous process improvement,
- What measures are meaningful for a large organization.

This book is organized into two major thrusts. Part I (Chapters 2 to 8) provides a tactical framework for deciding what project metrics to use. Part II (Chapters 9 to 14) provides a strategic framework for continuous process improvement.

IS THIS BOOK FOR YOU?

The role of project manager is central to software development, maintenance, and enhancement. Of all the people involved in software, they derive the greatest benefit from using metrics. If you are a project manager, then this book is written for you. We should take a wider view of projects than just development and maintenance, though. Many people are also involved in process improvement. If this is your role, then this book is written for you, as well.

This book substantially extends the concepts and examples presented in *Software Metrics: Establishing a Company-Wide Program*. [1] That book describes many of the fundamentals of metrics in the context of Hewlett-Packard's initial widespread use of them. Both HP and the software industry have made significant progress since then, and this book is evidence of that progress. As a result, it is more of an advanced text. While it has been written to stand alone, you may want to refer to the first book for some definitions and introductory material.

THE TACTICAL APPLICATION OF SOFTWARE METRICS —
PROJECT MANAGEMENT

Part I of this book focuses on the use of software metrics by project managers. Such use represents the tactical application of software metrics. Simply stated, you must

- define the right product,
- execute the project effectively,
- release the product at the right time.

Figure 1-1 shows how Chapters 2 through 8 are organized to guide you from initial project planning through project execution. Each chapter states a central thesis. These key theses are developed and illustrated by practical examples.

All projects begin with a dream. We imagine how pleased the users of our product or service will be when it is complete, and we look forward to the satisfaction of a job well done. It is the job of the project manager to translate the dream into reality. This starts with tentative plans and estimates, and it builds as the details of what must be done, with what resources, become clearer.

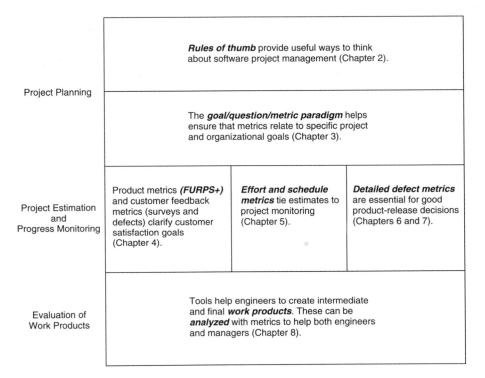

Figure 1-1 The tactical application of software metrics.

Software metrics help to clarify those details. It is natural for us to think in terms of size, effort, complexity, and time. When we are able to apply these numerical measures to the components of a project, it is easier to imagine what the constraints are and what it will take to satisfy them. Some of the metrics used in this book are KNCSS (thousands of non-comment source statements), engineering months, cyclomatic complexity (a metric based on the number of paths through a given piece of source code), calendar months, and defects.

While these seem simple, they form the basis of a powerful set of graphs and heuristic examples that are explored in later chapters. From these, you can learn to plan and manage better.

THE STRATEGIC APPLICATION OF SOFTWARE METRICS — PROCESS IMPROVEMENT

Over the years, the application of software metrics has evolved from tentative experiments to accepted best practices based on repeatable successes. As more people and organizations have adopted metrics, metric usage has evolved to become a strategic advantage. Part II of this book focuses on the use of software metrics to improve processes. Figure 1-2 shows how Chapters 9 through 14 are organized to discuss the strategic issues facing software organizations. The discussion starts with the people issues that all organizations must face when collecting data. It then moves on to the use of failure analysis techniques to identify high-leverage opportunities. It closes with a discussion of validation of best practices and justification of widespread change.

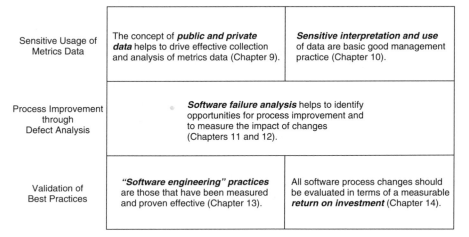

Sensitive Usage of Metrics Data	The concept of **public and private data** helps to drive effective collection and analysis of metrics data (Chapter 9).	**Sensitive interpretation and use** of data are basic good management practice (Chapter 10).
Process Improvement through Defect Analysis	**Software failure analysis** helps to identify opportunities for process improvement and to measure the impact of changes (Chapters 11 and 12).	
Validation of Best Practices	**"Software engineering" practices** are those that have been measured and proven effective (Chapter 13).	All software process changes should be evaluated in terms of a measurable **return on investment** (Chapter 14).

Figure 1-2 The strategic application of software metrics.

RECENT TRENDS THAT ENCOURAGE AND INFLUENCE METRICS USAGE

Some recent trends are influencing the level of interest in metrics, the relative ease of data collection, and the nature of the data that is collected. Let's review four of these before we move on to Part I.

Software Process Maturity

Several years ago, the Software Engineering Institute (SEI) was created. One group at the SEI introduced the idea of a software process maturity model. For them, the model was a way to convince companies who develop software for the U.S. Department of Defense to improve their delivered software.

The model consists of five levels. Development at each level is more organized and better managed than at lower levels. The premise is that better software will be produced with fewer resources as your process becomes more mature. Figure 1-3 shows that metrics play a key role in an organization as it matures from an initial state to an optimized one. [2] The "result" part of the figure says that immature organizations operate at high risk and low productivity and quality.

Level	Characteristic	Key Problem Areas	Result
Optimizing	Improvement fed back into process	Automation	**Productivity & Quality**
Managed	(quantitative) Measured process	Changing technology Problem analysis Problem prevention	
Defined	(qualitative) Process defined and institutionalized	Process measurement Process analysis Quantitative quality plans	
Repeatable	(intuitive) Process dependent on individuals	Training Technical practices – reviews, testing Process focus – standards, process groups	
Initial	(ad hoc/chaotic)	Project management Project planning Configuration management Software quality assurance	**Risk**

Figure 1-3 SEI software process maturity model.

The model is a very useful way to illustrate some of the strategic issues facing anyone who collects metrics data. It is easy to understand and believe in. It has been highly successful in motivating many managers at least to say "I want our software practices improved." At the same time, though, this motivation can lead to disappointment. Many managers look at this view of the model as a simple checklist for easy success. They visualize a rapid progression up the maturity ladder to the point where they can brag about their level.

It is the organizational orientation of the SEI model that limits rapid progression. Parts of an organization can move and change rapidly. For example, individual projects and project managers can rapidly understand and apply the tactical applications of software metrics described in Part I of this book. They can even assume a leadership role in moving an organization to adopt the strategic applications of metrics described in Part II. Entire organizations take longer to change.

The SEI also introduced in-depth evaluations called "assessments." These summarize organizational strengths and weaknesses and numerically place an organization on one of the five model levels. Early results from these assessments have shown that the industry is still quite immature. They show that few organizations were beyond the "initial" level of the model, and that no assessed organization was beyond the "defined" level. [2] With such results, it is difficult to quantify the cost of greater maturity or to know whether the benefits justify the cost. It is also difficult to know which particular level is most appropriate at a given business stage. These differences will only be resolved when organizations have made the transitions and measure the benefits. These are issues that the techniques described in Part II of this book directly address.

In summary, some of the issues that the SEI model raises (along with where this book helps to resolve them) are:

- Few organizations can claim high process maturity. (Chapters 3 and 13)
- What improvements toward greater maturity are really justified? (Chapters 11 and 14)
- Is there a checklist for process improvement? (Chapters 2, 12, 13)
- At what process maturity level are metrics required? (Chapters 4, 5, 6, 16)

Software Tools and Environments

Another recent trend is the creation of many new CASE tools. The large, emerging market for CASE is in response to software developers trying to fulfill their customers' insatiable demand for more software, faster. Some of these tools are valuable, but expectations for many others will not be met. Part I includes examples that were derived from outputs of several CASE tools.

Software metrics can help to sort out the good from the bad and the ugly. We will discuss the measured successes not only of some CASE tools, but also of some other best practices. In these discussions you will probably see data that sounds more conservative than the claims that are sometimes made. This is because it is difficult to generalize such claims to all environments and organizations. Chapters 12 and 14 will particularly help you to translate costs and benefits to your own organization.

Object-Oriented Approaches

In recent years, object-oriented analysis, design, and programming have shown promise for major improvements in software development. While these techniques are based on sound principles, they are still changing and adapting as their usage spreads. As a result, few measurements have been taken, and it is even more difficult to back up any claims for major improvement than it is for many CASE tools.

Some examples of metrics application to object-oriented projects are shown in Chapter 5. These illustrate that metrics for such projects are useful, even though they don't prove any compelling overall project results, yet.

Similar statements could be made about other promising new techniques and technologies. Whether object-oriented techniques or any others will prove to be measurably better or not remains to be proven with software metrics. What is encouraging is that there is strong pressure for metrics that apply to object-oriented projects. This is a good sign that metrics have proven their value for both project management purposes and for validation of best practices.

SOFTWARE METRICS PROGRAMS

Hewlett-Packard initiated a widespread software metrics program in 1983. At that time, there were limited published papers and books on the subject, expecially in terms of industrial practice. Since then, there has been an increasing popularity of software metrics. It is clear that many companies have initiated strategic programs, and their shared experiences have helped the software industry to progress more rapidly.

Some people argue that Hewlett-Packard's successes are unique to our company culture, that other cultures are much more resistant to the use of measurement. It is possible that our culture has helped to contribute to our success, but I resist crediting it too much.

Recently I spoke with a manager who had gone to another company after working for Hewlett-Packard. The manager had been active in our metrics efforts, so it was natural to initiate metrics in the new group. The company culture was quite different from ours, so the manager was a little surprised to encounter significant resistance from the engineers. On the other hand, it only took about two months of patient reinforcement to bring the engineers around to the level of trust necessary for success. Now, they are enthusiastic about the use of metrics and what they are learning.

Success is not guaranteed, though. Howard Rubin has tracked the implementation of metrics in information systems organizations. His data (Figure 1-4) shows that only about one-fifth of the attempts to start a program resulted in documented success. He defines a "success" as:

- the measurement program results are actively used in I/S organizational decision making,
- they are communicated and accepted outside of I/S,
- the program lasts longer than 2 years. [3]

So why don't we see more reports of success? The reason may be the same as why we don't see all projects succeed, or why many new businesses fail. Success takes good planning and follow-through, patience, leadership, and hard work. As my friend who went to another company learned, you have to

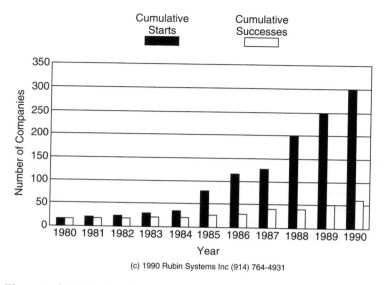

Figure 1-4 Rubin data base (Measurement program starts and successes).

convince people of the importance of measurement, *and* you have to follow through by building an environment of trust with consistent, correct use of data.

In *Software Metrics: Establishing a Company-Wide Program*, we included a chapter on "The Selling of Metrics." You can update its sales pitch with the figures and stories in this book to help you to sell metrics to people in your organization. Building an environment of trust starts with understanding the issues of "public and private data" covered in Chapter 9. Chapter 10 extends the ideas by describing many real situations, both positive and negative, that have occurred in organizations as they used metrics.

Finally, Chapter 16 contains an update of HP's software metrics program.

CONCLUSION

This chapter has outlined the structure of this book and given you some idea of what you will learn in the rest of the book. The structure is intended to lead you from immediate needs (data that will help you to know if your project is on track), to understanding the data-collection process and the proper use of metrics, to specific recommendations for process improvement.

The next chapter simply states many basic concepts that metrics have helped to establish. You should recognize most of them, although the specific numbers that you have heard may differ somewhat. Notice that they span the entire lifecycle and they form the basis for good project management practice.

BIBLIOGRAPHY

1. Grady, R., and D. Caswell, *Software Metrics: Establishing a Company-Wide Program*, Englewood Cliffs, NJ: Prentice-Hall, Inc., 1987.
2. Humphrey, W., D. Kitson, and T. Kasse, "The State of Software Engineering Practice: A Preliminary Report," *Eleventh International Conference on Software Engineering*, *ACM*, (May 1989), pp. 277–288.
3. Rubin, H., "How to Configure Your Measurement Dashboard," *Conference Papers of the ASQC International Conference on Applications of Software Measurement*, San Diego, CA, (Nov. 1990), pp. 125–132.

Part One

The Tactical Application of Software Metrics – Project Management

Project Planning	**Rules of thumb** provide useful ways to think about software project management (Chapter 2).		
	The **goal/question/metric paradigm** helps ensure that metrics relate to specific project and organizational goals (Chapter 3).		
Project Estimation and Progress Monitoring	Product metrics **(FURPS+)** and customer feedback metrics (surveys and defects) clarify customer satisfaction goals (Chapter 4).	**Effort and schedule metrics** tie estimates to project monitoring (Chapter 5).	**Detailed defect metrics** are essential for good product-release decisions (Chapters 6 and 7).
Evaluation of Work Products	Tools help engineers to create intermediate and final **work products**. These can be **analyzed** with metrics to help both engineers and managers (Chapter 8).		

2

Practical Rules of Thumb for Software Managers

*Thesis: Use metric **rules of thumb** to double check your project plans.*

As we grow up, we are told many things by adults. Some of these are sound advice, based on real dangers and practical experience. "Don't talk with strangers." "Be in before dark." "Look both directions before you cross the street." Others seem to be based more on superstition and hearsay. "If you spill salt, throw a pinch over your left shoulder." "Don't break a mirror, or you will have seven years of bad luck." "Don't handle frogs, or you will get warts."

Often it seems like we offer software developers the same types of advice. Some of our recommended practices are based on experience, while others are unproven, based on wishful thinking. How can we distinguish one from the other?

Measurement in any field accompanies a transition from its early stages toward scientific refinement and maturity. For the field of software, metrics help us to examine trends and do useful experiments. Over the years, many useful guidelines have evolved. These give us some idea of how far we have come and yet how little we still know. This chapter gives a short list of these guidelines, and it introduces the use and benefits of metrics for project management. Later chapters expand on the brief introductions given here.

PROJECT AND PRODUCT DEFINITION _____

Before a project is even defined, we are under pressure to predict what resources we need and how long we will take. Software metrics aren't going to provide a magical solution to answer these important business questions. They do, however, provide rules of thumb that experience has shown are useful.

- Projects created primarily from reused software take about one fourth the time and resources of those that are new. [1,2]

There is no substitute for experience. This applies to the code that is used, the designs that are applied, and the people who are doing a project. The measurements that show reused software takes one fourth the time were averages for many projects, but it doesn't take much imagination to see how important the experience aspect is for a project during its definition phase. Where it is possible, reuse proven software designs and components. The other pieces, those that your team has no prior experience with, will be the hardest to predict and will cause the greatest schedule problems.

- Projects invest about 18 percent of their total effort during specifications/requirements (about 19 percent during design, 34 percent during coding, and 29 percent during test). (Chapter 5)

These values are the averages of 125 Hewlett-Packard projects. Various other organizations have measured these percentages, and their results vary by plus or minus 10 percent. The data is easy to collect and, once collected, represents an interesting insight into how an organization does business.

A project manager can use this type of data as a sanity check against project estimates for whatever portion of the project remains. If your project has taken a lot of effort during the early phases, you are wise to learn from your experience and plan for a lot of time during the later phases. It is important to note, though, that projects with a large amount of reused code sometimes have shorter implementation phases. These will distort the average percentages given above by making percentages for other phases longer.

DESIGN _____

The use of software metrics is still new, especially in design activities. Results of measurements from design activities are encouraging, but still preliminary. The most useful guideline is exciting and no longer preliminary.

- 50 to 75 percent of all design errors can be found with inspections. [3,4,5,6] (Chapter 11)

Design inspections are particularly important, since design defects are frequent and their cost is quite high if they are not found early.

Like most guidelines, this one must be interpreted in context. It is likely that your organization is doing some form of design inspections today. If so, they may not be able to achieve a 50 to 75 percent *improvement*. Nevertheless, most organizations are not yet achieving the potential savings that design inspections can provide, so implement a strategy to do effective design reviews.

It was tempting to place the next rule of thumb in the previous section. It involves code estimates, and most managers know that project estimates are often stated in terms of how much code will be produced. As a result, there is often strong pressure for code estimates during early project definition. This is quite unrealistic, though. We wouldn't ask a contractor who is building our house to order the lumber before the architect has drawn up the plans. Why would we ask our engineers to commit to us the amount of code before they have done the design?

- An average project delivers about 350 NCSS per engineering month (engineering time includes all design, implementation, and test to produce all deliverable non-comment source statements for a project). [1,7]

This figure is loaded with caveats and guaranteed to raise blood pressure. A lot of people fear the counting of code as a productivity indicator. What is the primary assumption? It is certainly that of what is being counted. Your numbers may differ from those above because you count differently. What is important is that you consciously measure data related to the function that you are delivering (as NCSS is), and that you measure consistently. The value above is the *average* of 135 Hewlett-Packard projects.

At the end of the design phase, the above rule of thumb becomes critical. At this point project managers must make a size estimate. Not only is it expected for project management, but also because size is a critical parameter against which to measure progress for the remainder of the project.

Again, a reminder that code reuse will improve your ability to deliver (and will improve your organization's statistics). On the other hand, the code-delivery rate is mostly language independent, so the use of higher level languages will improve your ability to deliver equivalent functionality with fewer lines of code (without improving your organization's code-delivery averages). This is because one line of a higher level language generally contains more functionality than one line of a lower level language. Just make sure that you can suitably create your application with a higher level language, if you choose that strategy.

IMPLEMENTATION

By far, most software metrics research has involved the measurement of various aspects of code. This research is interesting, but may provide little value during real projects. Most of the research has been carried out in controlled, but theoretical, academic environments. As a result, it doesn't generalize well to practical industrial applications. One exception is "cyclomatic complexity." It is derived from an analysis of potential paths through source code. This metric has been validated in practical environments and is readily computed today by a variety of automated tools.

- Modules with a cyclomatic complexity greater than ten are more difficult to understand and have a higher probability of defects than modules with smaller values. [8,9,10] (Chapter 13)

Many organizations use a threshold value such as ten to trigger special inspections or tests. Use this approach to help control logic errors and to improve maintainability.

A word of caution — Because cyclomatic complexity is a measure of *control* complexity, it is a more valuable indicator for control-oriented applications than for data-oriented applications. It works for both, but data-oriented applications have other dimensions that must be considered as well.

Other code metrics are promising, but they haven't been validated as well as cyclomatic complexity. [11,12] It is worth pointing out that the rules of thumb given in the design section are valuable during implementation, as well. Code inspections are a very cost-effective way of uncovering defects. They also widen your team's understanding of their product and of techniques used by other people. The other guideline, having a good feel for the code-generation rate of your team, helps you to track progress and discover potential problems early.

TEST

We find ourselves correcting many of our earlier mistakes during the software testing phase. Unfortunately, much of today's testing is ad hoc and undisciplined after a project is already late. The next rule of thumb recommends the use of code coverage measures to increase testing efficiency and effectiveness.

- Typical testing without measuring code coverage only exercises around 55 percent of the code. With code coverage instrumentation, this can be raised to at least 80 percent without excessive additional effort. [13] (Chapter 13)

Tools that measure code coverage automatically insert counters into the source code of a system. When tests are executed, data is saved so that a histogram of all executed code is produced. This information helps us to identify other necessary tests to exercise the missed code.

- Projects created primarily from reused software experience only about one third the defect density (defects/size) of those that are new. [1]

Your testing time is a function of your quality and customer satisfaction goals, the number of defects that your process and your management tolerance allow, the number of people available for testing, and your ability to fix defects as they are found. The simplest way to reduce this time is to reuse already tested and proven software.

MAINTENANCE

When asked what percentage of time their people spend doing maintenance, the average response to a Hewlett-Packard customer survey was 75 percent. This value is also supported by others. [3,14] Stated a little more conservatively:

- We spend about 2 to 3 times as much effort maintaining and enhancing software as we spend creating new software.

There is a lot of dissatisfaction with this ratio. The next two rules of thumb help us to go beyond just planning to spend lots of time and effort to support existing software. What are some of the contributing factors to high maintenance cost? First, there are defects left in the software when we deliver it to our customers.

- You will find about one defect postrelease for every ten defects that you find prerelease during test. [1,15]

Second, software becomes more difficult to maintain as it matures. This is because changes often make software more complex, and eventually the personnel maintaining the software change jobs. This evolution leads to another rule of thumb:

- It takes 4 to 10 times longer to fix defects in large mature software systems than to make fixes before, or shortly after, initial release of a system. [7,16]

The longer that defects go undetected, the more they cost to fix, because additional people and organizations get involved, and the change process is more complicated. This applies throughout the lifecycle. Specification defects that aren't found until test or until after release are the most expensive (up to 100 times), followed by design defects and then coding defects.

Clearly, you must select and use processes that detect and eliminate defects as early as possible. This implies that you also must track defects carefully and analyze the sources of defects in order to understand which fixes will minimize your costs.

CONCLUSION

We have discussed some of the most useful results that metrics research has produced, including suggestions for usage and comments on limitations. The results were presented in the context of the traditional progression of a software lifecycle. This helped us to see that there is a heavy emphasis on cost and time aspects in many of our most accepted rules of thumb, and that this emphasis continues throughout the lifecycle.

We also saw a focus on numbers of defects and of methods for defect removal. This reflects the belief that our development processes are too costly because they are ill-defined and too defect prone. If we can eliminate the major sources of defects, software development will become more predictable and less expensive.

The guidelines for inspections, cyclomatic complexity, and code coverage represent three examples of experimentally validated techniques for discovering and removing defects. Their validation was only possible because measurements were taken across multiple projects using consistently defined metrics.

Thus the ten rules of thumb offer good illustrations of three different uses of software metrics:

1. project estimation and progress monitoring,
2. process improvement,
3. experimental validation of best practices.

The next four chapters focus on the most useful of these to project managers: progress monitoring. These chapters discuss three primary strategies that organizations follow. They are illustrated with useful examples that span the project life cycle with several that reinforce our rules of thumb.

Hopefully you will find that the guidelines given here more closely represent practical experience than they do "old wives tales," like those at the start of the chapter. They represent a foundation to build on, and each additional experimentally validated technique will help to build better development practices. They are a good sign that we are growing up.

BIBLIOGRAPHY

1. Grady, R. and D. Caswell, *Software Metrics: Establishing a Company-Wide Program*, Englewood Cliffs, NJ: Prentice-Hall, Inc., 1987, pp. 34, 65, 111, 112, 113.

2. Card, D., V. Church, and W. Agresti, "An Empirical Study of Software Design Practices," *IEEE Transactions on Software Engineering*, Vol. SE-12, no. 2, (Feb. 1986), pp. 264–271.

3. Boehm, B., "Industrial Software Metrics Top 10 List," *IEEE Software*, (Sept, 1987), pp. 84–85.

4. Fagan, M. E., "Advances in Software Inspections," *IEEE Transactions on Software Engineering*, Vol. SE-12, no. 7 (July 1986), pp. 744–751.

5. Jones, C., *Programming Productivity*. New York: McGraw-Hill Book Co., 1986, p. 179.

6. Myers, G., "A Controlled Experiment in Program Testing and Code Walkthroughs/Inspections," *Communications of ACM*, Vol. 21, no. 9, (Sept. 1978), pp. 760–768.

7. Boehm, Barry W., *Software Engineering Economics*. Englewood Cliffs, NJ: Prentice-Hall, Inc., 1981, pp. 40, 64, 150.

8. McCabe, T., "A Complexity Measure," *IEEE Transactions on Software Engineering*, Vol. SE-2, no. 4, Dec. 1976, pp. 308–320.

9. Walsh, T. J., "A Software Reliability Study Using a Complexity Measure," *Proceedings of the 1979 National Computer Conference*. New Jersey: AFIPS Press (1979), pp. 761–768.

10. Ward, W., "Software Defect Prevention Using McCabe's Complexity Metric," *Hewlett-Packard Journal*, Vol. 40, no. 2 (April 1989), pp. 64–69.

11. Curtis, B., S. B. Sheppard, and P. Milliman, "Third Time Charm: Stronger Prediction of Programmer Performance by Software Complexity Metrics," *Proceedings of the Fourth International Conference on Software Engineering*, (July 1979), pp. 356–360.

12. Rambo, R., P. Buckley, and E. Branyan, "Establishment and Validation of Software Metric Factors," *Proceedings of the International Society of Parametric Analysts Seventh Annual Conference*, (May 1985), pp. 406–417.

13. Herington, D., P. Nichols, and R. Lipp, "Software Verification Using Branch Analysis," *Hewlett-Packard Journal*, (June 1987), pp. 13–22.

14. Vessey, I., and R. Weber, "Some Factors Affecting Program Repair Maintenance: An Empirical Study," *Communications of the ACM*, Vol. 26, no. 2 (Feb. 1983), pp. 128–134.

15. Levendel, Y., "Reliability Analysis of Large Software Systems: Defect Data Modeling," *IEEE Transactions on Software Engineering*, Vol. 16, no. 2, Feb. 1990, pp. 141–152.

16. Moller, K. H., "Increasing of Software Quality by Objectives and Residual Fault Prognosis," *First E.O.Q.C. Seminar on Software Quality*, Brussels, Belgium, (April 1988), pp. 478–488.

3

Major Strategies of a Software Business

*Thesis: Use the **goal/question/metric paradigm** to ensure measurement relevancy and organizational support.*

Why does it take so many people to support software systems? Software development has evolved rapidly in the short time that computers have existed. With most products, such evolution is accompanied by creation of replacement products and obsolescence of old ones. However, the nature of software products is that they evolve through modification rather than replacement. Today, better design and implementation methods lead to higher initial software quality than in the past, but the quality of older products that have undergone continual change is often poor. Because we cannot economically replace all our old software, we must find better ways to manage needed changes. Until we do, software maintenance will continue to represent a large investment — and software quality will *not* improve.

In this chapter and the next three, we explore three strategies that organizations emphasize in the management of software. We'll discuss the pursuit of these strategies, when they apply, and what role they play in the evolution of software businesses. The strategies provide a convenient way to explore many metric examples that you can use to manage projects more effectively.

MANAGEMENT STRATEGIES

Many organizations responsible for the evolution of software systems seem to operate constantly in a reactive mode, fighting the flames of the most recent fire. Behind the visible sense of urgency, though, managers appear to emphasize one of three primary strategies:

- maximize customer satisfaction
- minimize engineering effort and schedule
- minimize defects

The final objective of all three approaches is customer satisfaction. So what is really meant by these terms? Let's build an initial understanding of the terms by looking at how these strategies pertain to the maintenance of delivered software. Maintenance includes fixing defects, enhancing product features or performance, and adapting to new hardware or external software. Of course, the items above are not unique to maintenance activities, but shifting priorities among the items is sometimes more frequent during maintenance than during initial product development. The following examples illustrate this.

Maximize customer satisfaction: (1) After initial product deliveries, development team members visit customer sites to train, observe operations, and isolate defects. (2) Special patches and workarounds are quickly found for defects and installed for individual customer installations. (3) Work on some defects is deferred to create an enhancement for one key customer.

Minimize engineering effort and schedule: (1) Resources are removed from maintaining/enhancing activities and assigned to new product development (to minimize new development schedule or cut total resources without hurting new development effort). (2) Resources are removed from new development to do maintaining/enhancing activities (to minimize defect-fix schedule). (3) Extended work times are used to complete an enhanced version in an unalterable schedule. (4) The amount of time taken to make fixes or run tests becomes so critical that only high-priority, customer-critical defects are fixed.

Minimize defects: (1) Besides fixing defects, engineers investigate the causes of defects. (2) Defects in the part of a product to be enhanced are corrected before a major new enhancement is attempted. (3) The original development engineers continue to fix defects and make product enhancements for at least six months after product release and before moving on to other new products.

Business Pressures

An organization that creates a new software product will often try to capture a new market. It will work closely with customers to define their product needs completely and correctly the first time, and it will follow up with quick responses to problems. Its initial success depends heavily on customer satisfaction. (Even internal MIS groups have to compete with non-MIS projects for the pool of available project money. In this sense, customer satisfaction is just as important as it is to commercial product or government-contract organizations.) As its products become accepted in the marketplace, the organization tries to increase its advantage. It maximizes the quality of all its product releases, and it gradually improves them with enhancements and better hardware and software connections.

On the other hand, when competitive products already exist, it is necessary to create unique features or new products. Organizations must balance engineering effort and schedules between new development and maintenance. Trade-offs are often made to decrease maintenance effort in favor of new development.

Thus business pressures encourage organizations to emphasize different strategies to be competitive. These pressures influence product features, product quality, timeliness, and the ability to satisfy all these needs more economically than the competition. Table 3-1 summarizes the major characteristics of these strategies. They form a framework to explore a wide range of project management examples in the next three chapters. This particular table fits the context of some typical HP product development divisions. You will have to mentally adjust some of the entries to match your own organizational frame of reference.

Metrics

Project measurements are a powerful way to track progress toward goals. Such data is often used in high-level management presentations. For example, the number of defects outstanding or the time to respond to defects are frequently cited when discussing postrelease software. The rate of generating code or product features is often tracked for prerelease software. Without such measures for managing software, it is difficult for any organization to understand whether it is successful, and it is difficult to resist frequent changes of strategy. *It is in the best interests of both managers and engineers responsible for software to help provide the data needed to choose the best balance among available strategies.*

THE GOAL/QUESTION/METRIC PARADIGM

Table 3-1 gives us some insight into why strategies change. What can we do to control those changes, or at least to adapt to them more readily? Victor Basili and his associates at the University of Maryland created a measurement and evaluation paradigm that we have found to be very useful for both new

MAJOR CHARACTERISTICS	MAXIMIZE CUSTOMER SATISFACTION	MINIMIZE ENGINEERING EFFORT & SCHEDULE	MINIMIZE DEFECTS
MAJOR BUSINESS FACTOR	Attempt to capture market share	Competitive pressures forcing new product development or cost control	Hold/increase market share
WHEN MOST EFFECTIVE	When initially entering market	When there are several competitive products or you sell more profitable products	When features are competitive and adequate market share is held
CHARACTERISTIC FEATURES	Customer communications, quick responses	Focus on delivery dates and effort	Analysis and removal of defect causes
MOST VISIBLE METRICS	Survey and interview data, product metrics, defects	Calendar time, engineering effort, defects	Failure analysis by module, cause, & severity; size; code coverage
GROUP MOST LIKELY TO DRIVE STRATEGY	Development team initially, customer support later	Division or company management	Development team and/or quality organization
GROUP MOST LIKELY TO BE IN DIRECT CONTACT WITH CUSTOMER	Development team	Marketing/factory customer support	Field support organization
POTENTIAL DRAWBACKS IF FOCUS TOO RESTRICTED	Process of developing products may not improve	Defect backlog can get unmanageable; customers and developers frustrated	Defects may be fixed that are not cost effective

Table 3-1 Major Strategies of a Software Business

development and maintenance. [1, 2, 3] The basic principle behind the paradigm is that each organization or project has a set of goals. For each goal there is a set of questions that you might ask to help you understand whether you are achieving your goal. Many of these questions have answers that can be measured. To the extent that the questions are a complete set, and to the extent the metric data satisfactorily answers the questions, you can measure whether you are meeting goals. The relationships among goals, questions, and metrics are shown in Figure 3-1.

Hewlett-Packard's Software Metrics Council [4] defined a set of software maintenance metrics using the goal/question/metric paradigm. The complete HP list consisted of five goals, 31 questions, and 35 metrics.[5] After creating the list, it became clear to us that such a list was too complicated to easily use. Table 3-1 was created in response to this complexity. The three strategies are a simpler way of looking at the entire list, and they make it easier to group metrics into sets of measurement guidelines that can be realistically followed.

Does this mean that the goal/question/metric paradigm isn't useful? Not at all. We were tackling a highly generalized problem that spanned many organizations. The paradigm certainly helped us to get to a solution. Similarly, we have used the paradigm very effectively to tie project measurements to both project and divisional goals. It is this use that is most exciting to project managers. In addition, once we developed Table 3-1, we could see that it provided a valuable framework within which to test our progress reports for consistency with larger organizational goals.

I have chosen to include the results of our maintenance metric brainstorming. They emphasize the complexity of software maintenance and provide a convenient reference for almost thirty examples in the next three chapters. The original list has been reorganized here. The five maintenance goals have been collapsed into three goals that match the three major software business strategies.

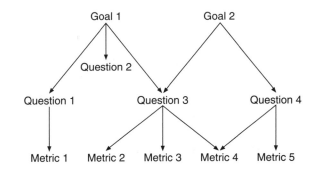

Figure 3-1
Measurement
and evaluation
paradigm

The "metrics" in this chapter are the result of brainstorming sessions, so some are not precisely defined and should be considered general approaches to measurable feedback. It is easy to imagine different ways of expressing answers to questions depending on whether the answers are being prepared for top management, project management, customer engineers, or people responsible for process improvement. Of course, few of the questions only apply to maintenance, but maintenance is so often ignored that it is useful to preserve the questions and metrics in their initial Metrics Council form. The numbers in parenthesis after the questions are figure or table references for examples shown later.

GOAL: MAXIMIZE CUSTOMER SATISFACTION

Q1. What are the attributes of customer satisfaction? (4-1)
  M. Functionality, usability, reliability, performance, supportability (FURPS+, defined more completely in Chapter 4)

Q2. What are the key indicators of customer satisfaction? (4-2)
  M. Survey data, Quality Function Deployment (QFD defined more completely in Chapter 4)

Q3. What aspects result in customer satisfaction? (4-2, 4-3)
  M. Survey data, QFD

Q4. How satisfied are customers? (4-4)
  M. Survey data, customer visit data, number of customers severly affected by defects

Q5. How do we compare with the competition? (4-2)
  M. Survey data, QFD

Q6. How many problems are affecting the customer? (4-5, 4-6, 6-8)
  M. Incoming defect rate
  M. Open critical and serious defects
  M. Break/fix ratio (count of defects introduced versus count of defects fixed)
  M. Postrelease defect density

Q7. How long does it take to fix a problem (compared to customer expectation and commitments)?
  M. Mean time to acknowledge problem
  M. Mean time to deliver solution
  M. Scheduled versus actual delivery
  M. Customer expectation (by severity level) of time to fix

Q8. How does installing a fix affect the customer?
  M. Time customer's operation is down
  M. Customer's effort required during installation

Q9. How many customers are affected by a problem? (and how much?)
  M. Number of duplicate defects by severity

Q10. Where are the bottlenecks? (4-6)

M. Backlog status, time spent doing different activities

GOAL: MINIMIZE ENGINEERING EFFORT AND SCHEDULE

Q11. Where are the resources going? Where are the worst rework loops in the process? (5-1, 5-10, 6-6)

M. Engineering months by product/component/activity

Q12. What are the total life-cycle maintenance and support costs for the product (and how distributed by time and organization)? (5-10)

M. Engineering months by product/component/activity

M. Engineering months by corrective, adaptive, perfective maintenance

Q13. What development methods affect maintenance costs?

M. Prerelease records of methods and postrelease costs

Q14. How maintainable is the product as changes occur? When do I give up and rewrite? (5-11)

M. Incoming problem rate

M. Defect density

M. Code stability

M. Complexity

M. Number of modules changed to fix one defect

Q15. What will process monitoring cost and where are the costs distributed?

M. Engineering hours and cost

Q16. What will maintenance requirements be? (5-6)

M. Code stability, complexity, size

M. Prerelease defect density

Q17. How long does it take to respond to (fix) a defect? Historically? With new processes? With resource changes? With complexity and severity variations? For each activity in process? (5-8, 5-9, T5-2, 6-2)

M. Calendar time, process and module records

Q18. How can we predict cycle time, reliability, and effort? (5-5, 5-7, 5-8, 5-9, 6-1)

M. Calendar time

M. Engineering time

M. Defect density

M. Number of defects to fix

M. Break/fix ratio — historical averages

M. Code stability

M. Complexity

M. Number of lines to change

Q19. What practices yield best results? (5-2, 5-3, 6-4)

    M. Correlations between prerelease practices and customer satisfaction data

Q20. How much do the maintenance phase activities cost? (5-4)

    M. Engineering time and cost

Q21. What are major cost components? What aspects affect the cost? (5-1, 5-2, T5-2)

    M. Engineering months by product/component/activity

Q22. How do costs change over time? (5-3, 5-4, 5-10)

    M. Track cost components over entire maintenance lifecycle

GOAL: MINIMIZE DEFECTS

Q23. What are key indicators of process health and how are we doing? (4-4, 4-5)

    M. Release schedules met, trends of defect density, serious and critical defects

Q24. What are high-leverage opportunities for preventive maintenance? (6-5, 6-6)

    M. Defect categorization

    M. Code stability

Q25. Are fixes effective? Are unexpected side effects created?

    M. Break/fix ratio

Q26. What is the postrelease quality of each module? (6-5)

    M. Defect density, critical and serious defects

Q27. What are we doing right? (5-2, 6-4, 6-7)

    M. Defect removal efficiency (ratio of prerelease defect density to postrelease defect density)

    M. Break/fix ratio

Q28. How do we know when to release? (5-6, 6-1, 6-2, 6-3)

    M. Predicted defect detection based upon prerelease records and postrelease defect densities

    M. Branch coverage

Q29. How effective is the development process in preventing defects? (6-4, 6-9)

    M. Postrelease defect density

Q30. What can we predict will happen postrelease based on prerelease data? (5-6, 6-5)

    M. Correlations between prerelease complexity, defect density, stability, FURPS+, and postrelease defect density; ability to make changes easily; customer survey results

Q31. What defects are getting through? What caused those defects? (6-6, 6-7)

M. Defect categorization

CONCLUSION

The three strategies of a software business help us to understand decisions that are often made. The goal/question/metric paradigm is useful in helping managers both to focus on relevant metrics and to examine data in an appropriate organizational context.

Each of the next three chapters explores one of the three strategies in depth. For each of these, graphs are shown that have proven practical at various times. Although the primary emphasis of the graphs is to give project managers a variety of useful tracking approaches, many of the examples also show how data is viewed for larger organizations. These help project managers to understand the context within which their graphs might fit.

The examples in each chapter are generally divided into early project activities, development activities, and postrelease activities. The graphs and charts are drawn from many different organizations in very different types of businesses. As a result, they are widely useful. *Remember that collection and analysis of this metric data does not depend upon the execution of any specific process of maintenance or development.*

BIBLIOGRAPHY

1. Basili, V., and H. D. Rombach, "Tailoring the Software Process to Project Goals and Environments," *IEEE Proceedings of the Ninth International Conference on Software Engineering*, Monterey, CA, (Apr. 1987), pp. 345–357.
2. Basili, V., and D. M. Weiss, "A Methodology for Collecting Valid Software Engineering Data," *IEEE Transactions on Software Engineering*, Vol. SE-10, no. 6 (Nov. 1984), pp. 728–738.
3. Rombach, H. D., and B. Ulery, "Improving Software Maintenance Through Measurement," *Proceedings of the IEEE*, Vol. 77, no. 4, (April 1989), pp. 581–595.
4. Grady, R. and D. Caswell, *Software Metrics: Establishing a Company-Wide Program*, Englewood Cliffs, NJ: Prentice-Hall, Inc., 1987, pp. 44.
5. Grady, R., "Measuring and Managing the Software Maintenance Process," *IEEE Software*, (Sept., 1987), pp. 35–45.

4

Project Management to Maximize Customer Satisfaction

Thesis: Drive customer satisfaction goals from a combination of product metrics (FURPS+) and customer feedback metrics (surveys and defects).

I have worked for a variety of managers and groups in HP. It's interesting to reflect on the various strategies that we followed, because three of them stand out in my mind as strongly characterizing the three major strategies introduced in Chapter 3. See if their descriptions help you to better understand an "organizational mood" for the measurement examples in each of the next three chapters.

In the first of these divisions, we had successfully introduced a new product line and were about to extend the key concepts of these products into a less-familiar application area. Our lab manager recognized the danger of not understanding our future customers' needs, so arrangements were made for every engineer and manager in the lab to participate in at least three customer meetings or visits. In addition, one of these had to include a tour of a customer's work environment.

At the time, this seemed like a huge investment. Of course, it was. It was an investment in providing the whole organization with a deep understanding of our customers' needs and with how to maximize customer satisfaction.

Maximizing customer satisfaction is easiest to pursue when the product team has close ties to customers. Examples include many MIS projects and projects with small-volume products. For other products, it is necessary to provide very efficient communication links from the customers through the various layers of a sales and support organization to get the needed data and feedback. In some ways, overemphasis of customers' current needs can result in a short-term viewpoint. The examples in this chapter must be supplemented by other measures to make more long-term process and product changes.

MAJOR CHARACTERISTICS	MAXIMIZE CUSTOMER SATISFACTION
MAJOR BUSINESS FACTOR	Attempt to capture market share
WHEN MOST EFFECTIVE	When initially entering market
CHARACTERISTIC FEATURES	Customer communications, quick responses
MOST VISIBLE METRICS	Survey and interview data, product metrics, defects
GROUP MOST LIKELY TO DRIVE STRATEGY	Development team initially, customer support later
GROUP MOST LIKELY TO BE IN DIRECT CONTACT WITH CUSTOMER	Development team
POTENTIAL DRAWBACKS IF FOCUS TOO RESTRICTED	Process of developing products may not improve

Table 4-1 The strategy of maximizing customer satisfaction.

This strategy depends on understanding customer needs and beliefs. It is a very powerful way to positively affect later products. The metrics here are:

- product metrics,
- survey data,
- counts of unresolved critical and serious defects,
- calendar time by phase and activity (emphasis on times customers experience problems),
- defect and enhancement request counts,
- break/fix ratio (count of defects introduced versus count of defects fixed).

We most often see analysis of this data early in the life of a project, but the following examples show that an emphasis on customer needs can span the entire lifecycle.

ORGANIZING CUSTOMER NEEDS

There are several models of quality that are useful when considering which attributes are most important for a particular product. [1, 2] Hewlett-Packard uses the FURPS+ model* shown in Figure 4-1 to help developers establish priorities and to define the priorities in measurable terms. [3] The letters stand for the categories: functionality, usability, reliability, performance, and supportability. Your use of such a model to define measurable product goals will help you to achieve better customer satisfaction.

Functionality	Feature Set Capabilities Generality Security
Usability	Human Factors Aesthetics Consistency Documentation
Reliability	Frequency/Severity of Failure Recoverability Predictability Accuracy Mean Time to Failure
Performance	Speed Efficiency Resource Consumption Thruput Response Time
Supportability	Testability Extensibility Adaptability Maintainability Compatibility Configurability Serviceability Installability Localizability

Figure 4-1
Components
of FURPS+.

---

*The "+" was added to the FURPS+ model after several campaigns in HP to extend the acronym to emphasize various specific attributes. For example, many divisions still refer to the model as "FLURPS." The "L" is used to emphasize the importance of building localizability into products. This is the ability to easily change products to satisfy the needs of languages other than English. Rather than have endless debate, and different versions around the company, a compromise was made to use FURPS+.

Customer Murmurs

Another recent method, successfully used in Japan for hardware products, is QFD (quality function deployment).[4] Many of the techniques used in QFD hold promise of application to software products, as well. One of the most important elements of QFD is to represent the "voice of the customer." Figure 4-2 shows a simplified example of a QFD planning matrix. This particular matrix addresses the upgrade of an existing engineering effort tracking and reporting system from a batch-oriented approach to a distributed, on-line approach. The left side of the matrix lists the customer requirements, while the top gives pertinent product design characteristics. In this example, the customer requirements are organized using the FURPS+ model to help insure that all the major categories are being considered.

The form of presentation quantifies the extent to which a customer need is met. The weighted values provide insight into which features should be emphasized during development and test. For example, the third voice of the customer item (the third row) is "track by phase and project component." The current system gets a rating of 2 out of the possible 4, and this value is mostly provided through the "strong" relationship to "data collection sheets." One of the proposed new features is "phase information." This addition would increase the value of this row to the maximum of 4. The total customer value for features in this table is 50. The current system value of 12 reflects the relationships shown in the left part of the matrix. The improved system value of 44 reflects the entire matrix.

Later steps in the QFD process provide additional information by assigning weighted values to all the planned product features and by providing a way to quantitatively compare product attributes to those of competitive products or systems.

It is easy to see that 12 out of a possible 50 points for the current system was poor. In fact, despite support by upper management for this particular system, the users were so unhappy with it that they wouldn't even consider it as a basis for an upgrade to a new system. The current system was thrown out.

Surveys and Interviews

So far we've seen ways to organize information about customer needs. There are two primary sources for the data — surveys and interviews. One HP group has developed several guidelines for creating surveys:

- Define what the goals are for the survey, what questions must be answered, how the data will be analyzed, and how results will be presented. State or graph sample conclusions.
- Test the survey and your method of data analysis before sending it out.

	Product Features / Voice of the Customer	Customer Value	Current					New Features							Current System	Improved System
			Data collection sheets	Collection sheet processing	Data correction processing	Validation routine	Monthly summary reports	On-line interface	Phase information	Component update routine	Help screens	Configurable expected data	Local data entry	Installation software		
F	Graphical output	3						⊙							0	3
	Tabular output	5					⊙								2	4
	Track by phase & project component	4	O						⊙						2	4
U	Components easy to change	4			Δ					⊙					1	3
	Data & graphs on-line	5						⊙							0	5
	Minimal eng. effort to report data	5	⊙												4	4
	Learning time < 1/2 hour	5	Δ				Δ				⊙				3	4
R	On-line data changes by project manager	4						⊙							0	4
	Data deviations automatically flagged	3										⊙			0	2
P	Data/graphs available Mon. for previous week	5											⊙		0	5
	Access to system < 10 sec.	4						⊙							N/A	4
S	Installation by project manager < 30 min.	3												⊙	N/A	2
	Totals	50													12	44

⊙ = Very strong relationship

O = Strong

Δ = Weak

Figure 4-2 A QFD matrix diagram for upgrades to an engineering effort tracking and reporting system.

- Ask questions that require simple answers, preferably quantitative or yes/no.
- Keep surveys short (preferrably one page).
- Don't send surveys with other material so they won't get lost in the shuffle.

- Make them very easy to return (for example, a fold and seal, prestamped form).

You should formulate at least one question from each of the FURPS+ categories when preparing customer surveys. Customer interviews are generally more accurate than written surveys. However, they might be biased if you don't make sure that you interview enough different customers to get a meaningful distribution. Many of the above guidelines are as true for interviews as they were for surveys. Refer to [5] for additional recommendations on doing effective surveys and interviews.

Ownership of Customer Data

Sometimes "ownership" of customer-related data can be an issue. Is it your job, as a project manager, to gather and analyze this data? Different projects organize this differently, but successful project managers make sure that it gets done. If you manage a small MIS project, you might personally collect and analyze this data. If you manage a project in an organization that includes a marketing department, you may need to work with a product marketing manager to successfully identify your customer's needs. Just remember that in both of these extremes, your development success depends on getting this data and understanding it.

DEVELOPMENT _____

One of the most common ways to track product development is to graph size against time (for example NCSS versus calendar time). Another way that emphasizes customer needs is to track FURPS+ attributes against time. Figure 4-3 shows an example of a project that specified 35 FURPS+ attributes early in the project. For example, 15 of the attributes specified key functionality that was needed. Eight others were usability attributes, like the form of user interface, the type of help, how interactions could be interrupted, and how screens could be configured. A major reliability goal specified how recovery from abnormal terminations would be supported.

Like the R&D manager who set up our customer visits, this project manager used this graph to emphasize customer needs throughout development and test. The team never lost sight of what their customers had told them was important. Some of the attributes were tested against measurable goals, while many were counted as complete when an appropriate function or capability was present. Only a few of the attributes required special effort and tests to measure.

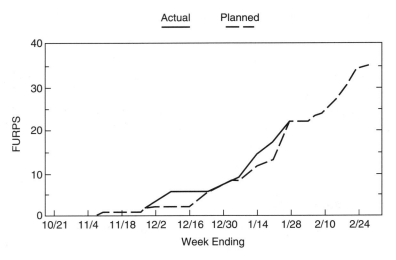

Figure 4-3 FURPS+ - planned versus actual.

POSTRELEASE

Responsiveness to Key Customer Problems

Another key aspect of ensuring customer satisfaction is responsiveness. For example, the two categories of HP defect reports that represent the problems of most concern to customers are "serious" and "critical." A serious problem is one where the customer is able to use a product but is severely restricted. A critical problem is one where the customer is unable to use a product, resulting in a critical impact on their operation.

When customers have these problems, they expect a timely response. Figure 4-4 shows how one division at HP has represented data and weighted it to insure that activities' priorities are rated appropriately.

When a customer finds a serious or critical problem, a site is placed on "alert" status. If no workaround is found quickly, the field organization declares the site "hot." The graph in Figure 4-4 also shows the results of improved responsiveness by the division.

Similar graphs help control maintenance activities for a product line or customer relationship. For example, a goal can be set for response time to resolve critical and serious problems with any key customer account. This provides a much tighter coupling between setting customer expectations and achieving customer satisfaction. The key point is to establish the desired metric and consistently measure the appropriate part of the process.

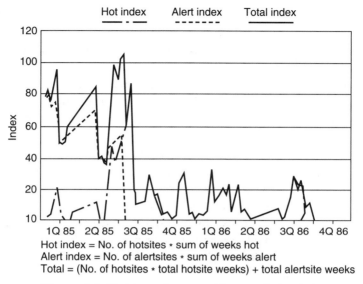

Hot index = No. of hotsites * sum of weeks hot
Alert index = No. of alertsites * sum of weeks alert
Total = (No. of hotsites * total hotsite weeks) + total alertsite weeks

Figure 4-4 Division software problem resolution index.

Defect Tracking

Figure 4-4 addresses the most important defects visible to customers. To maximize customer satisfaction, it is also important to deal with all the other defects that are day-to-day nuisances (not serious or critical, just annoying). The graph in Figure 4-5 is a useful way to monitor all the defects. This particular example is an aggregate view for a large organization, but there is no reason it can't be used for a single project.

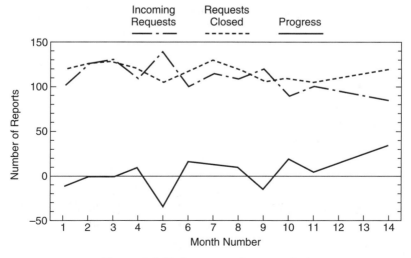

Figure 4-5 Defect report closure analysis.

   The line labeled "progress" is the difference between the incoming defects and those that were closed. It's a good way to see a cumulative trend, and you can even set upper and lower boundary limits to trigger special actions.

   This organization supplemented the defect report closure analysis with the bar chart shown in Figure 4-6. They considered this important, because defects weren't counted on the closure analysis until their existence was acknowledged as a "known problem."

   When a customer submits a service request, it goes through several steps. A support group in marketing first reviews it to make sure that it isn't a duplicate of a previous request. They also check to see if there is a workaround or fix available. They then pass it to the lab for classification. The lab tries to reproduce the problem and finally puts it into one of several "known problem" states: critical, serious, medium, low, or enhancement. As a result, a large backlog of defects in either the "lab" or "marketing" states could create customer dissatisfaction.

   Tracking a combination of Figures 4-4, 4-5, and 4-6 helps insure that you are aware of potential problems both in the areas of defect backlog and high-impact defects.

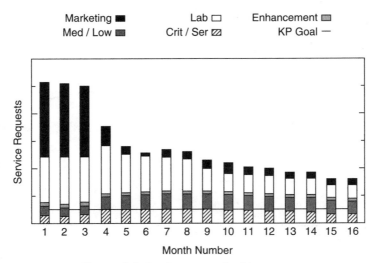

Figure 4-6 Service request backlog status.

effective during the middle part of a project — after you have defined your product well, and before you've entered final test. One set of metrics particularly applies to this strategy:

- engineering months by product/component/activity,
- engineering months by defects/enhancements,
- defect and enhancement request counts,
- counts of remaining critical and serious defects,
- calendar time by phase and activity,
- code stability (percent of code changed),
- size (NCSS, tasks, objects, components).

These measures switch from the emphasis of the previous chapter to much more of a process-oriented emphasis. Supplement the effort and time data in the following examples with process improvements in costly areas. One approach is to improve the most time-consuming activities. Another approach is to focus on the areas where defects appear most often, or on the defects that take the most effort. The next chapter discusses these last two process-improvement areas.

MAJOR CHARACTERISTICS	MINIMIZE ENGINEERING EFFORT & SCHEDULE
MAJOR BUSINESS FACTOR	Competitive pressures forcing new product development or cost control
WHEN MOST EFFECTIVE	When there are several competitive products or you sell more profitable products
CHARACTERISTIC FEATURES	Focus on delivery dates and effort
MOST VISIBLE METRICS	Calendar time, engineering effort, defects
GROUP MOST LIKELY TO DRIVE STRATEGY	Division or company management
GROUP MOST LIKELY TO BE IN DIRECT CONTACT WITH CUSTOMER	Marketing/factory customer support
POTENTIAL DRAWBACKS IF FOCUS TOO RESTRICTED	Defect backlog can get unmanageable; customers and developers frustrated

Table 5-1
The strategy of minimizing engineering effort and schedule.

INVESTIGATION AND DESIGN COST FACTORS

One of the most fundamental time and effort metrics is engineering hours by activity. Figure 5-1 shows such a breakdown by development activities. This information is relatively easy to collect, and yet it can be quite valuable for a project manager as a check against other estimating methods. The more information that you have about past projects, the more relevant these percentages become. For example, we see different percentages for three different classifications in the figure. We would see other patterns if we looked at the data by size or by implementation language. These variables and others are used by various estimation tools to determine project effort and schedules. The better you understand their influence in your particular environment, the more accurate your estimates will be. It isn't the estimation tools that provide the accuracy, it's your understanding of the variables as they apply to any given project.

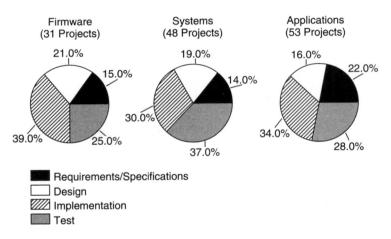

Figure 5-1 Percent engineering hours by phase.

Another important aspect that is popular today is the effect of software reuse. Figure 5-2 shows the relative rates of generating code for the same software types as in Figure 5-1, and it adds the category of reused code. The definition of reused here is one that was arbitrarily made for HP's Software Metrics Database (for a complete discussion, refer to *Software Metrics: Establishing a Company-Wide Program*. [1]). "Reused projects" are ones that were reported as consisting of greater than 75 percent reused code. Such projects included firmware, systems, and applications types.

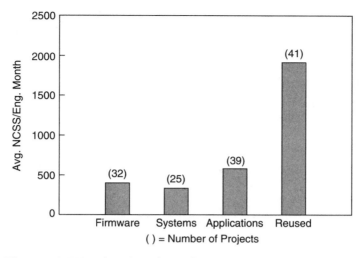

Figure 5-2 HP code volume by application class (137 total projects).

Learning Methods That Minimize Costs

Keeping accurate records of engineering time will help you to identify the best processes for future projects. For example, Figure 5-3 shows data from the Jet Propulsion Laboratories (JPL) for the average number of hours to find and fix defects using inspections. [2] The four inspection types shown are:

- R1 requirements,
- I0 high-level design,
- I1 low-level design,
- I2 source code.

On the surface, this data suggests that there may be no benefit to holding early inspections. There are several things to keep in mind, though. First, remember the rule of thumb given in Chapter 2. Defects introduced in the early phases of a project are expensive if they are not discovered until late in a project. They can cost up to 100 times as much to fix after product delivery than they would if you found them shortly after you introduced them. Second, different defect-finding techniques have differing degrees of success at finding specific types of defects. We will see an illustration of this in the next chapter. Third, JPL also measured the average time to find and fix defects during test. For the same environment as for Figure 5-3, it took them 5 to 17 hours during test to find and fix defects. [2]

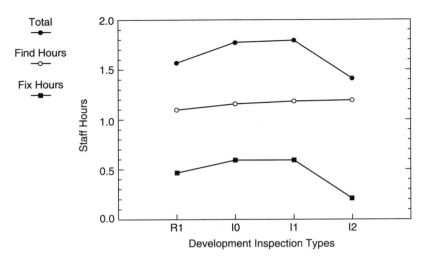

Figure 5-3 JPL resource hours per defect.

The JPL example shows how important it is to track time and effort data. Without data like this, groups often question the effectiveness of inspections. They argue that they don't have time for requirements or design inspections. They need to get to the coding phase quickly so that they can start uncovering and fixing the defects that they know will be there. The specific numbers that we've seen in this example may not be the same as yours, but the relative cost ratios should be large enough to convince you of the importance of early inspections (and other early development tools and techniques).

Let's close this discussion by looking at Figure 5-4. It shows a valuable method that one HP organization used to track the success of inspections (code inspections in this case). [3] After each inspection, they computed a return on investment by multiplying the number of "major" defects found times five hours (the lower JPL bound to find and fix defects in test) and by then subtracting the cost of the inspection. As long as the averages remained above the center line, they felt confident that their inspections were effective. This method is discussed further in Chapter 13.

Remember that if you don't track your project engineering time, you will neither learn the value of such techniques in your environment, nor will you be able to predict or track your projects with success.

TRACKING TO MINIMIZE DEVELOPMENT
AND TEST SCHEDULES

Tracking engineering time is useful during all phases of a project. This measure provides significant information that can help you to adjust resources and control schedules. For example, Figure 5-1 suggests that coding and test

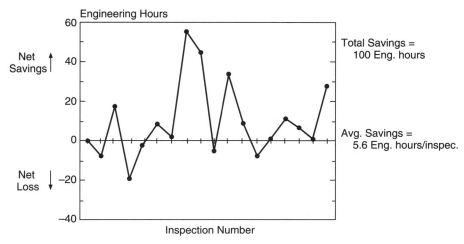

Figure 5-4 Tracking the effectiveness of code inspections.

represent 60 percent or more of the total effort. By tracking time during earlier activities, you can make very rough estimates for the expected duration of later activities. These can be very useful as comparisons to bottoms-up estimates that your people make.

Figure 5-5 shows how one project tracked other aspects of progress against time. [4] The project used an object-oriented approach to do their project. This allowed them to track deliverables earlier in their project than usual. First, they tracked classes. A class is a collection of one or more related objects. They also tracked what they called operations (these are sometimes called methods). There were an average of around 25 operations for each class in their project.

Although it is not shown in Figure 5-5, they also tracked non-comment source statements (NCSS). They had several reasons to do this. Their target application was in firmware, so NCSS gave them a way to check against physical constraints more easily than classes or operations. Many people also did low-level estimates using NCSS. Finally, tracking NCSS late in the project gave them a good feel for its stability.

Another primary concern when controlling costs and time is to test only as long as necessary to achieve a desired level of quality. This can be a particular strain on a project team, so there are a variety of techniques that attempt to predict when you reach such a level. Some of these involve monitoring the number of defects per hours of testing time [5], looking at the amount of test execution time between defects [6], and using past average times to find and fix defects. [1] Some of these will be discussed further in Chapter 7.

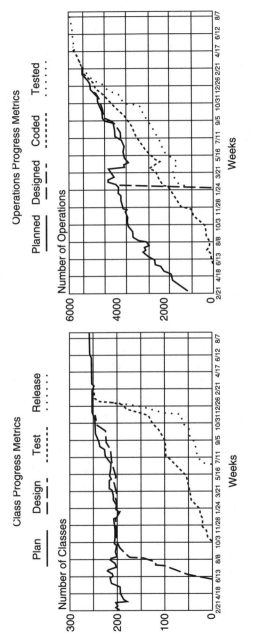

Figure 5-5

One particularly interesting example is shown in Figure 5-6. [7] This project tracked the number of defects against testing time with an interesting twist. They introduced 21 control defects into the product during final test. These were selected primarily from low-level design review results. Besides graphing the unknown defects (not shown here) against testing time, they also graphed the control defects (Figure 5-6) against testing time. In this example, time was expressed in terms of work shifts of the test team. They then used the number of residual control defects that they knew were remaining (one) to predict how many unknown defects were still present. After one year of operation, four defects had been found versus a prediction of three.

These are just two of many examples of metrics that provide visibility to project managers that help you to optimize project costs and schedules during development and test.

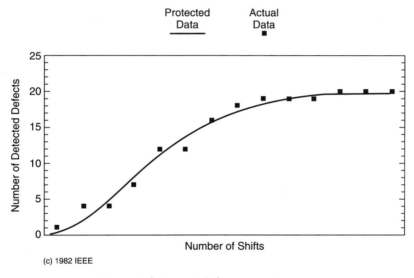

Figure 5-6 Control defect removal process.

POSTRELEASE COST FACTORS

There are many reasons for cost and schedule pressures. Nowhere are they more evident than in maintenance activities. In some cases, we must change software to run with new computers or peripherals. If there is no means to recover such costs built into our software product pricing, then this activity seems like a waste of resources. In other cases, we have aging products, and it seems wrong to invest too much in keeping them alive.

Information systems groups are probably torn more by cost and schedule pressures than any others. The nature of their applications is that they change and evolve to meet business needs. They seldom have the luxury of starting from scratch, so there are constant pressures to make do with fixed staff. For all these different reasons, a wide variety of metrics and graphical views have evolved that may be appropriate for your organization. Again many of these depend on tracking engineering effort and schedule components.

Incoming Defect Rates

In the previous chapter, we saw a graph that tracked both incoming and closed defects. That example was for a mature product. Another example of the incoming rate of defects is shown in Figure 5-7. [1] It shows the incoming defect rate for a product for one year after initial release. After initial product use began, defect reports increased until there was a known backlog of the most common defects. Reports then decreased and stabilized (more or less) to a constant rate until a new product release occurred. Combined with other data, this information helped managers to plan the staffing required for the product. This type of "hump" incoming pattern is quite typical.

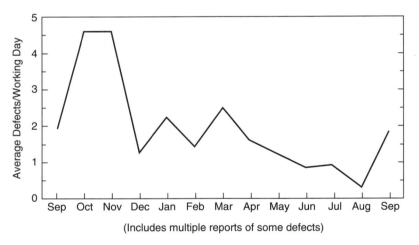

(Includes multiple reports of some defects)

Figure 5-7 Postrelease defect stability.

Task Completion Rates

Figures 5-8 [1] and 5-9 [8] illustrate two views of engineering and calendar time in the maintenance of two products. The first shows the actual times to fix various defects versus the estimated times.

The predicted time to fix defects was reasonably accurate for estimates of 6 hours or under, but higher estimates were not as accurate. One important variable not included in Figure 5-8 is the percentage of *effective* hours available. The recorded times only included time spent fixing defects. For estimating

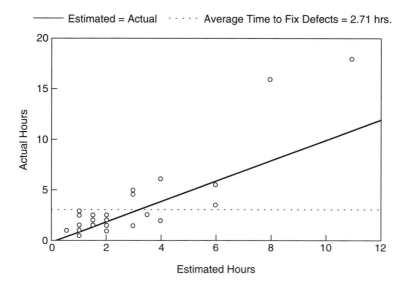

Figure 5-8 Defect fix times, estimated versus actual.

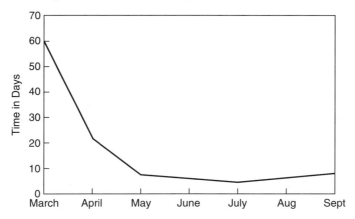

Figure 5-9 Average time to fix a service request (for an applications product).

purposes, they had to increase the average fixing time to around 4 hours to include time spent on other activities. The manager of this product line used this data to estimate schedules more accurately, and to measure how effective new tools or training were. They also could decide when to shorten schedules by creating an environment with a higher percentage of effective hours (even if only by arbitrarily limiting some of the nonproject related time temporarily).

On the other hand, Figure 5-9 shows fix times in calendar time (from when a person was first assigned to a defect until the fixed code was tested and returned to a control library). This form of tracking was useful during maintenance as a way to focus on the release schedule for a product update.

The figure shows the results of a concentrated effort at one HP division to reduce the time to get product updates through the release process.

The steps that they took are a model for process improvement. First, they set a fixed cycle time for updates that went to customers. The marketing group that dealt with customers set the order in which defects were fixed. Next, the lab created a sign-off form that specified the steps needed to fix each defect (quick fixes and workarounds were handled separately from this process). This form also captured the amount of engineering time spent for each step. From this data, they learned what the breakdown of time was for each task. These times were compared to each task's effectiveness. Last, the lab introduced one major process change per update cycle so they could monitor their total success. For example, it may have taken an engineer half a day to unit test a change. The lab found that few defects turned up during unit test if they conducted design reviews before making the changes. These defects were successfully caught by defect-specific tests, so they eliminated the unit tests.

When you use the approaches shown in Figures 5-8 and 5-9, remember that not all maintenance activities are corrective. The effort and time characteristics of changes made to improve products can be quite different from those for defect fixes. For tracking purposes, it is convenient to treat enhancements in two ways. First, some are major changes (in terms of time and effort) with most of the characteristics of new designs. Second, some are minor changes that can be grouped along with defect fixes. Generally, only minor enhancements are allowed for some period after initial product release, and major enhancements are done only after incoming defects have stabilized.

A good example of how maintenance activities evolve over time is shown in Figure 5-10. [9] Here we see how the work on an MIS system gradually shifted from initial development to a mixture of support and enhancements. Often organizations make basic business decisions to control the balance of resources among these different activities. In any case it is useful for project managers to understand the mix and what the trends are.

Complexity Increases Costs

For large software systems, minimizing effort and schedule must take into account the effect of complexity. Some years ago, Belady and Lehman proposed a law of software development. It said, "The entropy of a system increases with time unless specific work is executed to maintain or reduce it." [10] By entropy, they meant system complexity or lack of structure. Figure 5-11, taken from the same reference, shows increasing entropy for one large software product in the form of the fraction of modules handled for each new release over almost ten years. The larger the percentage of modules changed, the

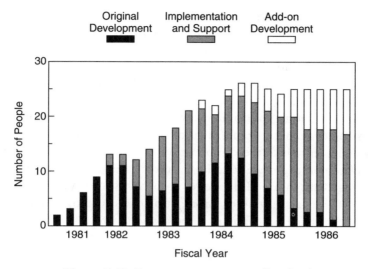

Figure 5-10 Procurement systems staffing levels.

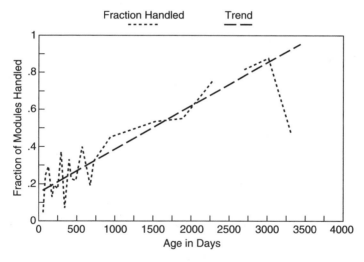

Figure 5-11 Modules handled as a function of system age (OS/360).

greater the probability that you will introduce new defects, and the more testing you will need to do to complete the job. At the 3000 day point, it appears that they undertook a major effort to control the number of modules changed for an update.

Looking at the percentage of modules affected is just one of several metrics that characterize maintainability. It is important also to look at incoming defect rates, individual module stability and complexity, test coverage, and other aspects to isolate the areas of the product that are the largest contributors to total maintenance costs.

These metrics don't apply only to large software systems. Sometimes you can change the entire working environment for yourself and a project team by focusing on complexity. Nathan Lowell tells a story of how he and a group that were maintaining a material control system written in COBOL transformed their environment. It had been characterized by emergencies and early-morning phone calls. They changed it into one where the system was much easier to maintain during normal human working hours. [11] They did this by measuring the cyclomatic complexity of their software and by making a conscious effort to reduce the complexity with every change. This gradual reduction of complexity made it easier for them to understand the code they were changing. This, in turn, led to fewer mistakes when changes were made.

This was not a short-term effort. It also wasn't triggered by some management directive from high up. It was a gradual process with a long-term goal that was very attractive to the team. It was a different way to approach a difficult job that helped the team change from a totally reactive approach to one that was proactive. Their efforts resulted in a system that cost much less to maintain, an environment that was much better to work in, and a greater sense of job satisfaction for the team.

So high complexity interferes with your ability to predict and control projects. By monitoring complexity in some form, you can identify warning signals that help you to anticipate your team's effort and schedules better.

Cost Trade-offs

Managers seek information on cost trade offs among methods that might be applied to either new development or maintenance. HP has improved quality in recent years by applying effective software-engineering methods to products during their development. These methods include structured analysis and design, the use of prototypes for products with extensive user interactions, design and code inspections, branch coverage analysis, testing-prediction models, and statistical quality control techniques.

The next example, analysis of engineering time, shows the potential value of these methods, whether they are used during initial development or during maintenance. Table 5-2 shows the relative amounts of time needed to fix defects as a function of defect introduction for two products.

You can see that the average times to find and fix defects are substantially more than the four hours discussed in the Figure 5-8 example. That example represented the early maintenance records of a small product (10 KNCSS). The data in Table 5-2 is from two very large, mature software products. The effect of defects on their maintenance is also very large. When you become aware of the potential downstream costs of as much as *two engineering months for each design defect* (project 1), the motivation to train

Phase Introduced	Project #1		Project #2	
	% Defects Introduced	Average Fix Time **	% Defects Introduced	Average Fix Time **
Requirements/ Specifications	–	–	3	575
Design	20	315	15	235
Implementation	75	80	65	118
Test	5	46	17	74
Total	100	125	100	142

** Time includes finding and fixing (units are engineering hours).
Defects mainly fixed during implementation and test phases.

Table 5-2 Engineering time versus defects for two software projects.

engineers to use good design techniques and design reviews becomes high. Only by tracking and analyzing engineering costs by different activities can you learn the facts to make the most cost-effective decisions.

Remember, a major goal in the maintenance phase is to balance responsiveness to customer needs against the need to minimize total engineering resources that don't create visible new sources of revenue.

CONCLUSION

Estimating and tracking engineering effort and schedule components is a key part of successful project management. Emphasizing metrics for them is most effective during

- design, implementation, and test activities,
- heavy maintenance,
- evaluation of best practices.

This strategy is most liable to people's misinterpretation. More will be said about this later when we discuss public and private data. For now, just remember that, in the minds of your people, there is a subtle distinction between collecting effort and time data to balance and predict project progress versus using the same data to hold their feet to the fire.

One sign of the goal to minimize engineering effort and schedule is high-level pressure for productivity. True productivity also includes other aspects such as quality, time to market, and long-term investments such as design for reuse. Make sure that both you and your people keep these other aspects in mind, also.

BIBLIOGRAPHY

1. Grady, R. and D. Caswell, *Software Metrics: Establishing a Company-Wide Program*, Englewood Cliffs, NJ: Prentice-Hall, Inc.,1987, pp. 88, 116, 128.

2. Kelly, J., and J. Sherif, "An Analysis of Defect Densities Found During Software Inspections," *Proceedings of the Fifteenth Annual Software Engineering Workshop*, Goddard Space Flight Center, (Nov 1990), p. 30.

3. Rodriguez, S., "SESD Inspections Results," (April 1991).

4. Benton, R., private communications, (March 1991).

5. Kruger, G. A., "Project Management Using Software Reliability Growth Models," *Hewlett-Packard Journal*, (June 1988), pp. 30–35.

6. Musa, J., A. Iannino, and K. Okumoto, *Software Reliability: Measurement, Prediction, Application*, New York: McGraw-Hill 1987.

7. Ohba, Mitsuru, "Software Quality = Test Accuracy X Text Coverage," *0270-5257/82/0000/0287, IEEE* (1982), pp. 287–293.

8. Horenstein, R., Presentation to Fourth Annual HP Software Metrics Council Conference, (Oct 1986).

9. Sieloff, C., Internal Hewlett-Packard Management Presentation, (Feb 1988).

10. Belady, L., and M. Lehman, "The Characteristics of Large Systems," *Research Directions in Software Technology* (ed by P. Wegner). Cambridge, MA: MIT Press, 1979, p. 114.

11. Lowell, N., "An Interview with Nathan Lowell," *Software Quality World*, Vol. 2, no. 2, (1990), pp. 1, 5-7.

6

Project
Management
to Minimize
Defects

*Thesis: Use **detailed defect information** to make product-release decisions.*

The mood of this chapter is set by an entire organization, rather than by a single manager. Several years ago, Hewlett-Packard introduced a new computer product line called Precision Architecture. Besides a new hardware architecture, this introduction involved major rewrites of a wide variety of our software. I'm not sure which individual manager first set our rigorous goals for minimizing defects, but this strategic focus influenced our reporting methods and decisions more than any other during the project.

This project involved hundreds of engineers whose activities had to be coordinated across multiple divisions and multiple physical locations. When we compare its focus with those of the last two chapters, we can see why the emphasis naturally tended toward minimizing defects. The minimum product FURPS+ (functionality, usability, reliability, performance, supportability) were set by existing products on our previous computer product platforms. For example, our customers expected our operating systems, compilers, networking software, and so forth to function as well or better than they had before.

Schedules were critical, because time to market was very important and the coordination complexity was high. Nevertheless, if we cut the schedule too short at the expense of delivering products with worse defect levels than in the past, it would have been readily apparent to our customers, and the risk would have been high. So while there were clear influences to maximize customer satisfaction and to minimize schedule, the strongest focus remained to minimize defects.

This chapter emphasizes improving processes by tracking, analyzing, and eliminating defects. The metrics are:

- count of prerelease defects,
- count of postrelease defects,
- count of remaining critical and serious defects,
- count of defects sorted by module and cause,
- NCSS (Non-Comment Source Statements),
- percentage of branches covered during test,
- calendar time by phase.

This strategy has the greatest process-oriented focus of the three introduced in Chapter 3, yet we can still see its practical application even by a single project manager.

MAJOR CHARACTERISTICS	MINIMIZE DEFECTS
MAJOR BUSINESS FACTOR	Hold/increase market share
WHEN MOST EFFECTIVE	When features are competitive and adequate market share is held
CHARACTERISTIC FEATURES	Analysis and removal of defect causes
MOST VISIBLE METRICS	Failure analysis by module, cause, & severity; size; code coverage
GROUP MOST LIKELY TO DRIVE STRATEGY	Development and/or quality organization
GROUP MOST LIKELY TO BE IN DIRECT CONTACT WITH CUSTOMER	Field support organization
POTENTIAL DRAWBACKS IF FOCUS TOO RESTRICTED	Defects may be fixed that are not cost effective

Table 6-1
The strategy of minimizing defects.

INVESTIGATION AND DESIGN ACTIVITIES _____

The best approach to minimize defects during early project activities is to understand customer needs. Use the metrics and techniques described early in Chapter 4 to gain this understanding and to prevent defects from occurring. Also use early inspections to help uncover any early defects that are introduced.

DEVELOPMENT _____

Project Tracking

One key approach to minimize defects is to record and track defects carefully throughout the lifecycle of a project. Figure 6-1 shows defects as they were monitored on a continuous basis for one small project. This data shows a clear linear pattern of defect discovery, and a reassuring trend of the open defects being quickly resolved. It is possible to calculate the number of defects fixed from the graph, and divide by the calendar time to determine the average elapsed time to fix a defect. For the data on the curves shown, it appears that the project staff was both finding and fixing only three defects per week.

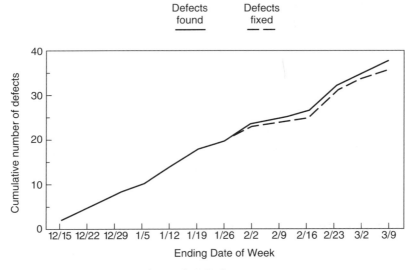

Figure 6-1 Defect status.

For large systems, the rate of change in trends may be more important than the trends themselves, because it shows the product's stability. Figure 6-2 shows the rates of change of both the incoming defects and the defects fixed for part of one large HP system. [1] The data only reflects the weekly incoming and fixed defects for the final time period of the project. You can imagine both lines extending from the chart off its left side and alternating with more defects found or fixed during any given week depending on what engineers were doing. Our experience has proven that products whose defect status slopes did not decline, as this example does, had poor quality after release.

Sometimes the pressure to release overcomes our better judgment. Just remember that this can be very expensive. One example of this was a software system that was released despite an absence of a clear defect decline like the one in Figure 6-2. The result was that a multi-million dollar update was required shortly after release and the product got a bad reputation for quality, as well. This is the kind of mistake that can cause the downfall of an entire product line.

These examples show that simple tracking of defects helps project managers of both small and large projects to make the right product-release decisions.

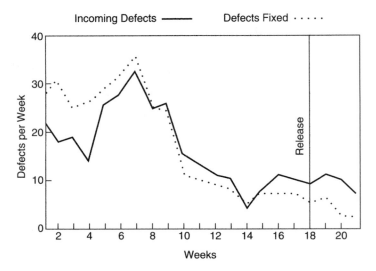

Figure 6-2 Project defect status.

Test Techniques to Minimize Defects

During both product development and maintenance, one primary concern is to ensure that you don't introduce new defects. An effective way to check this is to maintain suites of test programs and then continually update them as products change and improve. Figure 6-3 illustrates one of several ways needed to verify the tests' completeness. [1] It shows two levels of branch-coverage goals and the data for one part of an HP product. Branch coverage is measured by using a program that automatically inserts statements into the product's precompilation sources. These statements increment counters during testing to provide a histogram of what code parts were executed and what parts were not.

In the example, you can see a graph that summarizes the histogram results over many months time. It shows how the goals for coverage and the actual coverage get higher over time. The branch coverage decrease during the early part of the graph was caused by the addition of new code that hadn't been tested yet. This graph represents composite data during integration-level testing of all components. Unit-level testing is done earlier in the process, and the goal for unit-level coverage is 100 percent.

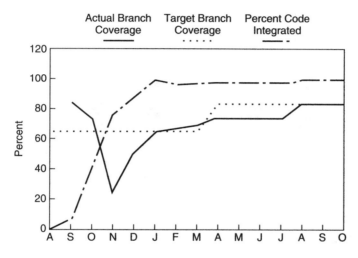

Figure 6-3 Branch coverage.

Branch coverage is only one test technique, though. One particularly interesting study compared the success of six common test techniques. These techniques were applied to known shapshots of two completed software projects. They showed considerable variation among the techniques at both the unit level and at the CSC (configured source code) level. The results are shown in Figure 6-4. [2] Each bar reflects the percentage of the total defects found by a team using a specific method. Since different teams used different methods on the same code, some defects were found by more than one method. While it is likely that results for other projects would be different, it seems clear that a combination of test techniques is necessary to ensure high-quality software.

Perhaps an even more disturbing result of the study was that the different techniques uncovered as many as 20 defects in the software that had never been previously found.

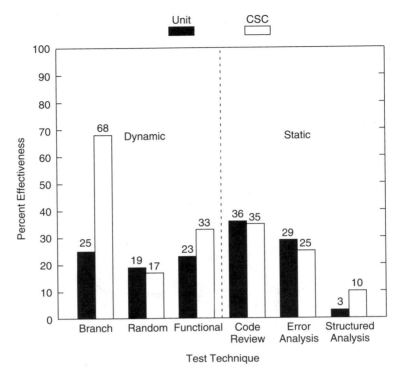

Figure 6-4 Descriptive comparison of test technique effectiveness.

POSTRELEASE

We saw a variety of postrelease examples in the previous chapter that support the strategy of minimizing defects. These help us to quantify how many defects we have and how much they cost to fix. On the other hand, they don't provide the information we need to change our processes to eliminate these defects permanently. Categorization of defects and analysis to uncover major causes satisfies this need.

Minimizing Defects Using Failure Analysis

Figure 6-5 shows a bar chart that addresses important questions about postrelease quality and how to maximize the engineers' success during maintenance [3]. Defect analysis showed that three of the 13 modules (24 percent of the code) accounted for 76 percent of the defects reported before release. This could have meant that these modules had simply been tested more thoroughly than the others. Six months after release, though, a similar analysis was done using data reported by customers. The results were that the same three modules accounted for a similar portion of the defects. This information

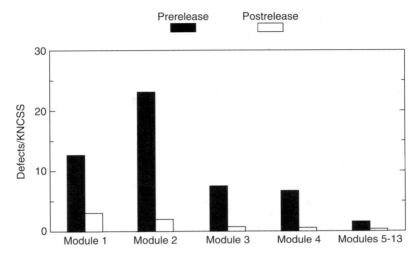

Figure 6-5 Defect analysis by code module.

helped managers to formulate a more thorough plan to test the three modules and long-term plans to rewrite the error-prone modules. Until then, the team was wise to exercise caution when considering enhancements to those modules, since their design was unstable or complex. Defect categorization is a powerful tool to help identify where work must be done and to predict where you can expect more defects to appear.

Another effective way to examine defect data is to analyze causes of defects. By identifying common causes of defects, you can take steps to limit the possibility of these problems occurring again. One organization at HP did such an analysis and found that more than one third of their defects were caused by a poor understanding of their users' interface requirements [3,4]. A Pareto analysis of these defects is shown in Figure 6-6. Each of the bars represented a different cause code. The codes were divided into three major groupings: A, user interface/interaction; B, programming defect; C, operating environment. Each number referred to a different defect type.

The organization responded to the data by changing their process to focus more specifically on user interface design (such as technical design reviews and evolutionary prototypes reviewed by representative customers). Refer to Chapter 9 of the book *Software Metrics: Establishing a Company-Wide Program* for a more complete discussion of their analysis [3].

Figure 6-7 shows three categories of defects before and after release for four successive releases of the same product after the organization had changed its user-interface design process. It shows that the organization now has few postrelease design errors. The percentage of defects found after release also dropped from 25 percent of the total for the first two releases to less than ten percent in the third and to zero in the fourth. While they were not completely successful in removing all sources of defects, they did improve their process so that the defects did not reach customers.

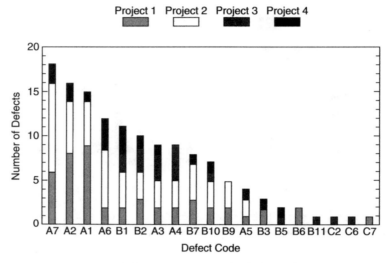

Figure 6-6 Pareto analysis of software defects.

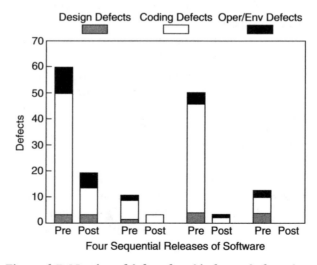

Figure 6-7 Number of defects found before and after release.

Top-Management Presentation

The graphs presented so far are most useful for project managers. The next two graphs help to present a top-management summary of a strategy to minimize defects. The first graph deals with measuring one aspect of customer satisfaction. Figure 6-8 is an example of data that receives monthly management attention in HP, because it summarizes how many unfixed critical and serious problems customers see.

The second graph (Figure 6-9) shows the postrelease defect density for the first 12 months after product release for one division's products. Better than any other visual representation, this graph summarizes whether all the other efforts to reduce defects are having a permanent, positive effect. The figure shows some progress toward higher quality at release in the last year and a half for product line 2. There are no recent data points for the other two product lines which would suggest whether they made similar progress.

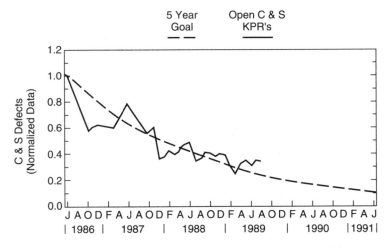

Figure 6-8 Division defect progress (critical and serious defects).

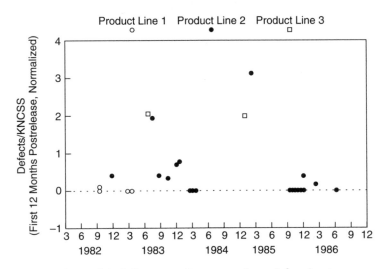

Figure 6-9 Software quality - postrelease defect density.

These last two graphs complement the earlier graphs by providing top-management views that are consistent with the strategy of minimizing defects.

These nine illustrations came from different projects, entities, and times. Measuring any one or two of them is useful, but the best results are achieved by tracking them all. Fortunately, the amount of data to collect is not a great burden. Many managers collect such data anyway, but graphs are helpful when it is important to *see* a trend.

CONCLUSION

Controlling software costs requires that an organization has a strategy (whether or not it is explicitly stated) and that the primary characteristics of the strategy and the most effective measures of its success are understood. Software metric data provides feedback of progress in meeting an organization's goals.

Figure 6-10 shows a simplified dataflow diagram of software development that summarizes relevant data for our three strategies. The metrics include size and complexity data from automated counters,

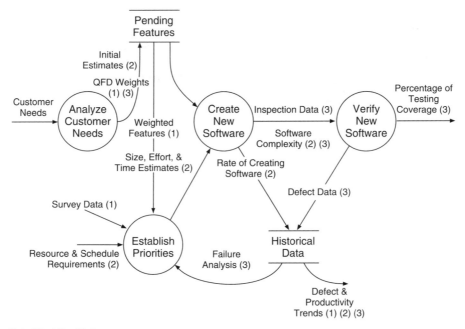

Data That Facilitates:
(1) Strategic Focus on Customer Satisfaction
(2) Strategic Focus on Minimizing Engineering Effort and Schedule
(3) Strategic Focus on Minimizing Defects

Figure 6-10 Simplified software management information sources.

engineering effort and time information collected manually, automated defect-tracking information, and information from customer surveys. The figure suggests that the fundamental job of software creation is not overly complicated.

Let us return to the opening question asked in Chapter 3, "Why does it take so many resources to support software systems?" The examples in the last three chapters suggest that both software development and maintenance are expensive because software products are complex, and project managers may be asked to change their focus to adapt to changing business conditions.

Figure 6-11 shows how the insertion of defects into our software and the continuous evolution of our software complicates the simple model shown in Figure 6-10. This diagram shows metrics that help project managers to understand and control a wide range of activities and choices. *It isn't the metrics that make the management tasks complicated.* Rather, we wouldn't have to measure so many process variables if we didn't have to respond to business needs in so many different ways.

Because the model only addresses data sources, it does not depend on any particular process for maintenance. On the other hand, evaluating the data provides useful checks against any of the three strategies, and the model provides a framework for data that supports better decisions. Conscientious use of this model will help achieve a proper balance among the equally important goals of maximizing customer satisfaction, minimizing engineering effort and schedule, and minimizing defects.

There are several aspects to remember when considering which strategy to use. Software metrics can only be *part* of a successful plan for development improvement. The metrics selected will help manage a business for many years, so they must be carefully chosen. No matter what strategy you pursue, you can effectively execute that strategy only if you understand the necessary product and process attributes. *That understanding requires software metrics.*

In the next chapter we will see that despite any primary emphasis you might use, you must consider inputs from all three strategies when deciding when you are done. In its discussion, we return to the goal/question/metric paradigm to visualize the role of software metrics in managing quality and testing.

Data That Facilitates:
(1) Strategic Focus on Customer Satisfaction
(2) Strategic Focus on Minimizing Engineering Effort and Schedule
(3) Strategic Focus on Minimizing Defects

Figure 6-11 Software management information sources.

BIBLIOGRAPHY

1. Sakai, B., Hewlett-Packard Software Metrics Council Meeting, (Sept 1987).
2. Lauterbach, L., and W. Randell, "Six Test Techniques Compared: The Test Process and Product," *Proceedings of the NSIA Fifth Anniversary National Joint Conference and Tutorial on Software Quality and Productivity*, National Security Industrial Association, Washington, DC, 1989.
3. Grady, R. and D. Caswell, *Software Metrics: Establishing a Company-Wide Program*, Englewood Cliffs, NJ: Prentice-Hall, Inc.,1987, pp. 110, 123–125.
4. Sieloff, C., "Software TQC: Improving the Software Development Process Through Statistical Quality Control," *Software Productivity Conference Proceedings, (April 1984), pp. 2-56 – 2-57.*

7

The Role of Software Metrics in Managing Quality and Testing

*Thesis: Use **detailed defect information** to make product-release decisions. (continued)*

When the SEI maturity model was introduced in Chapter 1, the point was made that few organizations are beyond the "initial" level of maturity. Extensive testing is one of the characteristics of the bottom levels of the SEI model. Testing is one way to reduce risk and to attempt to ensure quality, in spite of a process that produces unpredictable, widely varying results.

Of course, testing is not bad. It is often needed even in an optimized process. The primary difference is that an optimized process includes tests during the process and not just at the end. Such tests are at key process points. You test intermediate work products as you complete them instead of in a "big bang" at the end.

This chapter rounds out our discussion of useful techniques for project managers. It extends our thesis of using detailed defect information to make product-related decisions by tying defects back to significant project risks and through a discussion of testing models based on defects.

A FRAMEWORK FOR MANAGING TEST

The testing process can be characterized like any other process. It has inputs, it follows repeatable steps, and it produces a final output (a product tested against specifications and requirements). It is useful to set measurable goals to manage the testing process effectively. Some suggested goals are shown in Figure 7-1. The goals and metrics in the figure are all oriented toward people primarily responsible for testing, as will be the discussion throughout this chapter.

The inputs to the testing process come from the development process. We can most successfully apply our testing resources by understanding the product from the customer's perspective and by identifying potential problem areas exposed during development. In Figure 7-1, the left box represents the development process. "Metrics" from the development process that are useful for managing the testing phase include quality specification techniques such as FURPS+, QFD, and risk analysis. We can put the term metrics in quotation

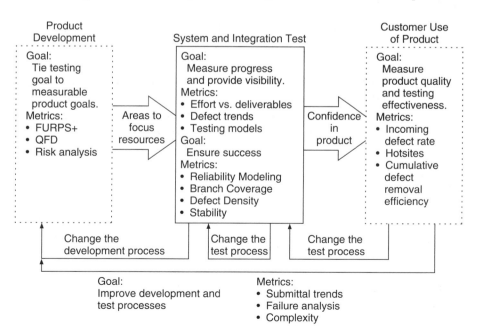

Figure 7-1 Measurable attributes for the testing process.

marks here, because none of these three examples necessarily provide quantifiable data. The intent is to *derive* usable testing metrics from the information that FURPS+, QFD, and risk analysis supply.

In our model, the center box represents the process of system and integration test. Here we see two management objectives: to measure and show progress in the development of a stable product of known quality. Defect data is most convenient to track, and various analyses of this data constitute testing metrics.

The box on the right of Figure 7-1 represents customer use of a product after testing is complete. It is then that we find out just how good our tests were in representing the customer environment and expectations. Again, defect data plays a prominent role in evaluating how successful both the development and testing processes were.

Below the boxes are several feedback paths that represent the opportunity to improve the development and testing processes by learning from past successes and mistakes. Here, measurements are more closely related to a fundamental understanding of process problems. The metrics in Figure 7-1 are explained in more detail in the next four sections.

DEVELOPMENT: TYING TESTING GOALS TO MEASURABLE PRODUCT GOALS

There are many kinds of tests that can be executed to help verify that a software system is operational. Unless these tests are prepared with some optimal customer perspective in mind, they may not be as effective as desired. Chapter 4 introduced the concepts of FURPS+ (functionality, usability, reliability, performance, and supportability) and QFD (quality function deployment). These provide one way to quantify the level of quality that you desire, particularly in the requirements and specifications stages of a project. The primary early test method used here is inspections. The metrics that you identify at this early stage will be useful throughout the life cycle of the product, though.

Figure 7-2 shows another example of a QFD matrix. [1] This one captures both customer experience with an existing prototype and direct customer feedback for proposed changes to the prototype. So this high-level view helps us to focus on the primary customer desires. The relative weightings provided in the matrix help to guide you in emphasizing which items must be well-specified and tested throughout product development.

Sometimes there are multiple customer perspectives. This can get confusing if you summarize them all in one matrix. In such cases, you need to extract subsets of data to see how well you match each subset against its

Figure 7-2 QFD matrix diagram for a project management tool.

Voice of the Customer — Product Features

Product Features	Customer Value	Current System	Improved System
Access control	2	0	2.0
Report customization	2	1.2	2.0
Database customization	1	.6	1.0
On screen selection	3	0	3.0
Track sub projects milestones & components	2	1.0	1.0
Propagation of checklist changes	1	0	1.0
Checklist templates for life cycle products	4	2.4	4.0
Add submitter field to checklist items	4	2.4	4.0
Component size metric	1	.6	1.0
Summary of project status	4	.8	4.0
Multiuser access	5	0	5.0
Easy status reporting	3	3.0	3.0
Convenient to do list	5	5.0	5.0
Simple paper checklist	4	4.0	4.0
Pert interface	5	1.0	5.0
STARS/DTS interface	2	.4	2.0
100% Feature execution and error generation	3	3.0	3.0
Sign on takes too long	3	0	3.0
Status roll up takes too long	5	0	5.0
Source controlled with RCS	2	0	2.0
Totals	**61**	**26**	**60**

Column feature groups:

Prototype Features: Process for conducting software evaluations (on-line or paper); Tool for tracking and reporting evaluation results (on-line or paper); Simple user interface; On-line maintenance of records using data input screens & DBASEIV tools; Structured framework for project & evaluation planning; Multi level commenting capability; Automatic roll-up of status for all levels; Manual status alarms at all levels; Customizable checklists, Templates for all evaluation types; Automatic versioning of checklists; Ensures compliance with key req'mts & standards; Tracks and controls key dependancies; Provides guidelines for developers; Tracks & controls prerelease discrepancies

New Features: New platform and demo with multi user capability; Create user defined reports; Customize checklists by adding items from existing checklists; Summary view of project status; Automatic status for project element dependancies; Data transfer between SET and common project planners; Data transfer between SET and HP defect tracking systems; Customer support and on-line help; Data security; On-screen select capability; Checklist templates for all life cycle tracks; User modifiable data base structure

Legend:
⊙ = 5-Very strong relationship
O = 3-Strong
△ = 1-Weak

requirements. For example, Figure 7-3 shows a high-level summary for three different target customers of one product. Such a summary can provide insights into potential weaknesses. In this example, the data suggests that product performance is a key customer concern. This summary is tied to a more detailed matrix where we can normally see which features or changes give us the greatest leverage to improve our product.

		Product Version A	Product Version B	Product Version C
	F	4	3.5	4
	U	4.5	4	3.5
Figure 7-3 FURPS+	R	3.5	3.5	2.5
customer evaluation	P	1.5	1.5	1
summary.	S	2.5	2.5	2

Another major input that development data can provide to the testing process is a risk analysis based on observed measurements. These can help to drive the kinds of tests that must be generated. For example, you can examine the results of design and code inspections to identify modules or functions that already seem error prone or overly complex.

There are also metrics that identify design or code complexity. Figure 7-4 shows a graph of defect density versus design complexity, from *Measuring Software Design Quality* by David Card with Robert Glass. It strongly suggests special testing of modules with high design complexity. [2] They define design complexity as a function of structural complexity based on fanout[2], data complexity based on the number of I/O variables, and procedural complexity based on the decision count. Other studies have shown similar relationships to metrics such as code size and number of control paths present in a program. [3,4]

These examples show that there are several metrics that are available from product development that are useful for planning what kinds of tests to produce and what areas to test. Besides providing insights for planning tests, QFD, FURPS+, and risk analysis methods such as measuring design complexity are also immediately useful for monitoring and controlling early development work products.

By correctly translating the content and emphases of QFD and FURPS+ to system specifications, you optimize your chances that you are developing and testing the *right product*. By reviewing your designs against these specifications, you provide traceability to your customers' original needs. Measurement of design complexity is one useful way to test that you are producing the *product right*. Together these methods help to reduce the risks of project cancellation or later expensive rework.

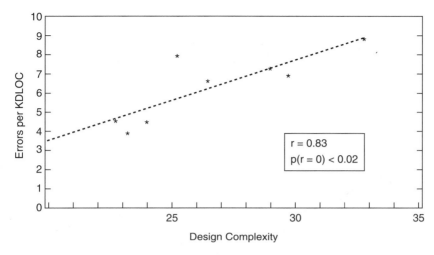

Figure 7-4 Design complexity versus defect density.

TEST: MEASURING PROGRESS AND ENSURING SUCCESS

By the time testing begins, a variety of useful data is available for measuring progress and ensuring success. A traditional management tool for monitoring progress is the PERT chart. This tool shows all major project steps and their interrelationships, and it is the most straightforward tool for monitoring progress. It has not proven to be effective by itself as a tool for software project management, though.

The best indicators of progress for system testing are discovered and fixed defects. The most basic use is to plot these against time, such as in Figure 7-5.

Graphs showing trends provide support for project-management decisions. For a stable process, the amount of time available for testing constrains the number of defects discovered. The curve is usually exponentially shaped with the top flattening as the most difficult to discover defects take more time. Defect fixes are usually constrained during the early stages of testing, because it is difficult to fix the defects as rapidly as they are found. The ideal fix curve is the opposite of the find curve, a decaying exponential.

The trends in Figure 7-5 are considerably different from the ideal, and they show how important it is to understand the assumptions in the ideal case and whether those assumptions apply to a specific project. The project shown in Figure 7-5 was large, with many isolated components and considerable overlap between development and testing. This helps to explain the long linear defect-finding shape. The increased rate of defects in September and the corresponding increased defect backlog were the result of integrating a large complicated part of the product into the system. It not only had defects of its

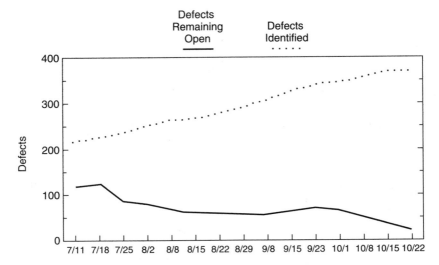

Figure 7-5 Defects identified/defects remaining open.

own, but it also exposed large portions of code that were not tested earlier. Nevertheless, the graphs were valuable to the project manager in understanding project progress and status.

Figure 7-6 shows a graph of the cumulative defects found for another project. [5] Cumulative test hours include all the engineering hours spent by the project team on testing. The graph follows the ideal shape much more closely than in our previous example. This data was taken from a project that used the Goel-Okumoto software reliability growth model. [6] This type of model extends the idea of simply monitoring the trends of defects found and fixed to attempt to control and predict the testing process more accurately. It does this by mapping the initial detected defects onto a formula that projects future defect-finding patterns.

Such models can be very useful, but they do depend on several assumptions. They assume that

  • data used in the model only comes from testing that occurred after system builds contained all the system code,
  • the testing resources for creating and executing new tests remain the same (both in terms of number and abilities of people) throughout test,
  • defects are fixed in a timely manner with no interference with testing.

The key to the use of both simple plots of defects and more sophisticated plots with a testing model is to apply good management judgment to the assumptions you make.

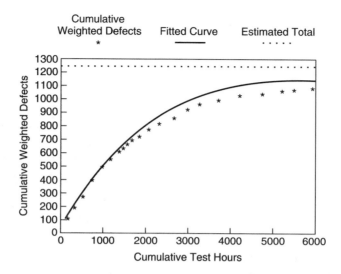

Figure 7-6 Cumulative defects found.

The following empirical model, defined by Henry Kohoutek of HP, falls somewhere between simple monitoring of defects and the use of formal reliability growth models. (The model and its use are explained in more detail in [7,8].) This model is similar to the formal models. It assumes the number of defects in the code is known (or estimated) and what the typical defect finding rates are, but it simplifies the mathematics necessary in the more formal models.

- 25 percent of defects are found and fixed in 2 hours per defect
- 50 percent of defects are found and fixed in 5 hours per defect
- 20 percent of defects are found and fixed in 10 hours per defect
- 4 percent of defects are found and fixed in 20 hours per defect
- 1 percent of defects are found and fixed in 50 hours per defect

Figure 7-7 shows another useful graph that is used with reliability models. It plots the ratio of test-writing time to defects found. You can expect the mean time to find new defects to start high if a test framework must be created. The mean time between defects will then decrease as problem areas appear and tests become more focused. The expected shape is a U-shape where initial test-writing time exposes few defects. A critical mass in the test suite is soon achieved that maximizes the number of defects found for the number of test-writing hours invested. The test-writing process gradually achieves a level of stability that is signalled by reduced defects per hours spent writing new tests.

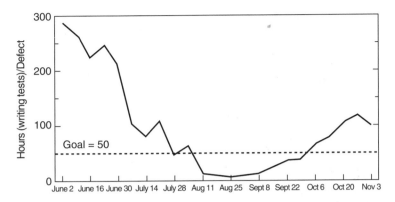

Figure 7-7 Mean time between defects.

In this example, we see that the project team set a completion goal based on the mean time between failures corresponding in the Kohoutek model to the region of the last one percent of defects in the product (50 hours/defect). Sometimes this goal is only based on critical or serious defects. Other times it is based on the discovery of any new defect. In either case, the goal includes investing additional engineering test hours until you spend more than some defined time period above the goal line.

Release Criteria

Ultimately, the testing process must end. The criteria used to judge the end point for testing software systems today vary widely and are often subjective. Because of the large variation in quality that this lack of standardization allowed, HP created a set of measurable criteria to certify that software products for some of its major systems were ready for release. [9] Release criteria such as these represent a balanced set of tests and a measurable baseline against which postrelease quality can be judged. The testing standards include agreed-to goals for the following criteria:

- breadth: testing coverage of user-accessible and internal functions,
- depth: branch coverage testing,
- reliability: continuous hours of operation under stress; stability; ability to recover gracefully from error conditions,
- remaining defect density at release.

We saw examples of branch coverage and stability in Figures 6-2 and 6-3. Figure 7-8 is an example of a defect density plot for one product that was included in a system.

Testing of large HP systems also includes multiple test cycles. We achieve three stages of completion and stability. Each has higher goals for breadth, depth, continuous operation, and defect density, as well as additional usability and performance tests at specific points. For example, the defect goal shown in Figure 7-8 allowed some critical or serious defects. This goal was for a test cycle before the final one.

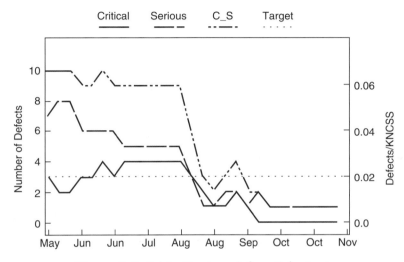

Figure 7-8 Critical/serious defects (lab view).

These goals allow us to integrate increasing numbers of components with known levels of quality. The overall collection of products is very unstable during early test cycles, but it is still usable, and internal lab teams have access to major combinations of the system. This process works well, because we set expectations properly regarding what types and levels of testing have been done.

CUSTOMER USE: MEASURING PRODUCT QUALITY AND TESTING EFFECTIVENESS

After release of a product, we learn how well we achieved the desired level of quality. As during the testing process, the primary management indicator is the incoming defect rate. Figure 7-9 shows three curves of incoming defects (in the form of service requests). They are for the first year after release of a major HP software system that used the certification and testing processes described in the previous section. [10] The number of defects in each case is normalized by the amount of code represented in thousands of non-comment source statements (KNCSS).

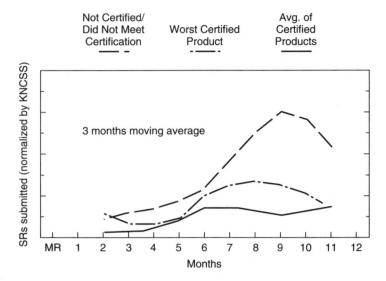

Figure 7-9 Postrelease incoming SR's submitted by customers.

The top curve represents several products that either were not certified or were released without meeting the certification criteria. These conditions were possible, because not all software-submitting entities were part of the same reporting structure. The bottom curve represents the average of a dozen certified products. The middle line shows that the defect rate of even the worst certified product was considerably better than the products that did not meet the certification standards. This graph shows that a combination of good development and testing processes will enable you to confidently predict a low incoming defect rate.

A narrower view of the incoming defect rate is that of hotsites. A hotsite is a customer site with a serious (severely restricted use of product) or critical (product unusable, critical impact on customer operation) problem for which no workaround has been found in a short time. Figure 7-10 shows the backlog of hotsites after two releases of a set of products. We can see that the backlog ramped up quickly, but was also quickly brought under control.

These two measures provide early feedback after product release and initial usage. A third measure, cumulative defect-removal efficiency, provides a total testing process measure. [11] It represents the ratio of defects found before release to the sum of those found both before and after release of a product. Capers Jones says that the typical cumulative defect removal efficiency for commercial U.S. software is a low 90 percent. [8]

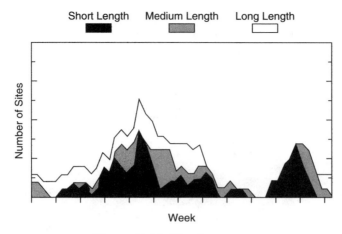

Short Length   Medium Length   Long Length

Figure 7-10 Hotsite status.

FEEDBACK: CLUES TO BETTER DEVELOPMENT AND TESTING PRACTICES

The metrics described thus far will help an organization to produce high-quality products. Still, the software processes used to build these products must be continually improved in order for companies to remain competitive. Data collection during and after the testing process plays a critical role in identifying areas for improvement.

One early sign of problems is bad or unplanned submittals to the testing process. In these cases, sources and/or documentation are incomplete or incorrect such that resubmission is necessary before progress is possible. The simplest metric to track is the number of planned and unplanned submittals. Figure 7-11 shows both for one organization. Most of the unplanned submittals here were due to resubmissions caused by problems in the submitted components.

A pattern of excessive or erratic submittals only quantifies the *symptoms* of one small set of problems, though. What we desire is the permanent elimination of entire classes of problems. The most effective way of accomplishing this is to track all types of defects carefully and investigate why they are introduced in the first place.

Chapter 6 introduced the subject of failure analysis. We can compare failure-analysis data against additional data that is available in order to anticipate whether such problems might exist in other products that are under test. These techniques lead to results such as the design complexity versus defect density graph that we saw in Figure 7-4. Obtaining complexity and defect data early in the development or testing process should influence strategies for testing or for what is submitted to testing.

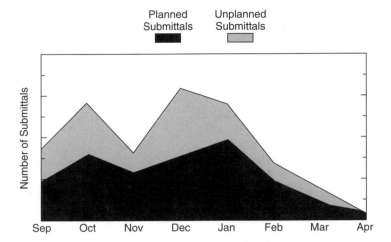

Figure 7-11 Product A submittals by months.

Historical data is useful to motivate a project or an organization to make measurements and to act on the results. Take, for example, the results shown in Figure 7-12. We tracked the number of defects in one product after release. Just over 20 percent of the code contained over 80 percent of the defects reported. After the product had been released for some time, we reverse engineered the source into structured design charts. We then analyzed one component of design complexity (fanout squared, as used in [2]) from the information that is normally available during the design phase. The results of this analysis are in Figure 7-12. They show that if the original design had been

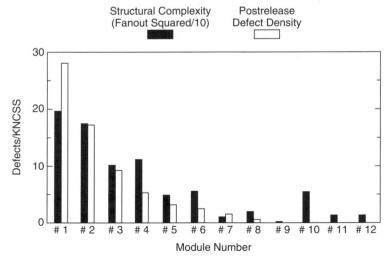

Figure 7-12 Defect analysis by code module.

measured, the relative expectations for defects would have been available very early in the project. At a minimum, these tendencies would have been useful to know before testing started.

The data for other projects might not line up as nicely as they did here, but such correlations are encouraging.

CONCLUSION

The cost and complexity of testing increasingly larger software systems is a major factor that affects our ability to deliver high-quality systems on schedule. Software metrics play a valuable role in managing the planning and execution of this critical phase of the development process. Detailed defect information is particularly important in decisions as we approach product release. This data must be examined in the context of project risks and incoming defect trends.

A model was presented that provides a framework for choosing meaningful metrics to manage the testing phase. It gave objectives and measures for managing four key aspects of any testing effort:

- establishing goals for testing,
- executing the testing process,
- measuring the results of the testing effort,
- changing the testing and development processes.

Project managers today seldom take the time to analyze data for more than one or two of the views presented in the last four chapters. And yet, they could make better decisions if they spent more time. There is a strong need for more complete automation of the data collection, analysis, and presentation process than is generally available. Such automation would include comparison of data against preset limits and automatic generation of exception reports, as well as generating many of the graphs shown earlier. The next chapter describes such a system more completely.

BIBLIOGRAPHY

1. Tier, G., Private communications, (Oct 1990).
2. Card, D. with R. Glass, *Measuring Software Design Quality*, Englewood Cliffs, NJ: Prentice-Hall, Inc., 1990, p. 55.
3. Curtis, B., S. Sheppard, and P. Milliman, "Third Time Charm: Stronger Prediction of Programmer Performance by Software Complexity Metrics," *Proceedings of the Fourth International Conference on Software Engineering*, (July 1979), pp. 356–360.

4. Rambo, R., P. Buckley, and E. Branyan, "Establishment and Validation of Software Metric Factors," *Proceedings of the International Society of Parametric Analysts Seventh Annual Conference*, (May 1985), pp. 406–417.

5. Kruger, G., "Project Management Using Software Reliability Growth Models," *Hewlett-Packard Journal*, (June 1988), pp. 30–35.

6. Goel, A., and K. Okumoto, "A Time-Dependent Error Detection Rate Model for Software Reliability and Other Performance Measures," *IEEE Transactions on Reliability*, Vol. R-28, (1979), pp. 206–211.

7. Kohoutek, H., "A Practical Approach to Software Reliability Management," *Proceedings of the 29th EOQC Conference on Quality and Development*, Vol. 2 (June 1985), pp. 211–220.

8. Grady, R. and D. Caswell, *Software Metrics: Establishing a Company-Wide Program*, Englewood Cliffs, NJ: Prentice-Hall, Inc., 1987, pp. 65, 82-95, 110, 112, 113, 159.

9. Davey, S., R. D. Classick, D. Lau, J. Loos, and B. Noble, *Spectrum Program Metrics and Certification Handbook*, HP Software Metrics Technology, Software Development Technology Lab, Information Software Division. Version 2.0 (Oct. 12, 1990).

10. Lau, Danny, "The Success of the Spectrum Software Certification Program," *HP Software Productivity Conference Proceedings*, (August 1988), pp. 109–117.

11. Jones, C., "Measuring Programming Quality and Productivity," *IBM Systems Journal*, Vol. 17, no. 1 (1978), pp. 39–63.

8

Work Product Analysis: The Philosopher's Stone of Software?

*Thesis: Use **work-product analysis** tools that both solve significant engineering problems and provide useful size and complexity data.*

It is an age-old dream to achieve perfection. An example from early times is the mythical philosopher's stone sought by alchemists to transform base metals into gold. In recent times, we have developed tools that have helped us achieve highly complex, yet highly reliable hardware. But, so far, the philosopher's stone for transforming ordinary software into easy-to-maintain, highly reliable software has been more difficult to find.

One attribute of software that makes it more difficult than hardware to produce with high quality is captured in its name. Unlike hardware, software components and designs are largely unconstrained by physical bounds. By contrast, the evolution of hardware components has been artificially constrained by the "hard" physical limits of packaging. There has been a natural migration of circuits that once fit on parts of a printed circuit board to fit onto chips, and this has aided the creative process by providing at least one limit on the introduction of complexity at each evolutionary step.

With software, we have no such constraints, and the greatest challenge of software project management is to limit the various intermediate and final products to the levels of complexity that are really necessary. This has led to the introduction of a wide variety of methods and life-cycle models. These help to decompose problems in logical ways that include intermediate steps where we can test whether the right thing is produced the right way.

WORK PRODUCTS AND METRICS

Figure 8-1 is a simplified version of the traditional waterfall model of the software life cycle. It shows examples of work products supported today by software tools that produce outputs of the life-cycle phases. (A work product is an intermediate or final output of software development that describes the design, operation, manufacture, or test of some portion of a deliverable or salable product. It is not the final product.) There are at least four ways that these work products encourage better standards for software components.

1. Each work product follows some form of standard representation that guarantees a degree of common terminology. Training engineers in their use encourages the use and sharing of the best practices and helps eliminate past problems.

2. Tool support allows automated checks and immediate feedback to engineers. This feedback most commonly takes the form of error messages and warnings.

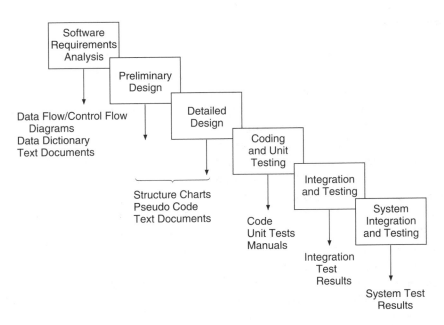

Figure 8-1 A waterfall development model with sample work products.

3. Common terminology simplifies inspections of work products by other team members. Inspections expose some defects that the automated checks cannot detect.

4. The tools can also generate metric data and sometimes calculate numerical figures of merit (or goodness). Both engineers and managers use the data to track progress. Unlike the automated checks that clearly identify defects, a figure of merit suggests the *probability* of defects occurring.

Software Metrics

People in the software field have experimented with metrics for virtually every form of work product since the earliest lines-of-code metric and later attempts to analyze code complexity. As new methods to represent specifications and designs have appeared, metrics have informally — and then more formally — appeared for each of them. For example, function points followed Hierarchical Input-Process-Output diagrams, [1] bang/design weight followed structured analysis/structured design. [2] (Bang and design weight are measures of functionality derived from dataflow-diagram and structure-chart representations of software.) And as computer power increased, people even created tools to classify the readability of textual documents (for example, the Flesch-Kincaid readability metric). [3]

Why is it that we need to attach numbers to these fragments of intellectual activity? Managers want to know if they are heading in the right direction at the right speed, and they want to know when they have successfully reached their destination. A manager's three primary objectives during development are to

- achieve measurable progress,
- provide project visibility for management review,
- ensure success.

Recognizing these general objectives, it becomes easier to see how metrics naturally derive from the methods we use. Take, for example, the lines-of-code metric. Very early in the days of software development, rules of thumb evolved like "People can code an average of eight lines per day." We needed such crude rules to achieve the objectives of measuring progress and providing visibility. Later, we measured many projects and many associated project variables, and we applied statistical techniques to improve our initial crude rules.

We've seen this evolution repeated for various other work products and metrics with varying degrees of success. Success has depended on the different ways that engineers and managers have used the tools.

Table 8-1 summarizes some of the tools and metrics available today and the development phases to which they apply. It includes work products for prototype code and data dictionaries, because they are widely used today, although they represent two cases where metrics research has been very limited (and so no metrics are shown).

THE ENGINEERING INTERFACE

In the past, engineers have expressed little need for metrics data, because the data was meaningful mostly to a project, not to an individual engineer. The engineers needed timely data which was tuned to the problem at hand.

Phase	Work Product	Tools	Metrics
Specifications/ Requirements	Text	Writing analysis	Flesch–Kincaid readability
	Spreadsheet	Quality function deployment (QFD)	Weighted customer needs
	Prototype	Fourth generation languages	–
	Dataflow diagrams	Structured analysis	Bang
Design	Text	Writing analysis	Flesch–Kincaid readability
	Structure charts	Structured design	Design weight, fanout ^{2}
	Data dictionary	Structured analysis/ design	–
	Pseudocode	Program design language	Cyclomatic complexity
Implementation	Code	Compilers, complexity analysis	Lines of code, cyclomatic complexity
	Unit tests	Code coverage	Percent coverage
	Manuals	Writing analysis	Flesch-Kincaid readability
	Performance tests	Ad hoc	Execution times

Table 8-1 Engineering work products, tools, and metrics.

Code Complexity

Consider the acceptance of one metric over time. In a 1976 article [4], Tom McCabe described a metric of cyclomatic complexity. It is derived from an analysis of potential paths through source code. Since then, several studies have correlated the McCabe metric with the probability of defects. One of these concluded that modules with complexity values greater than 10 were much more defect-prone than those with lower values, [5] while another determined that a complexity value of 14 correlated better. [6] However, other studies showed that defects correlated almost as well with code size. [7] Because the McCabe metric was derived from code, the acceptance of the metric was slow. It hardly seemed worth the extra effort of computing it.

At Hewlett-Packard, we repeated these studies involving code size, complexity metrics, and defects with similar results. More recently, however, we have used commercially available tools that not only provide the metric values but also a graphical representation of the analyzed code. The results have been much better. HP engineers found the visual images of complexity much more useful than the numeric values. [8]

The primary reason for this seems to be that the graph gives them information in a more useful form. A single number tells them only that they have a problem. The graph, and its cross-references to their source code, helps them understand the location of their problem and what some steps might be to fix it. The graphs excite managers, because their availability during the coding phase encourages engineers to produce more maintainable software. This is not to say that the numeric values produced by the tools are ignored: The McCabe metric provides managers and engineers a simple numerical figure of merit.

Figures 8-2 and 8-3 show two examples of modules from one product. One has a cyclomatic complexity of 10; the other is a much less acceptable 26. Engineers take pride in more structured-looking graphs. They know that it will be difficult to explain a graph like the one in Figure 8-3 to their peers in an inspection. They also know that the code for such a graph is undoubtedly more error-prone, difficult to test, and difficult to maintain than the one in Figure 8-2. Unfortunately, the code in question was created before the tools we now use were widely available.

Design Complexity

The challenge to the engineer is that the complexity identified in one work product often depends on or affects the complexity in another. For example, consider the flow graph in Figure 8-3. It represents the logic contained within

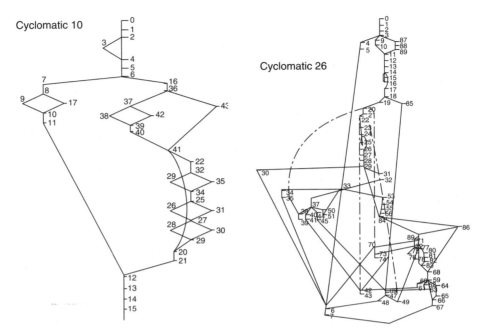

Figure 8-2 A program with acceptable complexity.

Figure 8-3 A program with high complexity.

the top box of the structure chart in Figure 8-4. One approach to reducing the cyclomatic complexity is to move parts of the module of Figure 8-3 to other modules, but this could easily increase the structural complexity of the total system.

The metric of design weight [2] also helps quantify the results of proposed changes. It is derived from the dataflow tokens at the boundary of a module, and the control-flow tokens. Design weight is a function of the token count associated with a module and the predicted number of decisions based on the data structure. This more global perspective complements the strictly modular one of the McCabe metric. Figure 8-4 gives the design-weight value of 654.55 that was computed by an HP tool for the module in question, and the values for the modules with which it communicates.

In the figure, a data couple represents a data value that is passed from one module to another. A control couple represents a flag or switch that affects the order of execution in another module. A hybrid couple represents a passed data value that is also evaluated by another module to affect the order of execution. A bidirectional hybrid couple is one that is both input to and output from a module.

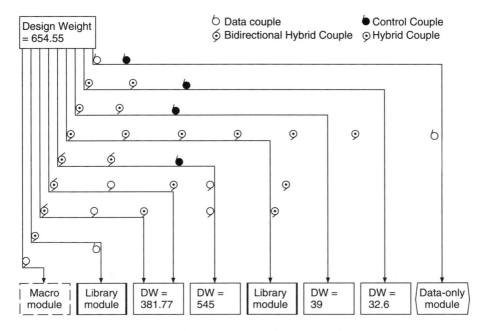

Figure 8-4 A structure chart with design weight analysis.

Our experience with design weight is not as advanced as with the McCabe metric. Initial investigations suggest that values of design weight greater than 200 potentially lead to complex code. This is supported by this real example. Even without knowing a "magic number" for design weight, a developer can see from the relative values shown in Figure 8-4 that it would be much better to move some of the code into a new module or to move code to the modules with weights of 39 or 32.6 than to the ones with much greater weights.

It may not even be necessary to measure design complexity in as sophisticated a way as design weight. The data shown in the previous chapter in Figure 7-12 suggested that simply measuring fanout[2] might give us a strong indication of potential problems.

The design decisions illustrated in this example are choices that engineers face daily. The advantage of these graphical tools and metrics is that they provide additional information to support the gut feelings of the engineer so decisions will be made more effectively. Having these two views helps the engineer finish a design for a product that will be more reliable and easier to maintain.

Testing

Consider another example that occurs later in the life cycle, during unit test. During test, an internal HP tool called a branch code analyzer reports on how well tests cover all the potential paths in a program.

Branch coverage was initially described and shown in Figure 6-3. The reports of the analyzer tell an engineer which parts of code were tested and how often they were tested. Combining this ability with a well-planned testing strategy helps us effectively validate software. Figure 8-5 illustrates a typical report from the analyzer.

Once again, the attractiveness of the tool to developers is a key to its success. One developer wrote,

> It is psychologically motivating to the programmer in that it gives instant feedback by way of the summary report that produces the final percentage value. After working to design and debug a large piece of software, I look forward to the final exercising of the code with the analyzer. It's a challenge to find ways to push the percentage up, and it has helped me to find bugs within my code that had not previously surfaced.

The use of this tool doesn't end at unit test, either. It has played an important role in HP system and integration testing for more than five years.

Procedure Name	# Times Invoked	Existing Paths	Number of Paths Hit	Percent of Paths Hit
File: print.c				
collect_range	391905	9	9	100.0
mystmcmp	72	6	6	100.0
* print_MA_table	0	21	0	0.0
print_MC_table	7	34	28	82.4
print_literal	3476	3	3	100.0
print_msg	712	13	8	61.5
print_page_listing	9	12	11	91.7
print_page_summary	2	10	6	60.0
print_prompt	30	15	14	93.3
print_range_status	3	44	24	54.5
print_ranges	17	7	5	71.4
print_test_pages	408304	12	12	100.0
user-collect_range	16348	11	10	90.9
valid_response	194	5	5	100.0
	821079	202	141	69.8

Figure 8-5 Typical branch coverage analysis.

Work-Product Analysis

Figure 8-6 shows the process of work product analysis during development. The work products represent the graphic and textual outputs of various life-cycle steps all the way from analysis of customer requirements through testing. Computers analyze these outputs for the responsible engineers, and other

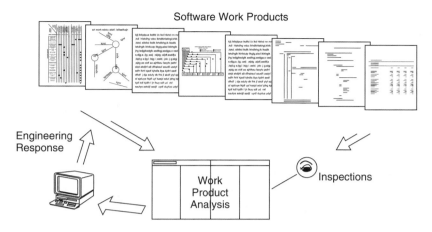

Figure 8-6 Work-product analysis.

engineers inspect these outputs. The feedback is timely and specific, and the complete working framework encourages well-documented, quality software products.

Automated work-product-analysis tools provide the benefits of standard terminology, automated checks and feedback, inspection aids, metrics, and numerical figures of merit. These benefits help both developers and managers of projects. However, the management approach to them all — and to the metrics particularly — must be nonthreatening if the tools are to be used successfully.

THE MANAGEMENT INTERFACE

There is a delicate balance between data used by engineers and the same data used by project managers. Unless the same data is used and interpreted under the same ground rules by both engineers and project managers, you run the risk of losing your engineers' confidence and thus jeopardizing the accuracy of the data.

It is the job of project managers to achieve the goals of measuring progress, providing visibility for management reviews, and ensuring success in a nonthreatening way. Their activities include

- estimating,
- planning,
- scheduling,
- tracking.

One of the greatest promises of CASE is the automated delivery of metric data to the project manager. Data that is often too difficult and time-consuming to obtain is crucial for making good decisions. Table 8-2 shows the relationships among the users of various metrics, how they use the data, and the most favorable timing availability of the data.

Primary User	Engineers	Project Manager	Project Manager	Project Manager/ Program Manager
Use of Data	Understand & Change Software Work Products	Identify trends & potential problem areas	Adjust schedules	Adjust plans, revise estimates
Optimum Timing	Seconds– Minutes	Hours	Weeks	Months

Table 8-2 Timeliness of metrics data.

The table represents a continuum of time that varies from real-time feedback to engineers to much longer sampling periods that are more appropriate to tracking and managing the activities of large teams. This helps you to understand why the most commonly available automated project-management tools — PERT programs and estimation tools — provide little support for project managers when schedules become tight and when they must convince others that the project is on track. These tools have update intervals of weeks or months, and it is difficult to keep their data current.

Project trend indicators are much more effective in alerting managers that events on a PERT chart need to change or that estimates are incorrect because of poor assumptions. Metric data is an invaluable supplement to these other tools for project managers. The integration of project milestone data and the data from various work-product-analysis tools into a convenient, accessible summary for project managers will provide a powerful capability for managing more effectively. Figure 8-7 shows an example of such a summary, which we call a project-management status table, as it might appear on a project manager's terminal. [9]

It consists of data from a combination of work-product-analysis tools, source-control tools, defect-tracking tools, and weekly reports by software engineers. Items shown with asterisks beside them violate limits that were predefined (by the project manager). These alert the project manager to potential problems as they develop.

Project Management Status Table

MODULE	FUNCTION	RESP. ENG.	STATUS	EST. NCSS	ACTUAL NCSS	CURRENT COMPLEXITY	DEFECTS	TEST COVERAGE
DISPLAY		D.C.	Test	390	442		8*	55
	MATCH				73	8	6*	96
	GETUSERSTRING				100	42*		100
	GETADDEDIT				64	25*	2*	32
	GETMAININPUT				56	5		45
	GETDELETEINPUT				53	7		60
	GETONELINE				36	11		100
	GETPLOTMENU				60	8		25
ARC		M.G.	Design insp.	60	0	72	4*	0
SUM		M.G.	Coding	100	209*	15*	3*	0
CRL		S.B.	Design	215	0	236*	1	0
SUB		D.D.	Test Done	250	1279*	10	4	85
			← Source Control System		← Counters	← SA/SD Tools Code Analysis Tools	← Defect Tracking System	← Code Coverage

Figure 8-7 Project management status table.

For example, the actual non-comment source statements (NCSS) for the module SUM are more than twice the original estimate. Why was the estimate off by so much? This might be a signal that the design was misunderstood or is changing. Some of the other flagged conditions shown in this example include design weights greater than 200, McCabe complexities greater than 14, and defect densities greater than 10.

Without the various tools to determine the data shown here and without a way to consolidate the data into an interface like the one shown in the figure, you can understand how difficult it is today for project managers to know the true status of a project and for them to make timely decisions. It is just not practical to manually gather all the data in a timely fashion. And without the data, project managers are operating blindfolded.

Figure 8-8 illustrates how the same sources of work-product analysis and inspections shown in Figure 8-6 provide tracking feedback to project managers — and do so as effectively as they do for engineers. Project managers use this data to make decisions that ultimately affect project schedules, plans, and estimates. The power is in the range of data automatically available from these new tools. This is data that the technically rooted project manager has always known was available but has never had the time and resources to obtain.

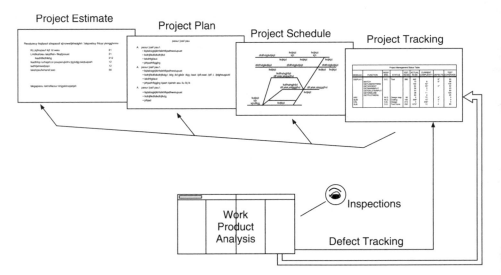

Figure 8-8 Project management use of work-product analysis.

MEASUREMENT TRENDS FOR THE PUBLIC INTERFACE _____

The project-management status table is a powerful concept, but the project manager will want it to be relatively private. The manager is probably the only person who can correctly interpret what might appear to be an excessive number of boundary violations without a lot of research. On the other hand, the data in the status table must be accessible on a per-engineer basis, or else the engineers might perceive it as a threat. Engineers must know the boundary-condition values ahead of time. The system should also probably notify them some time before the status table receives its periodic update.

Why would engineers perceive a project-management status table as a threat? Our experience shows that engineers don't mind quality-criteria targets and the collection of data to achieve their goals as long as they participate in setting those goals and agree with them. But, when data collection and interpretation are hidden from them, they will wonder whether the groundrules have changed without their being informed. (These issues are explored in more detail in the next two chapters.)

A project manager can also derive various trends from stored data and present them publicly. These are useful to both the team and to others who need regular status updates, like senior management and customers. Some of the graphs in this section's figures are automated by-products of the tools that support a status table. Others are derived from a combination of that data and other data that the project manager must learn by being in close touch with the development team and its activities. The graphs in this section are all real graphs from actual projects. Unfortunately, when the graphs were drawn, an automated status table did not exist. This cost the project managers extra effort and time for data collection, analysis, and presentation.

The first graph, shown in Figure 8-9 and taken from *Software Metrics: Establishing a Company-Wide Program*, [9] is simply a plot of engineering output (code in this case) against time. Is the output being produced in proportion to estimates?

There are other measures that you can use for plotting engineering output besides code, including percentage of weighted functionality complete, bang, design weight, and function points. Graphs of each of these measures are effective in showing progress, since they show actual output against planned output. Of course, their success depends heavily on the accuracy of a projected end point.

Graphs of output versus time are generally by-products of work-product-analysis tools. A necessary complement to these graphs comes from a defect-tracking system, although defects are all too often accurately tracked only *after* product release, not before. The most natural time to require accurate

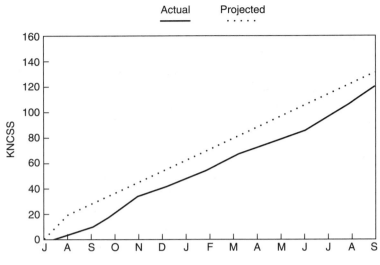

Figure 8-9 Total code generated.

reporting of defect data before release is after formal testing begins. Despite people's sensitivity about making mistakes, engineers today more readily accept that accurate defect reporting for system-level and integration-level testing is necessary in order to coordinate the change efforts of many engineers.

Nevertheless, reporting defects is labor-intensive, and project managers must be ready to devote their energy to encouraging the timely recording of accurate defect information. This is particularly necessary when the development team must double as the testing team. An automated defect-tracking system is the cornerstone of an integrated development environment, and plots of its data can provide several trends that project managers might want to monitor.

One trend that is highly useful to project teams is a graph of defects against time. An example is repeated from the previous chapter in Figure 8-10. Such graphs are easily generated when an automated defect-tracking system is available. These graphs show both the trend of defects discovered and the trend of defects that remain unfixed (open). In the later stages of a project, these trends are just as important as the trends of output versus estimates are during the earlier stages.

Perhaps the most difficult time for a project manager is the period early in a project when no code or prototypes yet exist. During this creative period in a project, it is very difficult to quantify design size. As a result, progress often seems to alternate between slow and rapid as engineers overcome conceptual blocks. Thus, plotting design progress can be frustrating.

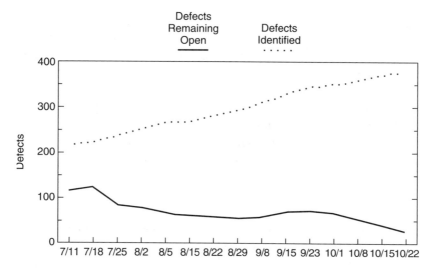

Figure 8-10 Defects identified/defects remaining open.

An alternative way of looking at progress during this period is to calculate the number of design defects that you *expect* to find during inspections, and to plan and plot the inspections (design reviews) necessary to find these defects. Figure 8-11 shows an example. The estimated number of design defects and the time to find them during inspections are based on past historical data. These are described more fully in Chapter 11.

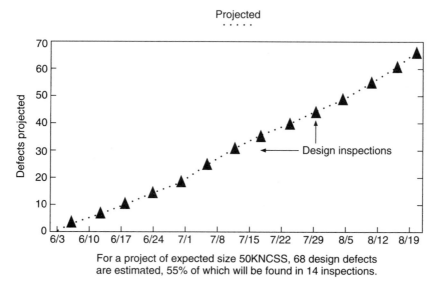

For a project of expected size 50KNCSS, 68 design defects are estimated, 55% of which will be found in 14 inspections.

Figure 8-11 Tracking design inspections by predicting the number of design defects.

Inspections can help a team to remove conceptual blocks, because even informal inspections encourage clarification of issues and discussion of different approaches. The purpose of the plot is to encourage holding the inspections on a predetermined schedule. You must take care to ensure that the team understands and agrees with this type of scheduling, and you must be flexible enough to postpone some formal inspections and to replace them with informal ones. Defects are not formally reported during *informal* inspections.

The inspections example is an unusual one, but it illustrates two points about work-product analysis and project management. First, it emphasizes that inspections remain an integral part of work-product analysis. It will be a long time before we eliminate them. Second, it emphasizes how useful it is to begin systematic defect tracking as early as possible. Such tracking normally starts after formal testing begins. Here formal inspections really represent the first appearance of *formal* testing in the development process.

The idea in Figure 8-11 of graphing defects over time is not particularly different from the approach used in Figure 8-10 — it is simply done at a different time period during the development process.

How do the examples in this section compare with the alternatives that past project managers used without the benefits that recent tools and environments provide? Figure 8-12 compares automated and manual tracking and reporting methods. The top half of the figure shows information that has often driven past decisions. The bottom half shows typical information now available to drive decisions. In both cases, the information is lined up with the relevant parts of the life cycle.

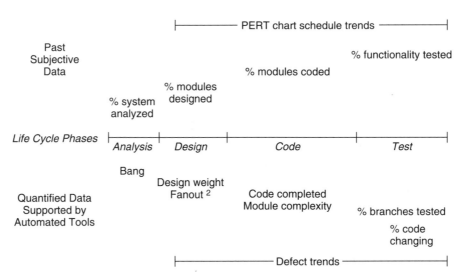

Figure 8-12 Conceptual model of old and new ways of reporting project progress.

Common methods of displaying progress in the past included a PERT chart and reports of percentage completion. PERT charts are not useful without up-to-date data from the programming environment. Reporting percentage completion also has its weaknesses: Perhaps no other words are as capable of striking terror in the hearts of project managers as "I'm 90 percent done" (it sometimes seems as if programs are 90 percent done for months). Yet, without measurable work products, we depend totally on subjective guesses of completion. The best results will occur when PERT charts and completion estimates are backed up by the solid data and trends that metrics supply.

The examples in Figure 8-12 of metrics supported by automated tools must continue to evolve as our development methods continue to change and improve. They already offer substantial clarity over past subjective methods, however, in quantifying and showing progress.

CONCLUSION

The complexity of developing software and of the organizations required to develop and support it continue to increase. Work-product-analysis tools help to measure and control development complexity, and data from these tools can be brought together to reduce the complexity of project management. Unlike the past manual use of some of these methods, the tools used today finally provide a sense of control to developers and managers alike.

Perhaps these tools and environments are like the mythical philosopher's stone that would turn lead into gold. The ability to do automated software work-product analysis certainly holds promise for helping engineers to recognize and reduce unnecessary complexity and for managers to receive more timely feedback about progress and quality.

Our experience with work-product-analysis tools and data in real projects shows that the combination of tools, methods, and metrics results in improved product reliability and more maintainable software. Whether the evolution of these tools will proceed far enough to reverse the long-term trend of increased complexity and help start eliminating process steps without sacrificing high quality remains to be seen.

One thing does seem clear: The automation that we are seeing provides accurate data to plot trends for project managers. These graphs have never been readily available in the past. This alone will help managers to make better, more informed decisions. Even if we don't yet have a software philosopher's stone, perhaps we have uncovered some philosopher's pebbles.

BIBLIOGRAPHY

1. Albrecht, A. J., "Measuring Application Development Productivity," *Proceedings of the Joint SHARE/GUIDE/IBM Application Development Symposium, Share*, Chicago, IL: (Oct. 1979), pp. 83–92.
2. DeMarco, T., *Controlling Software Projects*, New York: Yourdon Press, 1982, pp. 80, 106.
3. Losa, J., J. Aagard, and J. Kincaid, "Readability Grade Levels of Selected Navy Technical School Curricula," *Report No.: TAEG-TM-83-2*, Naval Training Analysis and Evaluation Group, Orlando, FL., (Feb 1983).
4. McCabe, T., "A Complexity Measure," *IEEE Transactions on Software Engineering*, Vol. SE-2, no. 4, Dec. 1976, pp. 308–320.
5. Walsh, T. J., "A Software Reliability Study Using a Complexity Measure," *Proceedings of the 1979 National Computer Conference*. Montvale, NJ: AFIPS Press (1979), pp. 761–768.
6. Rambo, R., P. Buckley, and E. Branyan, "Establishment and Validation of Software Metric Factors," *Proceedings of the International Society of Parametric Analysts Seventh Annual Conference*. Germantown, MD: (May 1985), pp. 406–417.
7. Curtis, B., S. B. Sheppard, and P. Milliman, "Third Time Charm: Stronger Prediction of Programmer Performance by Software Complexity Metrics," *Proceedings of the Fourth International Conference on Software Engineering*, (July 1979), pp. 356–360.
8. Ward, W., "Software Defect Prevention Using McCabe's Complexity Metric," *Hewlett-Packard Journal*, Vol. 40, no. 2 (April 1989), pp. 64–69.
9. Grady, R. and D. Caswell, *Software Metrics: Establishing a Company-Wide Program*, Englewood Cliffs, NJ: Prentice-Hall, Inc.,1987, p. 31, 216.

Part Two

The Strategic Application of Software Metrics – Process Improvement

Sensitive Usage of Metrics Data	The concept of **public and private data** helps to drive effective collection and analysis of metrics data (Chapter 9).	**Sensitive interpretation and use** of data are basic good management practice (Chapter 10).
Process Improvement through Defect Analysis	**Software failure analysis** helps to identify opportunities for process improvement and to measure the impact of changes (Chapters 11 and 12).	
Validation of Best Practices	**"Software engineering" practices** are those that have been measured and proven effective (Chapter 13).	All software process changes should be evaluated in terms of a measurable **return on investment** (Chapter 14).

9

Public and Private Data

*Thesis: Use the concept of **public and private data** to drive your decisions on how to collect and analyze data.*

When I give software metrics talks, I usually close with a warning that metrics are not consistently enough defined that anyone should consider using them to measure and evaluate people. After one such talk, I was approached by an excited executive. He had seen how metrics would help his operation to manage software much better, but he had missed my closing message. He concluded that, with metrics, he could measure his software people for the first time in the same way that he measured his manufacturing output. What he didn't realize was that his enthusiasm to measure his *people*, instead of his processes, would probably cause his implementation of metrics to fail.

When Debbie Caswell and I wrote *Software Metrics: Establishing a Company-Wide Program*, we specifically included a chapter called "The Human Element" to address this problem. [1] In it, we recalled many stories that emphasized the sensitivities of people to measurement. This chapter appears to have struck a resonant chord, for we have received many compliments and thanks for it. In fact, when I give talks, people always want to hear more such stories. Sometimes I think that they enjoy hearing these "tabloid horror stories."

In this chapter and the next, we will explore the first of several strategic aspects of metrics implementation: people issues. We'll first look at how people react to data collection, and then we will develop 12 software metric "rules of etiquette" from real project experiences.

PRIVATE DATA

In "The Human Element," the focus was on change and how people adapt to it. Equally important is an understanding of who owns what data and when it is appropriate to share the data with others. We have included a class exercise on the identification and use of public and private data in a Software Metrics class taught in Hewlett-Packard for many years. We found the concept of public versus private data to be very helpful both as a learning tool and as a ground rule in everyday practice. It provides students with a framework that helps to ensure the correct use of data. The exercise also provides a convenient opportunity to air students' concerns over potential misuse of data. The terms "public" and "private" data help the class to internalize how and why people react to measurement the way they do.

Defect data is one common example of data that people prefer to be private. People just don't like to find out that they did something wrong, and they hate it even more when other people also know. The question that we like to pose to the class is "How do we analyze defects to improve processes rather than to blame people?" We are looking for a way to instill in the class an attitude toward problem-solving instead of finger-pointing.

There are various times when defect data is made public. For example, people outside of the project team learn the number of customer-found defects after a product is released. Even earlier, after a software product enters final test, the number of defects becomes public to other groups. At these times, the project manager (and, hopefully, the developers) have said, "We're done; we think that this code is clean."

Private data becomes public at well-defined handoffs or transitions. When such a handoff exists, developers know that they are accountable for defects that are found later. That doesn't mean that they are any more comfortable with these defects. Often the causes of defects are still beyond their control. Should they be individually accountable, even at these points? Yes, and no.

Inspections

One of the most powerful techniques that we use in developing software is inspections. We can look at an inspection as a handoff, similar to the later transitions to final test or release. At each inspection, developers also know that they are accountable for defects that are found, but when defects are found during inspections, they won't be found later by customers. Also, when inspections are properly run, these defects only become public to the inspection team. So these defects are less embarrassing than defects that are found later. At an inspection, there is less of a tendency for developers to be defensive than when confronted with a mistake under pressure. It is easier for them to try to understand their mistakes and to prevent them from occurring again. Defect data prior to inspections is private to individuals. After inspections, the data is public, although still only to the project team.

Another important benefit of inspections is that there is an implied transfer of accountability from the individual to the team. After an inspection team has approved a design or a module of code, that *team* shares the "blame" if customers find additional problems. Developers and managers should also be motivated to hold inspections, because it is a proven fact that inspections help find problems that even the best developers overlook.

We've been using inspections as a typical example of a handoff point. The key idea is that data changes from being private to public *at some agreed-upon handoff* between an individual and some larger group, usually a project team. Even then, some data that is known beyond individuals still remains private to a project.

DATA THAT IS PRIVATE TO A PROJECT

Whereas individuals are particularly sensitive to defect data, project teams are also sensitive to time data. This sensitivity is just as natural, because an entire team is accountable for delivering a product. The software industry's record for delivering products on schedule isn't particularly good, either. It's not surprising that management asks for detailed estimates and regular reassurance that a project is on schedule.

So team progress is generally held private to the project team, except when the manager is called upon to report at status meetings. Then our software managers often apply the well-known software engineering principle of information hiding. This principle normally applies to writing software. In that context, it says that a software module should only provide information at its interfaces that other modules require to do their jobs correctly. In the management case, the interfaces refer to project communications to management and other relevant organizations. These are groups who do have a need to know project status.

Management Information Hiding

How does stretching the analogy to information hiding apply here? Consider our earlier discussion of inspections. An inspection is a process where a group of peers reviews a software work product against its earlier form of the requirements or design. We can interpret a project review as *an inspection of*

project progress against the design of a project (the project plan). The reason that
"information hiding" often occurs during a project review is that our plans
seldom include projections for many metric values that become available as a
project proceeds. For example, detailed module size breakdowns are usually
not included in a project plan. Relative expected complexity of the modules is
almost never included. The expected number of defects and when and how the
team expects to find them are not included. These are all values that are
frequently measured and plotted for projects in Hewlett-Packard, though we
seldom see them in project plans.

When this data is not considered in the planning process, it means that
there is no prior buyoff by the team members on what we might expect of such
numbers. It also means that no expectations have been set for management. In
order to avoid discussion of these topics, some managers give a subjective
assessment of progress: "We're 50 percent done with this part, 75 percent with
that part, and 90 percent with the rest."

A better approach is to define what will be tracked early during project
planning. Decide what trends can be displayed that the team and management
will believe correctly displays progress. Include these in a visible project plan
and provide regular updates using these trends.

It doesn't make sense to say that all "management information hiding" is
bad. It is neither desirable nor practical for everyone to know everything about
a project that the project manager knows. Information hiding crosses the line
from desirable to bad when it is a result of inadequate planning or concealing
relevant management issues. The symptoms of this are reports primarily
consisting of subjective data, sudden schedule shifts, and surprises.

In summary, data that is typically private to a project team includes
detailed estimates and actuals of number of modules, size and complexity of
modules, and projections for how many defects will be found and when. When
estimated values have been included in early project plans, the team feels more
comfortable with making both the estimated and the actual data public. Then,
snapshots of the data are included in project reviews, and public displays of
charts or graphs are posted. A key point here is that the team feels ownership
for the use and interpretation of this data, and the sharing of this data
generally results in a higher level of confidence in the project's progress for
everyone.

DATA THAT IS PUBLIC BEYOND A PROJECT

It is possible to further qualify access and use of data to increasingly larger
groups. For this discussion, we look at an entire R&D Lab. A typical Hewlett-
Packard R&D Lab is autonomous, has between 30 and 150 engineers, and
works on a single product line.

We have already seen that when data is shared, there is an acknowledgment of accountability for results, both at the private level and at the private-to-a-project level. A lab is accountable for its schedules, its budget, its quality, and the functionality of its products. So the metric values that are public within such an organization are calendar times, defect rates, project costs, and whatever measure of functionality that best applies. Note, though, that as we aggregate data more and more, we generally summarize more, and these public reports don't show some of the detail required by project managers and engineers for some project decisions.

Figure 9-1 shows typical examples of how experienced project managers believe that public and private data should be used.

PRIVATE (to-individual)	PRIVATE (to project team) (PUBLIC to team members)	PUBLIC (to company or lab)
Defect rates (by individual)	Defect rates (beyond indiv.)	Defect rates (by project)
Defect rates (by module)	NCSS/module	NCSS (by product)
Defects rates (under dev.)	Estimated NCSS/module	Effort (by project)
Number of compiles	No. of reinspections	Calendar times
	Defects/module (prerel.)	Defects/module (postrel.)
		Effort/defect (average)

Figure 9-1 Examples of public and private data.

Not all of these examples necessarily apply to all organizations, nor is the entire list comprehensive. Figure 9-1 does illustrate what managers can reasonably plan to measure and how the information can be used.

CONCLUSION

What information hiding exists in your organization? Is it all appropriate, or does it exist because your plans are incomplete or your processes are flawed? Thinking in terms of "public" and "private" data helps both managers and engineers to better understand who should have access to what data and how knowledge of the data should be applied. First, identify all the handoffs and transitions in a project's life. At each such milestone, identify which data will be available to a larger group that assumes responsibility for the success or failure of a project. Finally, make sure everyone understands how and when each metric will be used.

Remember that your decisions are only as good as the data on which they are based. Maintain the integrity of your data and honor the privacy of others' data when it is appropriate, and you will create an environment of trust where people will perform more effectively.

BIBLIOGRAPHY

1. Grady, R. and D. Caswell, *Software Metrics: Establishing a Company-Wide Program*, Englewood Cliffs, NJ: Prentice-Hall, Inc., 1987, Chapter 7.

10

Software
Metrics
Etiquette

*Thesis: Apply your best management **sensitivity to the interpretation and use** of software metrics data.*

One evening I was working late on a project that several of us on the HP Software Metrics Council had initiated. It involved some work with structure charts that one of my engineers had prepared. I managed to get about 30 charts ready for printout before I left for the night and started a job that would print them overnight.

When I came in the next day, I found that an engineer, who was also working late, had stopped the job in order to print something. I felt that it was rude of the engineer to stop it. This person felt it was rude of me to even start it. It turned out that the system that we were both using wasn't smart enough to prioritize printing jobs or to automatically assign higher priorities to shorter jobs so they could get through faster. As a result, the engineer would have had to wait a long time to get a printout, because of my job. I was used to other systems that automatically took care of that problem. All of the engineers who normally used the system had developed a mutual understanding to work around the problem. I had broken their rules of etiquette.

People who develop software sometimes seem to behave in peculiar ways. They have developed small subcultures that include certain rules of etiquette. When you examine these rules, you discover that they were developed to help them get their jobs done while getting along with other people, and their rules are no stranger than those in many other cultures.

Our discussion of public and private data was based on some of the human problems that we must deal with. One way to provide solutions to these problems is to generalize them into formal "rules of etiquette." Each of the following short stories is preceeded by such a rule that relates to the story and that is targeted toward a specific group of people: functional management, project management, and project team members. Managers, take note that while these rules are described as "etiquette," they really reflect basic good management practice. All the rules are summarized in a table at the end of the chapter.

Functional Management: Set clear goals and get your staff to help define metrics for success.

One lab created products that were integrated with products from several other labs. This lab had a poor reputation for meeting their schedules, so its manager asked for some way to graphically track schedule accuracy in order to emphasize the need for improvement to the lab.

They created the project progress chart shown in Figure 10-1. [1] Two ideas went into its creation. First, a schedule slip is the amount of time that a project schedule is moved out. Second, average project progress for a specific

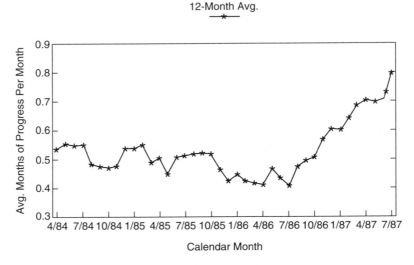

Figure 10-1 Development project progress.

time period is defined as one minus the ratio of the sum of all project slips divided by the sum of project elapsed times. For example, suppose you have a small lab with three projects. In a period of one month, the first project believes that it is on schedule (its schedule is unchanged). Its slip is zero. The second project had a bad month and the team estimates their schedule has to move out a full month. Its slip is one. The third project expects that they will slip one week for a slip of approximately one-quarter. The sum of the slips is 1.25. The sum of elapsed times is 3. Average project progress is therefore 1 - (1.25/3) = .58.

The graph uses a moving average to smooth month-to-month swings. When the lab first started plotting the graph (around the middle of Figure 10-1), they had enough historical data to show that they had only averaged about one-half a month of progress for every elapsed month. After monitoring the graph for a few months, the project teams gradually realized the importance of more accurate schedules, and they improved their accuracy to an enviable point.

The point could be made that all they did was to start padding their schedules. This is the wrong point, though. The reason that the lab manager asked for the data and had it visibly plotted was that partner organizations desperately needed better schedules in order to do their jobs right. The graph was a clear indicator for *what needed to improve. They wanted to improve the lab's ability to have accurate estimates and to communicate their confidence level to their partners.* In contrast, a different goal might be one to reduce schedules. They would have to look at an entirely different graph to measure their progress toward such a goal.

Let's apply the goal/question/metric paradigm to this example. The goal was to improve schedule accuracy. The questions that the graph addressed were, "How accurate are our schedules?" and "Are our schedules improving?" The metric data was taken from information that was already tracked.

Focusing on any single piece of data can cause it to improve at the expense of others. In order to protect against this, this lab also tracked product metrics (like functionality, usability, performance, and so forth) and reliability metrics. In addition, they took steps to improve the scheduling process and to add better checks and balances to that process than in the past. These steps were designed to prevent the scheduling pendulum from swinging too far in the direction of making schedules too long.

Project Management: Provide regular feedback to the team about the data they have helped to collect.
Project Team: Do your best to report accurate, timely data.

A lab created a simple program to capture engineering hours via keyboard entry to some standard screens. This allowed the lab manager to find out where the lab was spending its time, and typing the data into the computer would theoretically make it easier for people to record their times. After the system was in use for several months, the managers looked more carefully at the accumulated data. They discovered that one of the engineers had done a masterful job of automating inputs to the system, but not the hours really worked. This engineer had decided that the data was not important to the organization and wasn't going to be used. Let's contrast this story with another.

A second lab created a database to store engineering hours. They used a simple paper form that people filled out each Friday that captured the time spent for different activities. A clerk entered the data into the database, and a weekly report summarized time by activity. Charts were displayed and people were reminded when they had forgotten to turn in the form. They were also reminded of the decisions that were made from the data. In both stories, there was a potential for reporting bad data, but this second lab had done a much better job of showing the engineers how the data was used and of explaining its importance. As a result, the information was more accurate and decisions were more effective.

Functional Management: Don't allow anyone in your organization to use metrics to measure individuals.
Project Team: Help your managers to focus project data on improving your processes.

We sometimes see misrepresentation of data even on an organizational scale. A third lab used the products of a fourth lab during a long development cycle. During this time, the third lab found problems that they tried to report via the defect tracking system. People from the fourth lab wouldn't acknowledge the problems found by the third, and so the third lab chose to track the defects of the fourth lab under the umbrella of their own defect responsibilities, rather than lose the information.

What was happening there? The environment of the fourth lab was one of fault finding. People weren't willing to even record defects in their own divisional defect tracking system, because such information was ultimately used against them. As a result, their relationships with other labs deteriorated.

Their knowledge of what defects were or were not fixed was poor, and they lost their ability to make good decisions based on data.

It is critical for us to provide the right environment for tracking the data that we need. We must sell the people involved on the importance of accurately recording the data. We must also convince managers to use the data in a nonthreatening way. Showing both managers and engineers how to use the data is a necessary step.

Functional Management: Set clear goals and get your staff to help define metrics for success.

I'm constantly amazed at the number of companies who don't seem to have a formal mechanism to track defects. This information is one of the keys to process improvement. Figure 10-2 shows one of many ways that defect information can be used to focus on process improvements. One organization used it to monitor a goal to reduce their defect backlog significantly. The first question they had to answer was, "What are the major components of the backlog?"

When a customer submits a service request, it goes through several steps. A support group in marketing first reviews it to make sure that it isn't a duplicate of a previous request. They also check to see if there is a workaround or fix available. They then pass it to the lab for classification. The lab tries to reproduce the problem and finally puts it into one of several "known problem" states: critical, serious, medium, low, or enhancement.

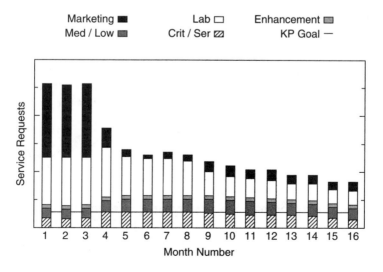

Figure 10-2 Service request backlog status.

The most obvious answer that the starting data in Figure 10-2 provided was that over three quarters of their defects hadn't been classified. As a result, it was difficult for the organization to know just how bad their problems were. They used this information to focus their efforts on first reducing defects in the marketing classification and then in the lab classification. The chart shows that their efforts were effective both at reducing the number of defects that were unclassified and at not increasing the defects in the other categories also.

This was a case where the decisions that were to be made were well understood. Let's look at how a lack of clear goals in another organization led to a virtual disaster.

Functional Management: Understand the data that your people take pride in reporting. Don't ever use it against them. Don't ever even hint that you might.

The support group in another organization tracked their version of the part of the chart in Figure 10-2 corresponding to marketing review. Reducing their service request backlog was just one of many goals that they had set. One month, the support manager decided to focus on that goal, and the group rallied to the task and ended the month with a backlog of zero.

The support manager proudly went to the next divisional staff meeting and presented a graph that showed the reduction to zero. The division manager thought about the results for a few moments and finally said in jest, "You know, I've never seen a group that has been able to reduce their backlog that way before. Maybe we have too many people working in the support area."

The problem is that no one in the room, including the support manager, interpreted the comment in jest. It's a sure thing that they will never report a backlog of zero again in that organization. Even worse, such a comment was demotivating to the entire staff, and the quality of reported data from all the staff will never be the same again. When your people feel that they are in an environment where data will be used against them, the data they report will be distorted and misleading.

Functional Management: Support your people when their reports are backed by data useful to the organization.

It would have been much better if the division manager had said "Excellent job. Now, in the next few months, I'd like to see us address the problem of . . ." With this comment, the division manager acknowledges that the organizational goals must be clarified and allows the team to remain motivated.

Project Management: Know the strategic focus of your organization and emphasize metrics that support the strategy in your reports.

Several years ago, we studied metrics for managing maintenance. We produced the set of major strategic elements of a software business that we first saw in Chapter 3. It suggests that any organization changes its primary focus as business conditions change, and that the kinds of things we measure must also change. It possibly helps to explain the reaction of the division manager in the last example.

The short-term strategy that the support manager was following was to maximize customer satisfaction. Even though the division manager spoke in jest, the fact was that the primary organizational strategy was to increase efficiency by minimizing engineering effort. To pursue that goal, it would have also been necessary to look at how long it took to process the service requests, whether any of them shouldn't have been submitted, and other issues more closely related to controlling costs.

For example, the division manager would have reacted more positively to a chart that illustrated an increasing efficiency of closing service requests, instead of the one that was shown. Such a chart would have supported the strategy directly and would have left the impression that resources were wisely used.

It is important to know what the organizational strategy is. That strategy will drive the primary things that are measured, and it will also drive the kinds of decisions that will be made.

Functional Management: Don't emphasize one metric to the exclusion of others.

A key question that must often be asked is, "Is there any way that the data can show improvement when things aren't improving?" Often we see the software hero who fixes problems day and night. The hero's dedication is widely recognized and they are often praised and rewarded. The question that must be asked, though, is "Are these efforts a true indication of the value provided to the organization?" If our hero is also the person who created many of these problems, then perhaps other engineers who are less flashy are making a greater contribution. We see data that seems to show one thing when, in reality, it might be showing something else entirely.

One organization that I know of went through a long period when the developers were asked to work long hours during the week, plus Saturdays and Sundays. The manager of the group took great pride in the dedication of the staff. Top management gave encouragement, since they thought that they were achieving great productivity. Of course, they couldn't have been more wrong. After the initial enthusiasm wore off, the team was totally exhausted. They spent large amounts of time convincing each other that they were doing the right thing instead of doing it, and the long hours led to costly rework. So, while the number of hours spent suggested that the project was getting back on its schedule, it was really falling even further behind. They were managing by hours spent without realizing they were getting fewer returns for each hour invested.

Both of these examples suffered the same basic problem. They focused too heavily on a single metric and didn't track other indicators that would signal a problem even if data for the single metric looked good. The bottom row on the chart in Table 10-1 is a good reminder that there must always be a proper balance among our strategies and among the measures we use.

Project Management: Don't try to measure individuals.

My friend Brian Sakai has taught a Software Metrics class for many years in HP. He has a technique for remembering names that involves taking the list of students attending a given class and marking down row and column coordinates on the list. In one particular class, some of the students noticed these numbers. They became concerned because they thought that Brian was somehow grading them on different class activities.

We like this story, because it emphasizes how concerned people get when they feel that they are being individually measured. It especially helped that class to understand the importance of using team measures, and of trying to avoid measures that appear to focus on individuals.

Project Management: Gain agreement with your team on the metrics that you will track, and define them in a project plan.

In the "Human Element" chapter of *Software Metrics: Establishing a Company-Wide Program*, there is one story about a team that was particularly successful with their metrics. There were four aspects that contributed to their success: [2]

1. The means of measurement and level of effort it took were well-understood and minimal.
2. The team was measured and plotted, not the individuals.
3. The team agreed up front that the measurements were meaningful.
4. By going through the process before committing to a schedule, the team approved of showing the data publicly.

Major Characteristics	Maximize Customer Satisfaction	Minimize Engineering Effort & Schedule	Minimize Defects
Major Business Factor	Attempt to capture market share	Competitive pressures forcing new product development or cost control	Hold/increase market share
When Most Effective	When initially entering market	When there are several competitive products or you sell more profitable products	When features are competitive and adequate market share is held
Characteristic Features	Customer communications, quick responses	Focus on delivery dates and effort	Analysis and removal of defect causes
Most Visible Metrics	Survey and interview data, product metrics, defects	Calendar time, engineering effort, defects	Failure analysis by module, cause, & severity; size; code coverage
Group Most Likely To Drive Strategy	Development team initially, customer support later	Division or company management	Development team and/or quality organization
Group Most Likely To Be In Direct Contact With Customer	Development team	Marketing/factory customer support	Field support organization
Potential Drawbacks If Focus Too Restricted	Process of developing products may not improve	Defect backlog can get unmanageable; customers and developers frustrated	Defects may be fixed that are not cost effective

Table 10-1 Major strategies of a software business.

Notice the strong presence of the word "team" in the list. Remember our discussion of private data. It's most important attribute was that it was data before some agreed-upon handoff occurred between an individual and some larger group, usually a project team. This team agreed to make their data public, because the team was measured and not the individuals, and they had early agreement regarding what the measures were and how they were to be used.

Project Management: Provide regular feedback to the team about the data they help collect.

Our next story begins at a meeting shortly before the release of an internal tool. The group involved had done an excellent job of working with their customers to get early releases integrated into the process. It was now time to release the tool and move on to other things (as is our wont in software).

The project manager finished the review by stating that they had removed all the defects from the product. Because the product prototype had been in use for so long, the manager felt that the only support necessary was a small part of an existing support person's time. Of course, this was just what the lab manager wanted to hear. There were other projects that needed to be done. On the other hand, the engineers had some reservations. They knew that they had fixed all the previously discovered defects, but they also knew that defects were still being found.

The quality person timidly spoke up and asked, "What has been the defect trend for the last two months?" Well, they had found and fixed quite a few defects, but the incoming defect rate wasn't very different at the end than it was earlier.

Here was a case where the team was well aware of the defect trend. They had been working closely with the customers and didn't want to let them down now, just as they were finishing. And here was their project manager and their lab manager about to prevent them from fixing the last-minute problems that the team expected. This is a sure formula for disillusioned engineers and disappointed customers. Project managers must not only provide feedback to the team about their interpretations of the data, they must also be sensitive to how the team interprets the data.

Our story would have had a happier ending if the project manager had reviewed the data with the team before making the presentation to the lab manager. If they had, they might have agreed to a transition plan that included part-time support by one or two team members for several months. This would have been a small price to pay to prevent a disillusioned team and to preserve continued commitment to future quality.

Functional Management: Support your people when their reports are backed by data useful to the organization.

Sometimes organizational changes can lead to problems. Another lab embarked on an ambitious program to analyze their defects. An enthusiastic advocate for the program was found who started with an analytical model that the HP Software Metrics Council had defined. This person spread enthusiasm throughout the organization and provided training, tools, and encouragement. Within two months, many people were working towards the goals of the program, and they had categorized enough defects to form some initial conclusions.

This is when the benefits of their work began to be seen, and this is also when a reorganization led to a new manager for the lab. Rather then follow through with what had started so well, a new set of priorities were set. The advocate had a different role in the new priorities, so the failure analysis program quickly lost steam.

So here was a case where the people were excited and had collected some good information that gave them important insights into changes that should be made. The new agenda for the lab didn't include their changes, though, and the new manager didn't take the time to listen to and support the proposed changes.

Contrast these last two stories with the one that we looked at earlier about the project progress chart. The only difference is that the lab manager who asked for the project progress chart supported the changes that the data (and the people involved) stated. The goal of improving estimates was clear. The measurements helped the project managers to work toward the goal while receiving support from the lab manager. This is the formula that we seek for success.

CONCLUSION

These stories help to remind us that software development is still a very people-dependent and creative activity. We do not have automated processes to develop software yet, so people must collect, interpret, and own metrics data. There is a sensitivity at all organizational levels that we must recognize and accommodate if we expect our data to be useful. Perhaps we need to acknowledge these sensitivities by developing a formal code of behavior, some "rules of etiquette" when dealing with software metrics. Figure 10-3 suggests a set of rules derived from the stories in this chapter.

Functional Management	1. Don't allow anyone in your organization to use metrics to measure individuals. 2. Set clear goals and get your staff to help define metrics for success. 3. Understand the data that your people take pride in reporting; don't ever use it against them; don't ever even hint that you might. 4. Don't emphasize one metric to the exclusion of others. 5. Support your people when their reports are backed by data useful to the organization.
Project Management	6. Don't try to measure individuals. 7. Gain agreement with your team on the metrics that you will track, and define them in a project plan. 8. Provide regular feedback to the team about the data they help collect. 9. Know the strategic focus of your organization and emphasize metrics that support the strategy in your reports.
Project Team	10. Do your best to report accurate, timely data. 11. Help your managers to focus project data on improving your processes. 12. Don't use metrics data to brag about how good you are or you will encourage others to use other data to show the opposite.

Figure 10-3 Rules of etiquette for applying software metrics.

Some of us will have to unlearn beliefs and attitudes that we unconsciously hold. Most of us who grew up in the United States went to schools where we were graded in every course that we took. We can't help questioning whether there are parallels when confronted with software metric data.

The message for functional managers is that software metric values are different from grades. Many of our measures are results from engineering activities that only our engineers can accurately report. We don't base school grades on students' reports of their own success or failure. We base them on objectively measured results. Software metric values are different from accounting and shop floor data. Our software processes are not as well defined and repeatable as our manufacturing processes. Metrics represent an opportunity for an organization to understand itself and improve. The most effective thing that can be done is to build an atmosphere of mutual trust and respect for people's abilities to measure and understand the changes necessary to remain competitive.

Project managers play a pivotal role. They must own the data and decide which metrics should be public and which ones should stay private. Their normal responsibilities require them to produce the right high-quality product efficiently and on schedule. At the same time, though, they must be aware of the processes they use and they must help the organization to improve its processes. They have the best opportunity to understand the needs of both the organization and their people.

Engineers must understand how important it is for them to help their project managers to prepare effective plans. They also need to help their managers improve their development processes.

In some ways, all this advice seems obvious. It seems like simple management common sense and sensitivity. In other ways, it seems like an ambitious undertaking. My advice is that if you haven't started collecting metrics data yet, start small and focus on building the long-term trust and enthusiasm that are necessary for you to convert your ad hoc processes into optimized engineering ones.

Remember that metrics data are a strategically important part of process improvement. The analysis, validation, and justification techniques described in the next three chapters depend on you fostering professional, enthusiastic attitudes among your staff and collegues.

BIBLIOGRAPHY

1. Levitt, D., "Process Measures to Improve R&D Scheduling Accuracy," *Hewlett-Packard Journal*, (April 1988), pp. 61–65.
2. Grady, R. and D. Caswell, *Software Metrics: Establishing a Company-Wide Program*, Englewood Cliffs, NJ: Prentice-Hall, Inc., 1987, pp. 85–86.

11

Dissecting
Software
═══ *Failures* ═══

*Thesis: Use **software failure analysis** to help drive process improvement decisions and to measure the impact of those decisions.*

Nobody likes to be told that they made a mistake. It's only human not to want to be wrong. On the other hand, software engineers don't intentionally make mistakes, so if we can understand why mistakes occur, without "accusing" individuals, we might eliminate the root causes of those mistakes in the future. Unfortunately, discussions about software defects are confusing because different people describe them from different perspectives.

This chapter discusses some of the terminology of these different views. It then examines some simple data collection and analysis techniques that help to identify causes of defects and point to areas where improvements can be made. Finally, it presents an example of justifying change based on the results of analyses.

"A defect is any flaw in the specification, design, or implementation of a product." [1] Such flaws cause managers to lose control by reducing their ability to predict when development or maintenance will be completed. Thus, we encounter another human trait. People like to be in control of a situation. The opportunity, then, is for software developers and managers to record sufficient defect data while analyzing and resolving defects to understand and remove the causes of those defects in the future.

DEFECT PERSPECTIVES

Figure 11-1 illustrates three views of a defect. Each of these views is characterized by its own terminology and focus. When users of a product have a problem, they know that they can't get their job done because the software product isn't working the way they expect it to. The level of their concern reflects how much their business is affected. Terms like "critical" or "serious" mean that they stand to lose substantial time and/or money if nothing is done soon.

On the other hand, people responsible for communicating defect information and status to and from customers refer to which component is at fault, whether a patch exists, and when a permanent fix can be expected. They must extract enough detail from customers to discover workarounds and to provide maintainers enough information to seek a permanent fix.

The third perspective is that of the people responsible for maintaining and enhancing software. They speak in terms of what code was at fault, the priority associated with correcting the defect, how difficult it will be to fix, and when to expect the fix.

If we draw an analogy to medicine, the patient describes their problem in terms of what hurts and how much. The nurse setting up the appointment must ask enough questions to tell the doctor enough to form preliminary conclusions and to determine how urgent it is for the doctor to see the patient. The doctor must run tests to discover the real cause of the ailment and must prescribe the correct treatment to heal the patient.

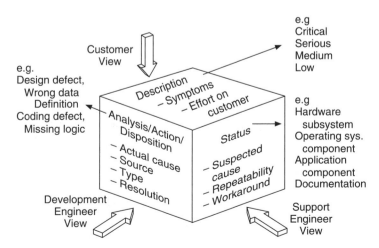

Figure 11-1 Defect cube.

DATA COLLECTION

The first step in diagnosing software defects is data collection. Most organizations already gather much of the necessary data. What is proposed is a program to use the data for a long-term quality improvement effort, not just to solve the current problems.

For example, there is always justifiable pressure to fix urgent problems. The goal is to maximize customer satisfaction (with an emphasis on timeliness, here). In pursuit of that goal, data is collected to optimize the flow of information from the customer about a defect (refer to Figure 11-2). Additional data is collected as engineers investigate the problem to provide information to the customer regarding status and possible fixes. Once customer satisfaction is achieved and the customer has a work-around or permanent fix for the problem, data collection shouldn't stop, though.

Submitter: Bruce Davis	Date submitted: 8/22/84
Company name: Hewlett-Packard	Dept.: SEL
Support engineer: John Michaels	Support office: Factory
Computer/system model: 3000/930	Identification no.: 0-13-821844-7
Defective software: MPE-XL	Release version: MIT X.B6.06
Severity (critical, serious, medium, low): Serious	
Workaround? (Y/N): Y	(easy/difficult)?: Difficult

Symptoms: System crashes with abort number of 1072. This has happened twice in the last week. At the time of the crash, there was one user on the system, mgr. official. The job running was newjobxl.

Figure 11-2 Simplified defect report.

If we want to *learn from past mistakes to improve development or support practices*, then a small additional amount of time must be spent to collect additional data. What are some of the questions that this long-term goal prompts? Some of questions we would like to answer are:

What development or maintenance process failed?

How often do such failures occur?

How expensive is it to fix such failures?

Which components are most subject to failure?

What process change will detect or eliminate these failures?

Figure 11-3 shows an example of the additional data needed for the defect first described by Figure 11-2.

Resistance to data collection when defects are being fixed is natural, because there may be a backlog of defects and strong schedule pressures. A common request is for additional automation aids to capture the information suggested in Figure 11-3, and until then, no data is collected. Such requests sometimes miss the point though, and fall into the trap of what we'll call the

Fixed by: Lynn Smith
Engineering hours to find and fix: 66   Date fixed: 9/19/84
Defect origin: Design
Defect type: Data definition   Modules changed: Disc_io, Table5
Category of defect   Other modules affected: Interx
  (missing, unclear, wrong, other): Wrong

How could this defect have been prevented or found earlier: Design walkthru;
more complete test coverage; more timely data dictionary updates.

Figure 11-3 Defect fix information.

"automation syndrome." In fact, it is unlikely that any entry of such data into an automated system would shorten the time involved on the part of the engineers reporting it. The problem with the "automation syndrome" is that it can prevent the collection of needed data for years if simple solutions and firm management don't prevail.

The question must be asked, "How much does collection of this *additional* data cost?" Let's take a typical product of 100 KNCSS (thousands of non-comment source statements). We have seen average postrelease defect densities from less than 0.1 to as high as 1 or 2 defects per KNCSS in the first year after release of a product. For the sake of calculations, let us assume a very high value of 1 defect/KNCSS. For our product, then, we would expect 100 defects in the first year. If we look at the data requested in Figure 11-3, it seems likely that it could be answered in ten minutes time. This time was validated at HP divisions where similar data was collected. This means that the total incremental engineering hours for our defect-plagued 100 KNCSS product would be slightly over two days (refer to Figure 11-4). Not a very large investment for such valuable data.

Product size	*	High Average Postrelease Defect Density	*	Time to Record Data	=	Engineering Cost
100 KNCSS	*	1 Defect/KNCSS	*	1/6 Hour/Defect	=	16 2/3 Hours

Figure 11-4 Sample calculation of the cost of collecting defect cause data.

Suppose your product is ten times as large, or that you want to do your analysis before product release (where we typically see about ten times the number of defects as in postrelease). Data collection time is always a sensitive issue, so just have the engineering team collect sufficient samples of defect data to yield an effective distribution of causes. This will be adequate as long as the sample size is large enough (probably 100-150 samples) and sufficiently random.

Provide a simple paper form to collect your data, and don't ask for so much of it that it becomes a burden. When the time comes to automate the process, you will already know which data is useful to collect, and you will also be able to specify an optimal solution.

Data Validation

When you initiate the collection of a new set of data, there are adjustments needed to people's activities and existing processes. It is particularly important at the start to include procedures to ensure valid data.

A common cause of invalid data is different interpretations of definitions. These are somewhat alleviated by proper training before collection begins, but all too often we incorrectly assume that everyone will interpret instructions in the same way. For example, two different HP divisions reported that many defects that were labeled as "coding defects" were really *caused* by changed requirements or design. The incorrect labeling occurred because the defects were *discovered or fixed* during the coding phase.

It is desirable to validate the initial collection of defect information with later interviews. These should be initiated by the project manager, or someone acting on their behalf. This will ensure that the data is accurate and it will emphasize the importance of accuracy to the engineers reporting the data. These checks should examine a large cross-section of the data in depth. Once this is accomplished, spot checks are probably all that are needed to ensure accurate data.

DATA ANALYSIS

In the previous section, the focus was on collection of valid data. The second step of this process is the analysis of the data that was collected. Again there is a danger that nothing will happen, because many managers have never taken the time to do such an analysis. They believe that the time involved will be too great. Perhaps this belief is as unfounded as the one about the data collection time.

What are the steps involved in a typical analysis? The following estimates assume that the analysis is begun with 100 one-page completed defect reports.

1. Sort the data collection forms by defect origin. Count the number in each group and total the number of engineering hours to fix the defects for each group. Arrange the totals in descending order of total engineering hours. (30 min.)

2. Calculate the average fix time for each of the totals from step 1. (5 min)

3. For the top two or three totals in step 1, count the defects sorted by defect type and multiply by the appropriate average fix times. Limit the number of types to the largest totals plus a single total for all others. (15 min.)

4. Add up the defects in each module. Get totals for the five most requently changed modules plus a single total for all others. (15 min.)

5. Review the defect reports for the defects included in the largest totals from steps 3 and 4. Summarize the defect-report suggestions for how the defects might have been prevented or found earlier. (1 hour)

Following this procedure, project managers would know several valuable facts after only two hours (and 5 min.) time. They would know what the most costly defects were, when they occurred, where they occurred, and the most likely steps to take to prevent their occurrence in the future.

Even two hours of a project manager's time are sometimes difficult to find. Other useful alternatives that have been successfully tried in HP are to use engineers from a quality or metrics organization or to hire a student from a local university to do the analysis. In both these cases, such analyses were a part of more extensive efforts to characterize software development.

A Model for Analyzing Defect Causes

Various reports have documented successful efforts to analyze defects, their causes, and proposed solutions. [2,3,4,5,6,7,8] But, the terminology among them has differed considerably, and the definitions could possibly mean different things to different people. In the fall of 1986, the HP Software Metrics Council addressed the definition of standard categories of defect causes. Our goal was to provide standard terminology for defects that different HP projects and labs could use to report, analyze, and focus efforts to eliminate defects and their root causes.

Fortunately, the IEEE had a subcommittee working on a standard for defect classification [9], so it was possible to start from their working documents. The IEEE definitions covered all phases of defect tracking in an extensive general way. These will undoubtedly be of value to the people supporting defect tracking systems. Unfortunately, the IEEE document at that time was very long, and too general to be applied specifically to any project. As a result, the Metrics Council extracted the material related to only defect causes and produced a metrics guideline that is easier to use. [10] Figure 11-5 illustrates a model of defect sources taken from the guideline, and Appendix A gives the definitions from the guideline.

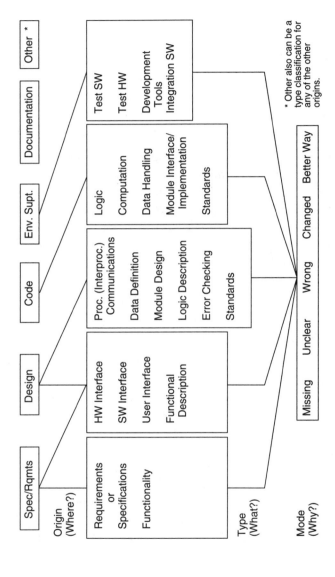

Figure 11-5 Categorization of sources of software defects.

The model is used by selecting one descriptor each from origins, types, and modes for each defect report as it is resolved. For example, a defect might be a *design defect* where part of the *user interface* described in the internal specification was *missing*. Another defect might be a *coding defect* where some *logic* was *wrong*.

An Example

Let us look at a specific example using the model presented in Figure 11-5. The data for this example is taken from a detailed study of defect causes done at HP. [6] In the study, defect data was gathered after testing began. Figure 11-6 shows step 1 of our five-step analysis procedure. The data is sorted by the primary origins of defects.

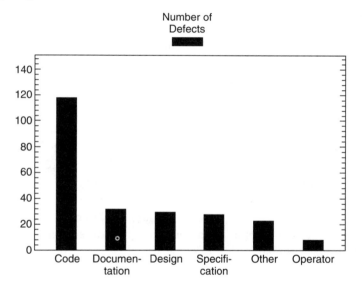

Figure 11-6 Distribution of defect origins.

Step 2 focuses attention on the causes of defects that cost the most to fix. The net cost of any given classification is represented by the total defects for the classification multiplied by the average cost to fix those defects. This study didn't accurately record the engineering times to fix the defects, so we will use average times summarized from several other studies to weight the defect origins. In particular, the average engineering cost to fix coding defects that are not found until testing is about 2.5 times their cost when they are found during coding. The factor for design defects is about 6.25, and the factor for specifications defects is about 14.25. [11] Figure 11-7 shows the relative costs to fix the defect population from Figure 11-6 when the weighting factors are

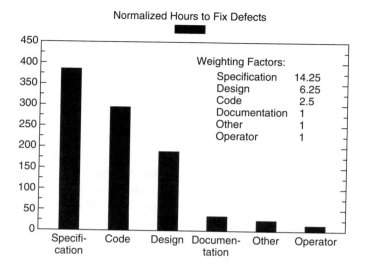

Figure 11-7 Weighted distribution of defect origins.

applied. For the sake of this example, the other origins are assumed to have a multiplier of one. We will normalize all fix times to assume that a coding defect fixed during coding takes one hour. The weighting factors then simply become engineering hours to fix the various defect categories.

The study from which this data was taken only provided defect type data for coding and design defects. Therefore, we will complete step 3 of our procedure with a breakdown of data for only coding and design. This is shown in Figure 11-8. It suggests that efforts should be focused to eliminate logic errors, computation errors, and process communications errors earlier than test.

We won't do steps 4 and 5 of our analysis procedure in this chapter other than to note that the assumption was that we would institute process changes to eliminate the root causes of those defects. It would be wise to consider your peoples' suggestions when planning these changes.

These brief examples show how easy it is to apply the analysis procedure to discover where changes with the greatest impact can be made. They also show how incomplete data can force us to make assumptions which might affect the accuracy of our conclusions. In this example we didn't have complete data regarding specifications defects or data detailing engineering hours for all defects. These are probably not serious drawbacks here, but be certain that you identify such uncertainties and their potential effects every time you do an analysis.

Here is an interesting note to conclude our example. The use of weighting factors in the analysis above emphasized working on eliminating causes of problems that *cost the most to resolve*. If the emphasis is to reduce the

Normalized Hours to Fix Defects

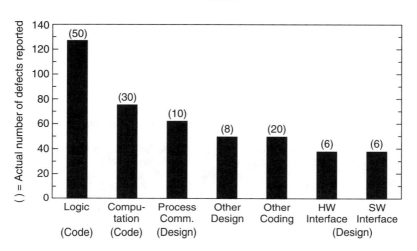

Figure 11-8 Weighted distribution of defect types. (Coding and design defects only.)

defect backlog as quickly as possible, then the effort must be focused on addressing those problems that are *easiest to fix quickly*. In that case, we would simply view the same data with a different goal. We would look for defect groups consisting of large numbers of defects that can be resolved quickly (e.g., documentation or some types of coding defects).

JUSTIFYING CHANGE

Once you have collected the data necessary to understand what changes you need to make to either the development or test processes, you encounter a very difficult step. This step is that of recommending and implementing change based on the discovered facts. It is difficult because humans are resistant to change. There are many facets to such resistance that span the entire change process. These are discussed in detail elsewhere, [1] so this section will focus on the first step in the change process only, that of initial justification of change. Recommendations for change take many forms, but most successful changes are based on a cost/benefit analysis built from components such as those outlined in Figure 11-9.

Most of the entries in the cost and benefit columns of an actual table would be represented by collected data. The remaining items would be estimates. The labels from any of the three columns can be used as item descriptors in the left column to add specificity. The entire table should be bound to a specific time period, such as one year or the duration of one project.

Generally you will construct a summary from an appropriate subset of items, costs, and benefits from Figure 11-9 that must be convincing by itself. For extra emphasis, it can be supplemented by benefits beyond the project and by more difficult to measure customer-satisfaction benefits and increased sales.

Items	Costs	Benefits
Training	Class costs Less time on project	Future expertise Consistency
Management	More management time	Less management time
Engineering	Start-up costs Data collection time	Reduced defect-finding times Reduced defect-fix times Fewer defects Fewer development engineers Fewer support engineers Shorter development and/or build cycles Reduced people cost per unit of output
Capital expenses	Purchased hardware Purchased software	
Time to market Job complexity		Product available sooner Less experienced engineers required

Figure 11-9 Considerations when recommending change and measuring progress.

An Example

Let's build a case for change based on data from studies done in HP. The change we will propose is to start design inspections. We won't make a strong case for the connection of this proposal to the analysis just done, because of some of the weaknesses in data capture. On the other hand, you will often discover that some form of inspection will be at least a part of your change proposals.

The first study evaluated various aspects related to design and code inspections. [12] It found

- optimum number of inspectors = 4 - 5,
- ratio of preparation/inspection time > 1.75,
- inspection rate = 300 - 400 lines of design text/hour,
- average number of defects found/inspection hour = 2.5.

Multiple studies documented when defects were introduced into software. These are discussed in the next chapter. They reported a range of from 9 to 54 percent design defects with an average of 35 percent. While this range seems disturbing at first glance, our experience has shown that for specific development methods used by one organization, the defect pattern does not vary significantly unless you change the methods. We will assume

- average number of design defects = 35% of total defects.

Figure 11-10 shows the results of combining the information from these two studies into a justification of design inspections for a 50 KNCSS project.

ANALYSIS OF SAVINGS FROM USE
OF DESIGN INSPECTIONS

Previously measured results (for various different organizations):

- Average prerelease defect density = 7 defects/KNCSS. [1]
- Average number of design defects = 35 percent of total defects. [Chapter 12]
- Optimum number of inspectors during inspections = 4 to 5. [12]
- Ratio of preparation/inspection time for inspections > 1.75. [12]
- Average number of defects found/inspection hour = 2.5. [12]
- Average percentage of defects found by inspections = 55 percent. [13]
- Ratio of cost to find and fix defects during test to cost during design = 6.25. [11] Note that we also assume that ratio applies equally to find times and fix times.

Assumptions:

- Training takes 8 hours * 6 engineers, and costs $275 * 6 engineers.
- Start-up costs are 16 hours * 6 engineers.

Design defects expected for a 50 KNCSS project:

$$50 \text{ KNCSS } * \frac{7 \text{ defects}}{\text{KNCSS}} * \frac{35 \text{ design defects}}{100 \text{ defects}} = 123 \text{ design defects}$$

Time cost to find the design defects using inspections (assume 55 percent might be found):

$$\frac{123 \text{ design defects} * 0.55}{2.5 \text{ defects found/insp. hour}} * 4.5 \text{ eng. } * \frac{(1.75 \text{ prep} + 1 \text{ insp}) \text{ hours}}{1 \text{ insp hour}} = 335 \text{ eng.hours}$$

Time to find the same 55 percent (123 * 0.55 = 68) of the design defects during test:

$$335 \text{ design eng. hours } * \frac{6.25 \text{ find/fix hours in test}}{1 \text{ find/fix hour in design}} = 2094 \text{ eng. hours}$$

Net savings:

2094 eng. hours − 335 eng. hours = 1759 eng. hours to find defects
1759 eng. hours * [1 cal. mo. /(6 eng. * 160 hours)] = 1.8 cal. months

Items	Costs	Benefits
Training	48 Engineering hours $1650	
Start-up costs	96 Engineering hours 0.5 Months	
Reduced defect finding time		1759 Engineering hours
Time to market		1.8 Calendar months

Figure 11-10 Cost/Benefit Analysis (of Design Inspections).

Note that neither costs nor benefits were specified for the item "management." For simplification we assume that roughly the same management time will be needed to introduce the new concepts to a project team as would have normally been needed to manage the additional engineering hours using the old techniques.

In summary, the introduction of design reviews seems to be very desirable. The benefits in this example totally overwhelm the costs, so why aren't inspections more widely used today? While there are many reasons that organizations have for not doing inspections, these reasons are all aspects of resistance to change.

Remember that while this example is based on real data, it is suspect since the data was measured by someone else and is derived from several sources. When preparing any justification, you will be faced with using a spectrum of data. You will have collected some data. People you know and trust will have collected some data. Some data will have been published by people whose methods and rigor allow you to assume that their results will apply for you, also. Finally, you will have to make some assumptions, just as we have in the examples in this book.

Your ability to justify change depends on your confidence in this spectrum of data and in your ability to explain any perceived difference between "unknown" sources and your environment. When you justify change, you must organize your arguments as clearly and persuasively as possible. You must also be prepared to continue trying to persuade the people involved until the change has occurred.

The example was selected to illustrate the process of justifying change. The core of the justification was the data recorded in previous studies of defects and the times taken to resolve them. You can use such published data to help guide your decisions, but ultimately you must also collect enough data that is specific to your process or products to verify that the problems you pursue are the most important ones.

CONCLUSION

Managers of software development cannot afford to simply continue producing and supporting products with the same old techniques and processes. The field is changing rapidly, and improvements in both quality and productivity are necessary to remain competitive.

The history of software metrics includes the continual application of basic scientific methods. We collect data and establish hypotheses for improvements. We take additional measurements to prove or disprove the hypotheses. And we revise our hypotheses accordingly and start the process again. The major problem of management without the use of data is that the hypotheses can never be really validated and appropriate changes institutionalized.

If we return to our medical analogy, software development without metrics is like medical doctors having to practice medicine without understanding the human body through dissections and autopsies. For over a thousand years before the fifteenth century, medical doctors were prevented from dissecting human bodies due to fear and superstition. When the rules against dissections were eased, great progress occurred in a relatively short time. We must experience a similar renaissance period in software development. Perhaps it is time that our schools began to teach "software autopsies."

The techniques described here for collecting, analyzing, and presenting data are simple, yet effective means to improve software development. We saw that the collection of a small amount of additional data can yield a large payback in terms of useful information that fits into a standard framework for analysis. We also saw a five-step process for data analysis that organizes this information to point to areas and methods for improvement. And a framework for justifying change to both management and engineers suggests how changes are proposed initially and justified.

What remains is for you to use these techniques as quickly as possible to promote positive change. The next chapter discusses such usage in a variety of different environments.

BIBLIOGRAPHY

1. Grady, R. and D. Caswell, *Software Metrics: Establishing a Company-Wide Program*, Englewood Cliffs, NJ: Prentice-Hall, Inc., 1987, pp. 82-95, 112, 224.

2. Endres, Albert, "An Analysis of Errors and Their Causes in System Programs," *IEEE Transactions on Software Engineering*, Vol. SE-1, no. 2 (June 1975), pp. 140–149.

3. Sieloff, C., "Software TQC: Improving the Software Development Process Through Statistical Quality Control," *HP Software Productivity Conference Proceedings*, (April, 1984), pp. 2–49 —2–62.

4. Hamilton, G., "Improving Software Development Using Quality Control," *HP Software Productivity Conference Proceedings*, (April, 1985), pp. 1–96 — 1–102.

5. Kenyon, D., "Implementing a Software Metrics Program," *HP Software Productivity Conference Proceedings*, (April, 1985), pp. 1–103 — 1–117.

6. Leath, C., "A Software Defect Analysis," *HP Software Productivity Conference Proceedings*, (April, 1987), pp. 4–147 — 4–161.

7. Nakajo, T., K. Sasabuchi, and T. Akiyama, "A Structured Approach to Software Defect Analysis," *Hewlett-Packard Journal*, (April 1989) pp. 50–56.

8. Mays, R., C. Jones, G. Holloway, and D. Studinski, "Experiences with Defect Prevention," *IBM Systems Journal*, Vol. 29, no. 1, (Jan 1990), pp. 4–32.

9. *A Standard for Software Errors, Faults, and Failures*, IEEE working group P1044, (March, 1987).

10. "Software Development Metrics Guideline: Defect Analysis," June, 1987.

11. Boehm, B., *Software Engineering Economics*. Englewood Cliffs, NJ: Prentice-Hall, Inc., 1981, p. 40.

12. Scott, B., and D. Decot, "Inspections at DSD — Automating Data Input and Data Analysis," *HP Software Productivity Conference Proceedings*, (April, 1985), pp. 1–79 — 1–89.

13. Jones, C., *Programming Productivity*. New York: McGraw-Hill Book Co., 1986, p. 179.

12

Investing
in Process
═ Improvements ═

*Thesis: Use **software failure analysis** to help drive process improvement decisions and to measure the impact of those decisions. (continued)*

One of my favorite childhood stories is the story of the poor Irishman who finds a leprechaun helplessly caught on a thorn bush. The Irishman takes the leprechaun off the thorn bush, but doesn't let go. The Irish know that if you are lucky enough to catch a leprechaun, it has to tell you where its pot of gold is. After much begging and pleading to be let free, the leprechaun finally tells the Irishman that the gold is buried under another particular thorn bush.

Now the Irishman doesn't have a shovel with him, so he ties his yellow kerchief to the bush to mark the spot. He then makes the leprechaun swear that it won't move the marker. When he returns with a shovel to dig up the gold, the Irishman unhappily discovers that the leprechaun has tied identical yellow kerchiefs to all the thorn bushes in the area. After digging for hours, he finally has to admit that he was tricked by the leprechaun.

Sometimes it feels as if we are like the Irishman. We know that our software development practices aren't doing the job very well for us, so we try different methods or tools, almost at random. This is like digging under all the thorn bushes to find the pot of gold. There is a better approach.

DEVELOPING YOUR PLAN _____

A method for identifying improvement opportunities was introduced in the last chapter. It uses failure analysis to find process problems. This chapter extends the method to help you decide what changes to make.

As you categorize defects, you will uncover a variety of symptoms. A typical first step will be for you to decide to do better or different inspections or tests. Often this is appropriate. The previous chapter contained a justification for design inspections to help you to start them.

Detection methods are only partially effective, though, and not as cost effective as preventive ones. Because preventive approaches cannot be measured as they are used (as defect detection approaches can), their proven effectiveness has generally not been well documented. As you make improvements, you will eventually have to consider introducing such processes, methods, and tools. This may seem more risky, but much of the potential risk comes from expecting too much of any single change. Most methods or tools were created to eliminate only certain types of problems. While they can help in various ways, don't assume that they will cure all your problems. Limit your expectations to those areas where you feel the most confidence.

A Variety of Problems

Figure 12-1 gives you some idea of how complicated the decision process can be. It shows the eight largest sources of defects for six different organizations. The different types of shadings reflect the origin part of the categorization model we saw in the previous chapter. The model is repeated here in Figure 12-2 to help your understanding.

We can immediately see from just looking at the shadings that the sources of defects vary greatly across the organizations. The middle two pie charts seem to be alike, but on closer inspection of the specific defect types, even they are dissimilar.

These differences are not surprising. If everyone used the same development environment and experienced the same problems, then we would have fixed those specific problems by now. It would be as if we knew which thorn bush hid the pot of gold. Instead, there are many different environments. While many proposed solutions to our problems apply to different situations, they don't necessarily apply equally well to all problems or all environments. This is why the data shown in Figure 12-1 for each organization is so important. Similar data for your organization will provide a measurable basis for decisions that you must make. By continuing to track your defect data, you can also measure how successful your solutions are.

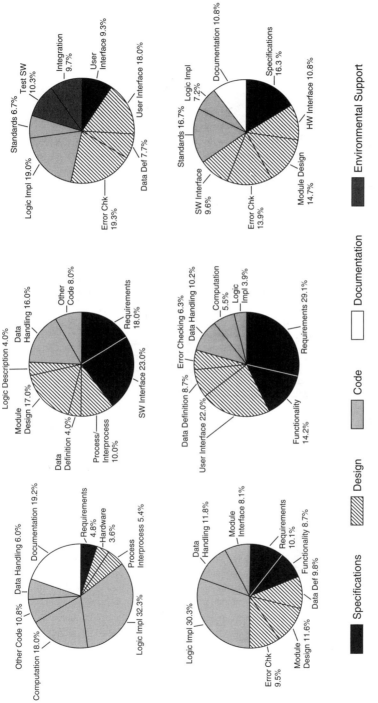

Figure 12-1 Sources of defects for six HP entities.

Specifications ▣   Design ▨   Code ▤   Documentation ☐   Environmental Support ▨

139

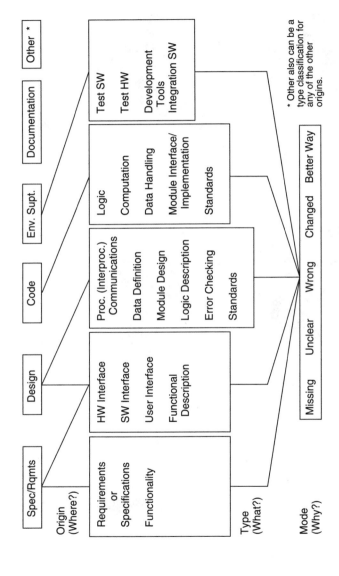

Figure 12-2 Categorization of sources of software defects.

A Variety of Solutions

Table 12-1 reintroduces the work-product analysis table (from Chapter 8), but adds a "needs addressed" column. The needs correspond to the defect types in Figure 12-2. The work products should be particularly good in eliminating the defect types listed in Table 12-1. For example, prototyping is often done

Phase	Work Product	Tools	Metrics	Needs Addressed
Specifications/ Requirements	Text	Writing analysis	Flesch–Kincaid readability	Functionality
	Spreadsheet	Quality function deployment (QFD)	Weighted customer needs	Requirements
	Object-relationship model	Object-oriented analysis		Functionality and functional descrip.
	Prototype	Fourth generation languages		User interfaces, requirements
	Dataflow diagrams	Structured analysis	Bang	SW and user interfaces
Design	Text	Writing analysis	Flesch–Kincaid readability	Module design, error checking, standards
	Structure charts	Structured design	Design weight, Fanout ^{2}	Module design SW interfaces, process commun.
	Data dictionary	Structured analysis/design		Data definition
	Pseudocode	Program design language	Cyclomatic complexity	Logic description
Implementation	Code	Compilers, Complexity analysis	Lines of code, Cyclomatic complexity	Logic implementation
	Code	Object-oriented compilers		Module interfaces
	Unit tests	Code coverage	Percent coverage	Module interfaces
	Manuals	Writing analysis	Flesch-Kincaid readability	Documentation
	Peformance tests	Ad hoc	Execution times	

Table 12-1 Engineering work products, tools, and metrics.

using a fourth generation language to clarify user interfaces and other types of requirements. Structure charts help to show module designs graphically. They also help to clarify process and interprocess communications by explicitly showing information that is passed from one module to another as control or dataflow tokens.

This table is not all inclusive. For example, inspections are not listed separately, because they can be effectively used with all the work products to help find defects. Some people will also disagree with the assertions made for some work products or tools. Use the table as one of several valuable resources. Others include suggestions your people make, recent success stories in the literature, and consultation from people outside your organization.

READING THE TEA LEAVES

Now that we've got an approach for analyzing defects and a model of how solutions are derived from the results of our analysis, we can have some real fun. Let's take the analysis results for seven organizations and explore several approaches for how we might choose to change their processes.

> *Apologia: Ideally, all these examples would represent detailed scientific experiments with carefully controlled variables and generalized conclusions. The examples shown aren't the ideal. They are all from the real world where there are limited resources and considerable pressures to produce products.*

> *The collected data is as accurate as the definitions and the framework permit. Each of the examples represents at least 100 data points. Some of the entities followed through on their changes. The results of these are described. Other changes are still in progress. Yet other changes will never occur, because reorganizations have occurred.*

Approaches to Decision Making

There are five approaches in this chapter to decide what process changes seem best. The "wedges" refer to parts of pie charts that show defect patterns.

- select the largest wedge
- select the easiest wedge
- select the largest normalized wedge
- select the largest combination of wedges
- select a combination of wedges based on confidence in a solution

Each approach is useful for different business conditions and patterns shown by your data. The examples illustrate some of the available options and help you to understand the decision-making process. Remember that while all the data came from real Hewlett-Packard divisions, these are hypothetical solution choices. In some cases they match the choices actually taken. In others, the divisions had good reasons to choose differently.

Select the Largest Wedge — Case 1

The first example is the pie chart shown in Figure 12-3. It shows data collected during system test for a firmware system that was over 100 KNCSS. The description of development methods includes a variety of defect detection methods, but it doesn't mention any particular defect prevention techniques or tools.

The first thing to look for in these pie charts is any significant or unusually high percentages. In Figure 12-3, we see a large percentage of logic implementation and computation defects. It seems unusual that these are so high, since the organization did quite a few inspections. Inspections are generally considered effective in finding logic and computation defects.

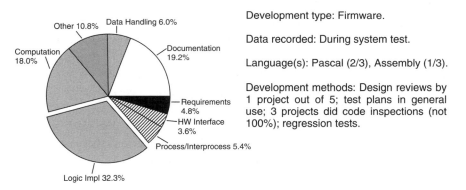

Development type: Firmware.

Data recorded: During system test.

Language(s): Pascal (2/3), Assembly (1/3).

Development methods: Design reviews by 1 project out of 5; test plans in general use; 3 projects did code inspections (not 100%); regression tests.

Figure 12-3 Case 1.

The large percentage of documentation defects is also unusual. These are not as costly to fix as the other development defects, but together with the logic and computation defects, they might suggest carelessness or inexperienced engineers.

The presence of hardware interface, process/interprocess, and data handling defects does not seem unusual for firmware.

So what should we recommend to this division? There are several possible approaches. First, the largest pie wedge is logic. Picking the largest wedge is a frequently chosen strategy. For processes that are in control (for example, processes monitored within statistical control bands [1]), this strategy is particularly appropriate. Indeed, this strategy is heavily used in manufacturing process analyses.

Second, we must remember that the relative costs to find and fix different types of defects vary. If we apply the multipliers that we used in the last chapter (refer to Figure 11-7), the relative size of the requirements wedge becomes larger. The restated values are shown in Figure 12-4. Still, logic remains the largest wedge.

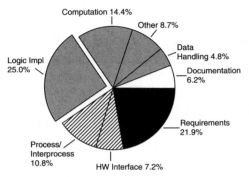

Development type: Firmware.

Data recorded: During system test.

Language(s): Pascal (2/3), Assembly (1/3).

Development methods: Design reviews by 1 project out of 5; test plans in general use; 3 projects did code inspections (not 100%); regression tests.

Figure 12-4 Normalized data for Case 1.

Third, we should look for combinations of wedges that might be addressed by a particular process, method, or tool. We've already noted that code inspections should be particularly effective in detecting logic and computational defects. It's not clear why these categories were still so large, since three of the five projects did some inspections. Nevertheless, better inspections are probably desirable.

Fourth, we must consider easy potential solutions or ones in which we have the most confidence. These are important considerations, because we are dealing here with organizational change. There is great psychological advantage in an organization achieving early success in a series of process changes. Here, logic defects also seem like an attractive target. Inspections are already done, so a good recommendation would be to introduce some new type of work product that would improve inspection success. Table 12-1 suggests that a complexity analysis tool, such as the one described in Chapter 8, would help. Such tools provide complexity metrics, and they provide engineers with graphical images that reinforce the messages that the metric data tells.

In this example, all the analysis approaches point at the coding defects as an opportunity for improvement. Our proposed approach is to introduce a complexity analysis tool and to improve our code inspection process. We can use the tool, as well as engineering inputs, to focus our inspections on complex or difficult code modules.

So our expectation is that the tool will help engineers directly to eliminate some logic defects by giving them a meaningful metric and graphical feedback. We should see these benefits even before inspections.

Printouts of code logic will also help inspection teams to focus their attention on the logic problem type, and they will also provide an alternative view of the code.

These seem like safe assumptions that we could sell to both our engineers and managers. An example justification is given in Chapter 14.

Review

Let's quickly review some of the key steps we took in this first example. First we categorized the defects and drew a pie chart showing the percentage of defects in each category. Then we tried four approaches to selecting which problem(s) to work on first. Finally we described how the chosen method would work to remove the defects.

The remaining examples focus on the different types of approaches and the resulting recommendations. As you read them, think through some of the other alternatives. See if you agree with the selected ones. Some of the choices will seem more obvious than others.

Select the Easiest Wedge — Case 2

Figure 12-5 shows the second case. Its pie chart looks quite different from the one in Case 1. Almost half of its defects are design defects, so this division clearly has major design problems. On the other hand, their specifications wedge is 16.3 percent. When you apply our weighting factors, that wedge represents a large opportunity (38 percent) for improvement. (Note that some divisions choose not to distinguish between requirements and specifications defects. In fact, our model definitions don't define any difference. This division did track the two separately. For them, requirements came first. Specifications were developed from the requirements.)

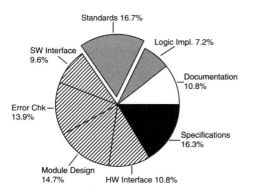

Development type: Systems.

Data recorded: During maintenance.

Language(s): C.

Development methods: SA/SD (design documentation not kept up to date), informal (not widespread) code inspections, branch coverage testing, regression testing.

Figure 12-5 Case 2.

As a first pass, though, let's select the standards wedge to attack. It has several characteristics that make it attractive. First, it should be much easier to address than the other problems. There are many standards defects, so standards must exist already. They may have to be clarified or rewritten, but these are tasks that can be done quickly.

Second, the presence of so many standards defects suggests that a broad-based training program in the basics of the technology being implemented would be quite valuable. Another benefit of such a training program could be to emphasize engineer motivation and organizational unity.

Our strategy is to have a small group of the most knowledgeable engineers spend no more than one week clarifying the standards documentation. One person would then prepare and give informal presentations. For this type of subject, we guess this will take no more than an additional month. Finally, we examine every standards defect that occurs in the future, and update the standards as necessary. We would then publicize both these changes and the significant absence of the defects compared with before.

Select the Largest Normalized Wedge — Case 3

Let's assume that our strategy for Case 2 quickly works. The pie chart would presumably change so that the standards wedge would decrease in size and the next largest category would now be shown as one of the top eight wedges. Figure 12-6 shows this new pattern. When we restate these percentages, specifications defects end up consuming almost 40 percent of our defect fixing time. This is not an easy problem to solve, but it is an area that has high potential payback. Note, though, that the data came from the maintenance phase. We need to keep in mind that process changes for this defect type will primarily apply to new products and not to the ones analyzed in Figure 12-6.

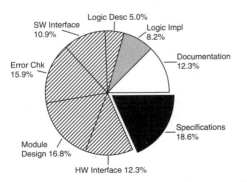

Development type: Systems.

Data recorded: During maintenance.

Language(s): C.

Development methods: SA/SD (design documentation not kept up to date), informal (not widespread) code inspections, branch coverage testing, regression testing.

Figure 12-6 Case 3.

Table 12-1 doesn't provide any suggestions, so here we depend even more on the suggestions of our team. One good way to generate suggestions is to have a brainstorming session. Figure 12-7 shows an Ishikawa or "fishbone" diagram [2] of what such a session might produce.

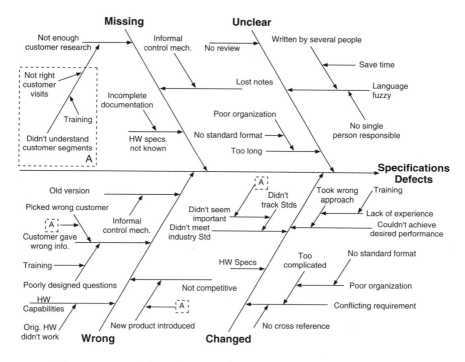

Figure 12-7 Fishbone diagram of the causes of specifications defects.

In a fishbone diagram, the main horizontal line represents the quality factor under examination. The "ribs of the fish" are diagonal lines that are brainstormed potential causes of the primary line. Notice that it is convenient to start the ribs of our diagram with the defect modes from Figure 12-2: unclear, missing, wrong, and changed. (The mode "better way" is typically selected as a choice when doing inspections during development. Since this data was collected during maintenance, better way is not included here.) Besides the convenience, this approach also provides additional quantitative information based on the number of reports of each mode. We can use these to help us decide which causes to address first.

For each of the diagonal lines, we then add additional lines that represent more detailed cause information. For example, one cause of specifications defects is that they are wrong. One cause of them being wrong was use of an old version. A cause of that was use of an informal control mechanism.

Eventually we end up with a set of potential causes of our problem. Some of the root causes for specifications defects that we see in this diagram are: unclear understanding of customer segments, poor version management, no document standards, lack of clearly assigned responsibilities, and hardware changes. Some of the brainstormed causes may not relate very closely to the observed defects. We must complete this exercise by returning to the defects and mentally testing these causes against the defects.

We have a multiprong strategy to address these problems. First we want our marketing group to set up customer visits for our engineers. These will be grouped by customer segments, and each group will give reports to the whole organization that stress the key customer needs for their segment. It will be Marketing's responsibility to collect all this information into a document for the organization that they will keep current.

Second, we will assign configuration management responsibility to one person. That person has the option of investigating and proposing an automated system for documentation or version control if that makes sense for the long-term.

Third, a task force will work with formats for specifications that will address the past weaknesses. The members of the team will be project managers, product managers, and key engineers. This assignment is a long-term one, although the team shouldn't have to meet often.

Note that these results and recommendations are specific to this division. It is very easy to imagine the same problem with a different solution in another environment. For example, one case might be that of a single contractual customer who can't specify their needs well. This situation might also result in many specification defects, but the causes and the solutions would be quite different. One consideration that this example also shows is that some solutions involve multiple groups and require several actions. It takes greater management commitment to execute such solutions than it does for the first two cases. On the other hand, the payoff is also higher.

Postscript — Cases 2 and 3

There is some follow-up data for these cases. This division did work on their standards defects as Case 2 proposed. Within six months, standards defects were down to less than 4 percent, and many of these were carryovers from the time when the process was changing. The other data patterns also changed somewhat, since their new data was collected during both test and maintenance as opposed to the original data being collected only during maintenance. Some of the changes in data patterns were probably because the testing process was more effective at finding some defect types than others. As a result, their data pattern was close to the one projected in Case 3. The pattern still reflected about 50 percent design defects, and the unnormalized specifications wedge was still 14 percent.

Select the Largest Combination Wedge — Case 4

So far, it has been relatively easy to choose the set of defects on which to focus. The remaining examples all involve combinations of wedges that are related to solution sets. A solution set is characterized by some particular methodology or tool set. Our first example is shown in Figure 12-8.

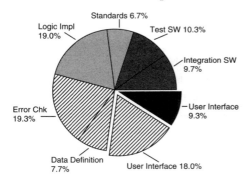

Development type: Applications.

Data recorded: Throughout development.

Language(s): Pascal and SPL.

Development methods: Prototype, scenarios, user walkthroughs, text design documents, thorough design and code inspections, regression tests.

Figure 12-8 Case 4.

This data is from an applications environment. We often expect user interface problems in an applications environment, so in that sense, this division is typical. When you combine the normalized values of the user interface defects, they make up close to 50 percent of the effort spent finding and fixing defects. We have to be careful, though. The normalization factors may not work here. This data was not collected after completion of the product. This division's process was an iterative one that focused on getting incomplete, early versions of the product to show to customers. Thus, they were detecting many of the user-interface errors much earlier than test.

This division should benefit from the iterative prototypes that they already produce, and the large number of user-interface defects implies that they did. They don't use a fourth-generation language for their development. Introducing one might help them to make changes to prototypes more quickly.

Of course, just making prototypes doesn't necessarily solve the problems. The prototypes must be evaluated by a carefully planned cross section of users. The users have to represent all the target market segments. They also must represent different classes of users like clerks, managers, systems administrators, operators, and so forth. The defect data here might clarify which types of users were least understood in the past.

This is an interesting example. Since they already use prototyping, our primary recommendation is that they work on their procedures for user selection and customer segmentation. This case is similar to Case 2 in this respect. The subject of market research is foreign to many engineering teams, so much of the responsibility for organizing this solution is marketing's. At the same time, the development team must work closely with the chosen customers to best internalize their needs. In applications environments particularly, new hardware is providing more flexibility than in the past. This leads to more choices for customers and more difficulty in pinning down a choice that is acceptable to their changing opinions.

Postscript — Case 4

We have follow-up data for Case 4, also. Remember that these examples came from various divisions. Based on their particular situations, these divisions sometimes decided to work on different choices from the ones picked here. Instead of focusing even more on user-interface defects, this division first selected the largest wedge, error checking. They introduced new standards for error handling. After their next release, error-checking defects were down over 40 percent, and with one more release they were down to almost zero. They are now trying to reduce their user-interface defects.

Select the Largest Combination Wedge —Case 5

Figure 12-9 shows the pattern for Case 5. Logic implementation defects are a single wedge of almost 30 percent, so one possible strategy to follow would be the same as for our first case. If we normalize the data though, software interface defects represent over 30 percent of the total. In fact, the normalized combination of specification and design origins are over three quarters of the total. This organization needs to focus its attention on defining and designing their products better.

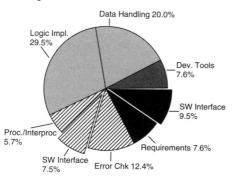

Development type: Systems.

Data recorded: During system test.

Language(s): C.

Development methods: A few inspections, branch coverage testing, certification process, regression tests.

Figure 12-9 Case 5.

Our strategy here is to use a combination of structured analysis methods, tools, and inspections to reduce software interface defects significantly. This approach also has strong potential for reducing the 20 percent data handling defects. We can expect this process to take two or three years to see significant measurable results. This is because we have to implement the process changes and go through at least one entire product lifecycle from analysis to system test before we can see how many software interface defects are detected in system test. As a result, this type of recommended change will require a strong sales job and a lot of management commitment and follow-through. There is a justification included in Chapter 14 for structured analysis if you find yourself in the position of having to do this sales job.

Select the Largest Combination Wedge — Case 6

Even before normalization, we see that the division represented in Figure 12-10 has significant front-end problems. Based on Table 12-1, they appear to be an ideal candidate for structured analysis/design. SA/SD directly addresses all the exploded wedges in the figure, and indirectly addresses data handling and requirements defects, as well. A byproduct of using SA/SD tools would be diagrams that could be used to aid inspections for the specific defect types that were problems in the past. They held no design reviews before, and one reason for this might be that they had no work products other than text documents to review.

As with the previous example, we can expect these changes to take some time before we see full results. On the other hand, the use of structured design and design inspections should immediately uncover defects of these types in inspections. This will help us to judge the eventual program success earlier than the testing phase.

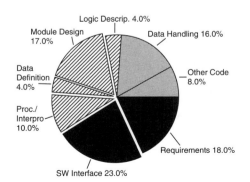

Development type: Systems.

Data recorded: During system test.

Language(s): C, Pascal

Development methods: No prototyping; no design reviews; code reviews (not 100%); regression tests (but not necessarily for fixes or enhancements); branch coverage; stress testing.

Figure 12-10 Case 6.

There are three justifications that explain how using SA/SD will yield the improvements that we expect to see. There are separate justifications for structured analysis and design in Chapter 14, and a justification for design inspections was given in Chapter 11. Remember to be careful not to double count defects when you combine justifications. For example, the design inspection justification assumes that we can eliminate 55 percent of all design defects. The SD justification assumes that we can eliminate 50 percent of a large subset of all design defects. The combination of structured design and design inspections might eliminate 75 percent of the module design and process/interprocess defects. But if you looked at the justifications separately, you might be tempted to count 100 percent (or more!) of the defects.

On the other hand, it is probably equally fair to assume that some small percentage of the requirements and software interface defects might be caught during design inspections. This would still be a definite improvement over not finding them until test.

Taken as a whole, this example represents one organization where we might cautiously expect to eliminate up to 50 percent of the sources of all defect-fixing time with one set of changes, even though the process changes would take a year or more. This would be quite dramatic.

Select a Combination of Wedges Based on Confidence in a Solution — Case 7

Figure 12-11 shows another division's data that was all collected during maintenance and enhancement activities. The point of data collection again must influence any approach that we take.

We begin to see patterns that we've seen before for which we already have proposed solutions. For example, the largest wedge is logic implementation, as in Case 1. The most design defects were module design, as in Case 6. There is a large error checking wedge, as in Case 4.

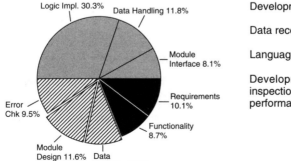

Logic Impl. 30.3% Data Handling 11.8%
Module Interface 8.1%
Requirements 10.1%
Functionality 8.7%
Error Chk 9.5%
Module Design 11.6% Data Definition 9.8%

Development type: Systems.

Data recorded: During maintenance.

Language(s): Pascal

Development methods: Some code inspections, stress tests, regression tests, performance tests.

Figure 12-11 Case 7.

We might attack the requirements and functionality wedges, but these are probably more important to new development than they are to maintenance. This division's product line is stable, and most of its new development is evolutionary. On the other hand, a large number of design defects suggests that the design is not documented well and is likely to get worse. For this reason, we can be more confident that changing our design process and retrofitting existing design documentation will help both existing and future designs. Table 12-1 suggests that structure charts and a data dictionary will help to eliminate module design and data definition defects.

Our strategy is to provide a structured design tool (that also has a data dictionary) and training for our engineers. Ideally, this tool can automatically do reverse engineering (produce design representations from existing code), as well. If it can't, then it will be difficult for the organization to find the necessary time to recreate accurate designs. Our expectation is that these changes will directly help us with the module design and data definition defects, and indirectly help reduce data handling and module interface defects.

Select a Combination of Wedges Based on Confidence in a Solution — Case 8

Our final example is from the data shown in Figure 12-12. It is from an applications environment, as Case 4 was. The two cases have almost identical problems with many design defects. However, this one has much more severe requirements and functionality defects.

Their methods of working closely with their customers early in their development are designed to try to overcome their problems. The strategy here is to refine the use of their iterative prototypes, and also to use QFD. The prototypes will help them to identify customer requirements correctly and to optimize user interfaces. QFD will help them to organize and rank their data so that they make the best decisions.

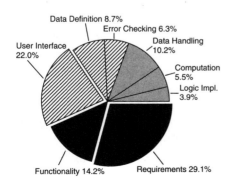

Development type: Applications.

Data recorded: Throughout development.

Language(s): 4GL

Development methods: Iterative prototypes, high-level DFD's and structure charts, data dictionary, design and code inspections, regression tests.

Figure 12-12 Case 8.

Our expectation is that these steps will take some time to pay off. On the other hand, the wedges for requirements and user interfaces are now 51 percent of the defect fixing time. In addition, the functionality wedge should also be partially affected by these changes. It represents another 14 percent of the current defects. Notice that again we can't necessarily use normalized times, because the data was collected throughout development.

Postscript — Case 8

This division combined the use of iterative prototypes with a commitment to process improvement. As a result, there were close to 40 percent fewer user-interface defects in their second release than there were in their first. While they didn't eliminate this defect type completely during development, they eventually found it unusual to get any user-interface complaints after other product releases.

On the other hand, they did not use QFD, so we have no way of knowing whether this technique might have helped them even more.

PATTERNS ACROSS ENVIRONMENTS

In this chapter, we looked at eight different "thorn bushes." We discovered that if we looked closely enough, no two of them looked alike. Maybe recognizing the differences between thorn bushes is the key to the Irishman's problem. It certainly holds promise for effectively choosing solutions to some of the problems experienced by these typical software development groups.

If we assume that these entities represent a cross section of all environments, we can do one last interesting exercise. Let's look at the data across environments to see if there are any general conclusions to draw. Remember that even though the pie charts only showed the top eight sources of defects for each, those eight represented between 70 and 94 percent of the various entities' defects. The total number of defects analyzed by these seven entities was 1721.

Requirements and design defects are major problems. Over the past two decades, a variety of people have reported this, but there has seldom been any detail about these problems. Requirements and design were the origin of over 50 percent of the defects in five of our seven different environments. After normalization (normalizing only those cases where defects were recorded in test or maintenance), they represent well over 50 percent of the defects for all but one of the cases. For that case, they account for almost 50 percent.

We saw logic implementation or logic description defects in all seven environments. Inspections are reported to help to reduce these. [3] CASE tools (like complexity analyzers, 4GL's, and branch coverage tools) will also help to reduce these defect types by providing better automated checks and better work products for inspections. This might be the case for data-handling defects as well. We saw these defects in five of the entities, and these included firmware, systems, and applications product areas.

Incorrect error checking was a common design problem. It appeared in five of the seven entities. It was very encouraging that one of the five also solved the problem with relative ease. This gives us some confidence that we might share this knowledge and achieve similar success. When we look at the normalized data, the potential improvement for such a change in the other four entities is a 15 to 20 percent decrease in fixing times.

The two reported applications entities both collected failure analysis data throughout development, and they both used prototyping. Unfortunately, we don't have their defect breakdowns for test alone. Otherwise we could make a stronger statement regarding which defects were prevented. These entities were the only two out of the seven to report user-interface defects among the top eight sources, though. In one of the entities, they reduced their prerelease user-interface defects almost 40 percent by using prototypes and other process changes. Their postrelease defect reduction was even better.

On the other hand, only the systems entities reported software-interface defects and module-design defects. For both categories, three of the four systems entities had sizable numbers of these defects.

Almost every defect type in our model appeared among the top eight defect sources of these seven entities. Even though the model was designed to be very concise, it is clearly complete enough to provide a useful frame of reference for failure analysis. We saw only two occurrences of the "other" category in the data from these seven groups. While the model fits well now, though, we expect that it will still have to evolve.

We can expect to see one more change as these groups make progress in eliminating root causes of defects. They will gradually change their focus from the engineering costs of fixing defects to calendar times spent on fixing defects. Software projects are seldom on or ahead of schedule, so defects that severely affect schedules have large paybacks if they can be eliminated. And when we switch to looking at time, we will also focus heavily on sequential processes. Our manufacturing experiences suggest that many sequential processes can be shortened or redesigned so they can be run in parallel with others. In both cases there is potential for shortening the time to market.

Improving Case Study Background Information

Our understanding of these examples has been limited by the available data. After reviewing them, we have a much clearer idea of why certain additional data is needed. You must collect this data when you apply these methods.

1. Describe your processes, products, and how well trained your people are.

2. Collect total project metric data for size, effort, and defects during test as a reference point.

3. Collect effort data for your particular process change as accurately as possible. Also record your best estimates of how efficient you were at the process. Remember that you are seldom as efficient the first time as you will be later.

4. Record failure analysis data as you did before you made process changes, so that you validate whether you prevented the targeted defects.

5. Extend your analysis to pay particular attention to those defect types that still occurred which you expected to be eliminated. Was there a flaw in the process change or in your implementation of it? Can you expect better results next time? Are there any differences in the product you are producing or maintaining that influenced your results?

6. Compute your final return on investment.

If you do these things, you will understand your results better. You will be better able to generalize your conclusions, and you will be confident of continuing your analysis to conquer other problems. None of the cases that we saw in this chapter adequately recorded this information. We can learn from these cases, though, and better understand what should be done in the future. An example is shown in Appendix B.

CONCLUSION

This chapter has brought together many of the concepts of metrics and process improvement. Software development environments have fundamental differences from each other. These differences are driven by product and business characteristics, as well as past practices. Metrics help you to characterize their similarities and differences. In particular, by analyzing defects you can gain important insights into your process problems.

You have an effective model for defect reporting and analysis. Once you've categorized your defects, there are various approaches to process changes. This chapter illustrated many defect patterns and five approaches for proceeding. The next chapter summarizes experimental results that support many of the recommendations made in this one.

BIBLIOGRAPHY

1. Grady, R. and D. Caswell, *Software Metrics: Establishing a Company-Wide Program*, Englewood Cliffs, NJ: Prentice-Hall, Inc., 1987, p. 10.
2. Ishikawa, K., *Guide to Quality Control*, Tokyo: Asian Productivity Organization, 1976.
3. Fagan, M., "Design and Code Inspections and Process Control in the Development of Programs," *TR21.572* IBM System Development Division, Kingston, N.Y., (Dec. 1974).

13

Elements
of Software
Engineering

*Thesis: Don't accept practices as "**software engineering**" until they have been measured and proven. Take those that have been proven and use them now.*

Ever since the term "software engineering" was created, our industry has struggled with what it really means. To some it means discipline. To others it is a useful way to select and organize subject matter for an educational program. To many software developers who were trained in other engineering disciplines, it reminds us to draw on useful techniques from those other disciplines.

People who attended the first conference that used the term in 1968 [1] saw a proliferation of software that was out of control and getting worse — the "software crisis." Since then, rapid change has continued, driven by hardware improvements and expanding demand. So the crisis is still with us. We should not get discouraged, though, because software engineering has made remarkable progress. In 1968 it would have been difficult to imagine some of today's common software systems and practices.

There are psychological implications to a term like "software engineering." For example, when HP started its metrics program, we struggled over what term to use for capturing time. We made a conscious decision to use the term "engineering months" instead of "man months" or "programmer months." This was because the metrics were part of a total program to improve our processes, methods, and tools. One of the goals for the overall program was to change attitudes and to encourage more of an engineering approach. Some cynical people point out that using such a title only sets higher expectations for pay. That's a risk that they should take, since the title also sets higher expectations for the approaches their people should take and the products they produce.

Many of the people doing software have also helped to propagate the term "software engineer." They like its use, because they want to be accepted as equals with other professionals. In the earlier days of software, people who wrote programs seemed different. What they did was mysterious, and what they produced was obviously not as valuable as something solid that you could touch and feel. In fact, it was difficult to get "real" engineers to do software, because they didn't want to move backwards in their careers. As the software field matured, these problems largely disappeared.

Like the field of software itself, the term "software engineer" has rapidly evolved from concept to widespread usage. By the middle of the 1980s, even the government acted to encourage software engineering discipline. They created the SEI (Software Engineering Institute) in order to remove some of the risk from software projects. One of the major contributions of the SEI is its five-level process maturity model. [2] It wasn't the first evaluative model, but it is the one that is gently forcing companies to look at their software practices from an engineering perspective.

ENGINEERING ROOTS

Engineers are people who apply scientific knowledge to provide practical, economic solutions to problems. They create structures, machines, and products. In contrast, a scientist searches for new knowledge and doesn't necessarily care whether it has a final use or not. A scientist might be fascinated with object-oriented technology, while an engineer would want to use object-oriented programming or an object-oriented database to solve a practical problem.

The name "engineer" was created in the Middle Ages. Latin writers first called the builders of battering rams, catapults, and other machines of war "ingeniators." [3] These early engineers were ingenious people. They often didn't have formal training, but they always had a knack for solving problems.

Engineering schools were created in the middle of the 19th century. Even then, much of the profession consisted of lone individuals applying common-sense rules. At the end of the 19th century, much of that changed. The development of electricity finally required the engineering profession to go beyond using only simple rules of thumb. They were forced to understand and apply more sophisticated scientific principles. This led the way for other engineering disciplines, as well.

As the engineering profession became recognized for its vast contribution to our society, high expectations developed. As a result, our expectations for software engineering start quite high. We look for the same type of discipline and mathematical foundations that are now part of other engineering fields. Yet many aspects of software are intangible. We invent new techniques and approaches and enthusiastically expect them to help us control our processes and results. All too often, we continue to use these methods without understanding whether they help or not.

Software metrics help us here, for at least some "software engineering" practices have been measured and proven effective in practical environments. Proven practices are referred to in this chapter as "fundamental principles." Many of these principles should sound familiar, because almost all of them were introduced earlier as "rules of thumb." We also have seen practical examples of how project managers apply them. *Various studies have provided evidence that the principles in this chapter work, and these principles are a starting point for planning any project.*

This chapter generally follows life cycle activities from the start of a project through the final testing of a product, except for the opening discussion on inspections, which apply throughout.

INSPECTIONS

The most important software engineering principle is that requirements models, designs, code, and other work products must all be reviewed. Following the practice of Michael Fagan, these reviews are called inspections. [4] Inspections can help us to uncover many defects before they become very costly or before they become so ingrained in a system that it is impractical to remove them. Equally important, inspections impose discipline. We must create inspectable work products at regular intervals that represent different views of parts of the final product. These work products have milestones on a project schedule, and the inspection milestones all provide objective, measurable feedback. Finally, inspections provide a way to educate the team and to encourage consistent best practices.

Early historical inspection reports emphasized significant results for code inspections. [4] We now have equally impressive results for many other work products. Figure 13-1 shows the average defect detection rates for six different types of work products at JPL. [5] The six inspection types shown are: R1 — requirements, I0 — high-level design, I1 — low-level design, I2 — source code, IT1 — test plans, and IT2 — test cases.

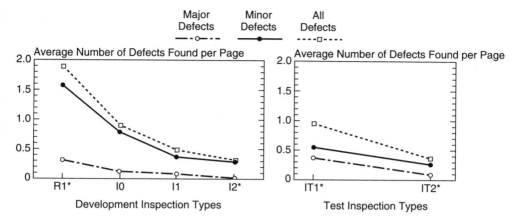

*At the alpha = 0.05 level of signifigance ANOVA F test showed a significant difference between the defect densities of R1 and I2, and between IT1 and IT2.

Figure 13-1 JPL defect density versus inspection type.

The figure suggests that early inspections are even more important than late ones. As your methods improve and your confidence grows, you might even consider eliminating some later inspections. We also saw JPL data earlier (Figure 5-2) that showed that inspection rates for different work products were constant at around 1.7 hours to find and fix a defect. The cost to find and fix average defects during final test was 5 to 17 times as much. [5] The cost ratio for one large HP project was 4.4 (the average efficiency of regular use, black box, and white box tests). The relative costs of their testing techniques are shown in Table 13-1. [6]

Testing Type	Efficiency (Defects Found/Hour)
Regular Use	.21
Black Box	.282
White Box	.322
Reading/Inspections*	1.057

Table 13-1 Comparison of testing efficiencies.

*Defect tracking system lumped code reading and inspections into one category. About 80% of the defects so logged were from inspections.

Other studies have measured other inspection parameters with favorable results. Table 13-2 came from one such HP study. [7] It gives values for team size, preparation time, and inspection rates. These can help you to plan and schedule effective inspections for your project.

	Average for One HP Division	Optimum for One HP Division	IBM™
Team Size	5.6 Engineers	4-5 Engineers	4-6 Engineers
Ratio of Preparation Time to Inspection Time	1.4	> 1.75	1.25
Inspection:			
– Code	360 LOC*/Hr	200-300 LOC/Hr	150 LOC/Hr
– Design	630 LOT*/Hr	300-400 LOT/Hr	250 LOT/Hr

*There were approximately 3 comment lines for every 10 NCSS
+LOT = Lines of Text

Table 13-2 Comparison of recommended inspection values.

As your project progresses, provide your team with immediate feedback to emphasize the value of inspections and to reinforce their active participation. Figure 13-2 is a simple example of the results of one inspection. [8] It shows several useful measures that are both meaningful by themselves, and when they are graphed against time. ROI was measured in terms of engineering time saved. In this ROI calculation, they used the JPL lower bound of five hours spent on defects found and fixed in test for every hour spent to find and fix defects in inspections. They only included "major" defects in the calculation. Fagan defined a major defect as one that would cause a product malfunction if it wasn't fixed. [9]

In a series of 18 inspections in this division, the ROI varied from 19 engineering hours lost to over 50 saved (also see Figure 5-3). About 70 percent of the inspections showed savings.

QUALITY CHARACTERISTICS

A software engineering principle that we didn't see in our earlier "rules of thumb" is that there are many software quality attributes. You are ill-advised to base your success on a narrow view of quality, for while you will undoubtedly achieve your narrow objectives, [10,11] your final product will be at risk.

Activity	Engineer Time	Moderator Time	Defects
Planning	30		
Overview	60	30	
Preparation #1	120		0 Major, 4 Questions
Preparation #2	60		4 Major
Inspection	120	60	1 Major, 12 minor
Total	390 minutes	90 minutes	5 Major, 12 minor
	6.5 hours	1.5 hours	

Return On Investment = (5 defects * 5 hours spent if found in test) - 8 hours spent
= 17 eng. hours saved

Effectiveness = 17 defects/8 hours = 2.13 defects found/hour

Finding Rate = 17 defects/.162 KNCSS = 104.94 defects/KNCSS

Inspection Rate = NCSS/elapsed hours = 162 NCSS/hour

Figure 13-2 Inspection result metrics.

Early in the development of software engineering, there were attempts to characterize quality. [12,13] We have already discussed HP's FURPS+ model in Chapters 4 and 7 and in *Software Metrics: Establishing a Company-Wide Program*. Let's extend that discussion to how you, as a project manager, can use it effectively during your projects.

First, use a list of quality attributes such as the one in Figure 4-1 as a checklist. You can think in terms of the goal/question/metric paradigm where the goal is "optimize delivered product functionality" or "optimize product usability," and so on. Some of the questions then are "What product functions do the customers need now?" "What functions do they take for granted?" "What functions would really excite customers?"

Second, select metrics that help you to know how well you are satisfying your customer's needs and wants. Recognize that you must measure your progress toward final, measurable product goals throughout product definition and development. While this may seem difficult, there are ways to do it. For example, Table 13-3 shows some for all the life cycle phases. [11]

Third, include these attributes in your quality plan, and document how you will test them during each phase of a project or during each inspection of a work product. For example, one project defined 33 FURPS+ goals (these were broken down into F=13, U=8, R=3, P=4, and S=5). [14] One of the FURPS+ usability attributes was that the product be:

	Investigation/ Specifications	Design	Implementation	Testing	Support
F	# target users to review spec or prototype % grade on report card from user % features competitive with other products # interface with existing products	% spec included in design # changes to spec due to design requirement # users to review change if needed	% designs included in code # code changes due to omissions discovered % features removed (reviewed by original target user)	% features tested at alpha sites % user documentation tested against product # target alpha customers	# Known Problem Reports sales act. reports (esp. cost sales) user surveys internal HP user surveys
U	# target users to review spec or prototype % grade on documentation plan by target user % grade on usability of prototype	% grade of design as compared to objectives # changes to prototype manuals after review	% grade by other lab user % grade by product marketing, documentation % original users to review any change	# changes to product after alpha test % grade from usability lab testing % grade by test sites	# User misunderstandings
R	# omissions noted in reviews of objectives (reliability goals) # changes to project plan, test plan after review	# changes to design after review due to error % grade of design as compared to objectives	% code changed due to reliability errors discovered in reviews % code covered by test cases # defects/KNCSS during module testing	MTTF (MTBF) % hrs reliability testing # defects/1K hrs # defects total defect rate before release ckpoints	# Known Problem Reports # defects/KNCSS
P	# changes to objectives after review % grade on objectives by target user % grade on objective by co-product managers	% product to be modeled defined modeled environment	performance tests achieve % of modeled expectations % of code tested with targeted ———— performance suite (module)	achieve performance goal with regard to environment(s) tested (system)	
S	# changes to support objectives after review by field & CPE	# design changes by CPE & field # diagnostic/recovery changes by CPE & field input	MTTR objective (time) ———— MTTC objective (time) ———— time to train tester: use of documentation	——————→ ——————→	same

Table 13-3 Examples of setting measurable objectives using FURPS for each life cycle phase.

User Tailorable

Goal: Tailor the interface to match the comfort level of the user in operating the product.

Customer Requirement	Ease of Implem.	Description
Must	Low	Provide one level of interaction and on-line support for errors.
Want	Medium	Allow both a "chatty" and "terse" mode.
Want	High	Change modes dynamically (e.g., Wordstar's™ interface).

A "must" represented a necessary feature to meet the goal, while a "want" was less necessary but still exciting to the customer. A complete list of attributes in this form helped the project team to make certain they created a system that met their customer's needs. It also helped them to understand where they could stretch and add some excitement to the product.

Part of clearly defining the goal included defining how they would measure their success at meeting the goal. They first defined how they would measure the quality attribute during final test. Then they could back up to earlier milestones and define how they would make similar measurements. For our tailorability attribute, this becomes:

Metric: Number of exceptions to (1) single-level interaction; (2) on-line error support.

Final Test: All user interactions and all error exits tested with final code.

Coding Phase: All code containing user interactions inspected for interaction level. All code inspected for error exits and how gracefully they handle on-line needs.

Design Phase: All designs inspected for interaction levels. All designs inspected for error exits and how gracefully they handle on-line needs.

By following this process, you define key project goals in a methodical, measurable way that help you to maintain customer focus throughout your project. These goals also provide a framework that helps you to anticipate and plan for evolving customer needs. You will find that the combination of inspections and quality attributes focused on customer needs will provide you with a valuable framework for project planning and implementation.

GRAPHICAL REPRESENTATIONS

Our third software engineering principle is to create and use multiple forms of work products, including graphics, throughout a project. Psychological research has shown that the human brain is very complicated. The left side of the brain (usually) processes verbal and written ideas and communications. The other side processes images and abstract ideas. [15] If we only create text versions of our documents and designs, we are limiting our potential for communication completeness, depth, and speed.

A variety of software engineering methods have been created to represent designs graphically. *Diagramming Techniques for Analysts and Programmers* shows many of these. [16] An article entitled "A Guided Tour of Program Design Methodologies" walks you through the same problem for functional decomposition, data flow design, data structure design, and programming calculus. [17] This particularly helps you to understand the application domains where these representations work best, and also shows you some of their inherent weaknesses. Remember that, despite some of their weaknesses, the pictorial work products help to reduce psychological complexity and aid getting valuable feedback when you show them to customers and use them during inspections.

One commonly used method is structured analysis/design (SA/SD). Various HP divisions have used SA/SD with differing degrees of success. Figure 13-3 shows the results from one 50 KNCSS firmware product where half of the product was designed using SA/SD methods, and the other half used existing methods. [18,19] The figure illustrates a dramatic reduction in defects. This study controlled variables well enough that we know differences weren't due to team makeup, component difficulty, or reuse aspects. In addition, the study found these defects much earlier in the process and, as a result, their productivity was 63 percent higher.

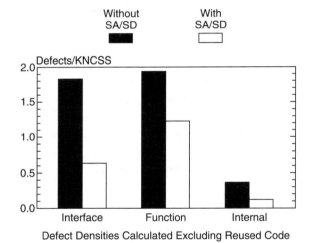

Figure 13-3
Effect of SA/SD methods
on defect densities
(for two comparable
firmware products).

People have used SA/SD for many years. If these results are so easy to obtain, why isn't SA/SD used by everyone? Perhaps another study explains the reason. A second HP division partially used SA/SD to develop an embedded systems product. [20] In their case, the part of the team using the SA/SD techniques experienced both advantages and disadvantages. Some of the advantages were: the project was easier to manage, the components seemed more likely to be reused, the team communications were slightly better, the functionality was better, and the product was more supportable. The disadvantages were: development time was longer, and they suspected that product performance would be worse.

Their results showed no defect density differences between the SA/SD and non-SA/SD product components. Because their results weren't as positive as the ones in the first study, SA/SD didn't become a standard part of their process.

So we are left with some uncertainty regarding SA/SD, but hopefully not for all graphical forms. There may not be a single method that works equally well for all application domains, but it seems likely that using one won't degrade your ability to produce good products. In fact, the repeated use of one of these methods is likely to provide significant improvements.

STRUCTURED DESIGN

Some software engineering design principles have been known and applied for many years. Structured design is a way to decompose a problem hierarchically and to partition it into smaller, single-purpose pieces. Structured programming introduces rules for program structure within modules. These methods were introduced to control increasing complexity that appeared as programs and systems grew in size. One study validated one of the underlying engineering basics of the structured methods: maximize cohesion, or module strength. [21]

A key principle of structured design is to maximize module strength. A high-strength module does one primary function. In *Composite/Structured Design*, Myers defined seven levels of module strength. [22] Card, Church, and Agresti tested this principle of module strength in a study that provides strong support for the practice of designing high-strength modules. For the study, programmers rated each module "they developed as performing one or more of the following functions: input/output, logic/control, and/or algorithmic processing." [21] Modules doing only one function were classified as high strength, two functions as medium strength, and three or more as low strength. Figure 13-4 shows that high-strength modules were significantly less error prone.

This classification technique is simple. It is easy to incorporate into module documentation, and it provides natural feedback to engineers regarding the complexity of their designs and the potential for defects. Project managers can also use these ratings as one decision criterion for types of inspections and tests.

MEASUREMENT OF COMPLEXITY

Our intuition strongly supports another software engineering principle: The most complex modules are most likely to have defects, and they will be the most difficult to maintain. We've already seen one measure of complexity in

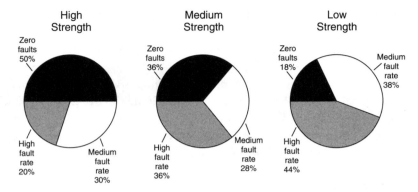

Figure 13-4 Fault rate for classes of module strength/cohesion.

this chapter — cohesion. Another measure discussed earlier in Chapters 2 and 8 is cyclomatic complexity. Cyclomatic complexity is a count of the number of different logic paths through a module. It was initially developed as a way of deriving the minimum number of test cases required to test a module.

Figure 13-5 shows a somewhat typical pattern of cyclomatic complexity for a product where no effort was made to control complexity. The figure also shows the limit of ten that Tom McCabe originally recommended. The first study that showed a strong correlation between cyclomatic complexity and defects was by Curtis, Sheppard, and Milliman. [23] A more recent study showed that modules exceeding cyclomatic complexities of 14 were more defect prone than those with lower complexity values. [24]

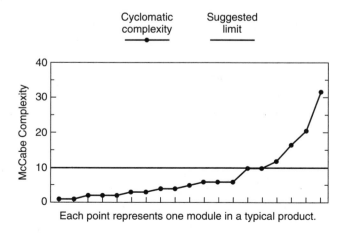

Figure 13-5 Typical pattern of cyclomatic complexity for a product.

In McCabe's original work, he also described the concept of essential complexity. This says that cyclomatic complexity will be naturally high for some structures (like Case statements). However, as long as you use the correct structured statements, the essential complexity of a module remains low. In fact, his company has automated the analysis of essential complexity. Their tool highlights the essential control flow of a module within the complete control graph of the module.

Cyclomatic complexity is a measure that helps you to recognize difficult parts of a product. You saw earlier that graphical images of this complexity helped engineers to control it (Chapter 8). You also saw that cyclomatic complexity acted as a team-unifier as a team improved the maintainability of a system (Chapter 5). These are all significant reasons to measure complexity to help you manage your projects.

METHODS OF VERIFICATION AND VALIDATION

There are many different ways to approach the verification and validation of software. But one underlying software engineering principle should be the same for all: the tests should model final customer usage of a product, result in a predictable level of quality, and be cost effective to develop and execute.

Several approaches were given in Chapter 7. Figure 13-6 shows another example. [25] This figure is taken from a firmware project that used the execution-time reliability model defined by John Musa. [26] Different reliability models make different assumptions about the testing methods that will be used and the timing of when defects will be found. By plotting the defects against time, you test the validity of a model's assumptions for your project. Generally, the defect discovery pattern converges toward values predicted by the model. This projection allows you to stop testing at an appropriate point with confidence in the quality of your software.

When using Musa's model, the number of defects found is plotted against the computer times spent executing different tests. The other approaches discussed in Chapter 7 were based on average times for finding and fixing defects and on times spent creating new tests.

All these models have one thing in common: They assume that your testing process is done in a defined, consistent way. This is a key principle that you must follow for your projects, as well. Select the model that best matches your product characteristics and development environment. Use the model's constraints to help control your process and to help you to predict your postrelease defect density.

The Drake article describes how the data shown in Figure 13-6 was used to predict a postrelease failure rate of 1.41 percent failures per year. [27] Such a failure rate predicts that if you ship a hundred units during the first year,

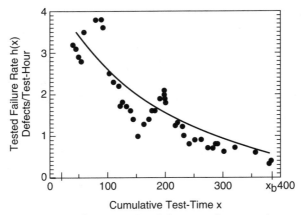

Figure 13-6 Terminal B failure rate from test data.

between one and two will require firmware changes. The actual failure rate turned out to be 1.58 percent. So we see that the failure rate model, like the model used by Ohba in the Chapter 5 example, was effective in predicting postrelease defect levels.

Another article by Ehrlich, Lee and Molisani [28] discusses the accuracy limitations of the Musa model early in the testing process. They found that the model was not particularly accurate in predicting when testing would be done until 60 percent of the total testing effort was complete. After that point, there was enough data that the schedule predictions were reliable.

One potential weakness of these reliability growth models is that they assume your tests exercise all parts of the software. To see if your tests meet this assumption, use a code-coverage tool. Examples of such tool use were given in Chapters 6 and 8.

Figure 13-7 illustrates the worth of such a tool. It shows the code coverage for 22 HP projects when they thought that they had tested their products thoroughly. When they ran the code coverage tests, they discovered that on average they had only exercised a little over half the code. We have found that it is not very hard to achieve 80 to 85 percent code coverage for systems or integration-level tests with the aid of a tool.

So reliability models and code coverage are two practical techniques to help you economically achieve a desired level of reliability. When you combine these with early plans for FURPS-like quality attributes, you will have a more "engineered" approach to verification and validation of your software.

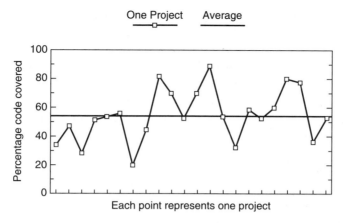

Figure 13-7 Typical code coverage before measurement.

CONCLUSION AND THOUGHTS ON PROJECT MANAGEMENT _____

Are the techniques in this chapter all we need to know about software engineering? Of course not. This book isn't meant to be a text book on software engineering. There is a lot more that could be said about lifecycles, documentation, coding standards, configuration management, reuse, and a variety of other subjects that are commonly taught.

The principles in this chapter have the unique property that they all have been validated with measurements in at least one environment, and we can use them to improve our chances for successful project schedules and products. In this sense, they are central to good software engineering practice. The more practices like these that you validate, the fewer experimental practices you will have to use for each new project. Also, you will get more efficient with the practices that you regularly use.

Many authors have claimed that individual programmer capabilities account for a difference of up to 25 times in productivity. Barry Boehm's Cocomo model includes a constant of 4.18 for such differences. [29] How does the use of these software engineering principles affect such individual differences in productivity?

One way of looking at all engineering disciplines is that their greatest contribution lies in the capture and standardization of knowledge and successful practices. Certainly some differences among software engineers today derive from the wide variation in their knowledge and application of best practices. There will always be differences in capabilities. It is our job as managers to minimize controllable differences through training and use of effective practices.

It is reasonable to assume that the same differences in capabilities exist among project managers. So how much of the programmer differences can be explained by differences in their managers? It has been suggested that programmer variation can be largely explained by the degree to which their learned knowledge happens to match the problem space. [30,31] So at least one critical engineering management skill is the ability to recognize a good match between an engineer's skill and background and the problems to solve.

Project management involves more than simply matching engineers to individual tasks, though. Developing software is often a sophisticated team activity, and this requires well-defined processes and skillfully coordinated teamwork. The engineering principles in this chapter span the entire software definition and development lifecycle, no matter what lifecycle model you use. They provide you with a framework that will help you to measure and manage more effectively. They also will help you to improve the productivity of your team.

You need to communicate to your team and to management how your processes, methods, and tools will be used, though. This will help to achieve their potential and make it easier to coordinate your team's activities. Figure 13-8 shows a guideline for a project plan that will help you to do this. Notice that it is an outline for either a presentation or a written plan.

The amount of detail that you need, and whether you even include all the suggested items in Figure 13-8 depends on various project risks. Table 13-4 summarizes four aspects of risk. When you scope a project, circle the applicable effort, size, support level, and coordination complexity choices. The criterion that appears farthest to the right determines whether the risk is "low," "medium," or "high." For example, even if a project has little code or few engineers involved, if it involves outside groups, it must be at least a "medium" size project. The bottom of the table gives recommendations for what type of project plan to do and for the target audience of the plan, depending on the risk level.

We have discussed a valuable set of software engineering principles to use and a guideline for how to plan your project to optimize your success. Will the combination of these guarantee your success? No, there are no guarantees, but software engineering provides discipline that should help. Through the application of these proven methods and practices, you can optimize your chances of success in solving practical problems with economic, effective techniques. Combining these principles with good planning and regular measured feedback offers at least a "limited warranty."

What and Why

Problem Being Solved or Opportunity
What is the primary focus (productivity, predictability, quality, and so forth)?

Product Description
Data sheet information, product environment, features, FURPS+ focus

Customers
Primary/secondary, how many, characteristics

Strategic Impact
Includes how effort supports strategy; also the lost opportunities if effort does not proceed; architectural context, business/operational context (e.g., IRP context), justification/ROI

How

Development Plan
Form of reporting status, reviews, checkpoints, metrics, quality objectives/means of verification, acceptance criteria including FURPS+ verification

Design Approach (optional in presentation with written project plan)
Methodology, tools, deliverables from design approach, audience for deliverables, support life

Project Standards (optional in presentation with written project plan)
Pointers to or brief description of: coding standards, interface standards, design standards, naming conventions, tools, configuration management, languages, testing process (hand-off criteria), backup/recovery (high-level detail)

Implementation Tactics (step-wise refinement of how to get to where you want to end up)
Sequence/decomposition of major deliverables, when and how many customers get them, steps that will occur, sequence, interdependencies, coordination with other groups, contingency plans

Packaging/Support Strategy
Documentation, training, packaging, implementation assist, maintenance plans, feedback mechanism, manufacturing and distribution

When and How Much

Phasing of Functionality
Items that are included in various deliverables/releases

Resources
People, hardware, software, space, expertise required

Schedule
PERT chart, Gantt chart

Issues
Technical, organizational, priority conflicts, timing

Figure 13-8 Project presentation/plan outline.

Risk	"Low"	"Medium"	"High"
Effort	0 - 6Eng. Mo.	6 - 18Eng. Mo.	>18 Eng. Mo.
Size	0 - 3KNCSS	3KNCSS - 15KNCSS	>15KNCSS
Support level (intended use of product)	Unsupported Internal	Supported internal with implementation assist	External customers
Coordination complexity	Internal to lab and local	Outside organization or geography	Outside vendors
Length of Project Plan	Slides only	Up to 10 pages	10 - 50 pages
Intended Use of Project Plan (users/reviewers)*	Proj. Mgr./ Sect. Mgr.	Multi-proj./ Multi-sect/Lab	>Lab

* The lab manager may identify additional parties for review where appropriate.

Table 13-4   Project plan scoping matrix.

BIBLIOGRAPHY

1. Naur, P., and B. Randell (editors), *Software Engineering: Report on a Conference*, Garmish, Oct. 1968.
2. Humphrey, W., D. Kitson, and T. Kasse, "The State of Software Engineering Practice: A Preliminary Report," *0270 5257/89/0500/ 0277*, ACM, (1989), pp. 277–288.
3. Furnas, C., J. McCarthy, and the Editors of LIFE, *The Engineer*, New York: Time Incorporated, 1966, p. 55.
4. Fagan, M. E., "Design and Code Inspections to Reduce Errors in Program Development," *IBM Systems Journal*, Vol. 15, no. 3 (1976), pp. 182–210.
5. Kelly, J., and J. Sherif, "An Analysis of Defect Densities Found During Software Inspections," *Proceedings of the Fifteenth Annual Software Engineering Workshop*, Goddard Space Flight Center, (Nov 1990), p. Kelly 11.
6. Tillson, T., and J. Walicki, "Testing HP SoftBench: A Distributed CASE Environment: Lessons Learned," *HP Software Engineering Productivity Conference Proceedings*, (Aug. 1990), pp. 441–460.
7. Scott, B., and D. Decot, "Inspections at DSD — Automating Data Input and Data Analysis," *HP Software Productivity Conference Proceedings*, (April 1985), pp. 1–79 — 1–89.
8. Rodriguez, S., "SESD Inspection Results," (April 1991).
9. Fagan, M. E., "Advances in Software Inspections," *IEEE Transactions on Software Engineering*, Vol. SE-12, no. 7 (July 1986), pp. 744–751.

10. Weinberg, G. M., and E. L. Schulman, "Goals and Performance in Computer Programming," *Human Factors*, Vol.16, no. 1 (1974), pp. 70–77.

11. Grady, R. and D. Caswell, *Software Metrics: Establishing a Company-Wide Program*, Englewood Cliffs, NJ: Prentice-Hall, Inc., 1987, p. 161.

12. Boehm, B. W., J. R. Brown, H. Kaspar, M. Lipow, G. MacLeod, and M. J. Merritt, "Characteristics of Software Quality," *TRW Series of Software Technology*, Vol. 1. Amsterdam: TRW and North-Holland Publishing Company, (1978).

13. McCall, J., P. Richards, and G. Walters, *Factors in Software Quality*, (Tech. Rep. 77CIS 02), Sunnyvale, CA, General Electric, Command and Information Systems 1977.

14. Mallette, D., "Release Management System: Product FURPS+," Version 2.0, (Feb. 3, 1988).

15. *ABC's of the Human Mind*, Pleasantville, N.Y.: Reader's Digest, 1990, p. 70.

16. Martin, J. and C. McClure, *Diagramming Techniques for Analysts and Programmers*, Englewood Cliffs, NJ: Prentice-Hall, Inc., 1985.

17. Bergland, G., "A Guided Tour of Program Design Methodologies," *IEEE Computer*, (Oct. 1981), pp. 126–150.

18. Tada, M. and F. Tsuruda, "Strategic Approach to Improve Quality in Analysis and Design Phases," *HP Software Engineering Productivity Conference Proceedings*, (Aug. 1988), pp. 259–267.

19. Nakajo, T., "A Case History Analysis of Software Error Cause-Effect Relationships," *IEEE Transactions on Software Engineering*, Vol. 17, no. 8, (Aug. 1991).

20. Fischer, B., and J. Jost, "A Comparison of Structured and Unstructured Methodologies in an Embedded Microprocessor Project," *HP Software Engineering Productivity Conference Proceedings*, (Aug. 1988), pp. 271–281.

21. Card, D. with R. Glass, *Measuring Software Design Quality*, Englewood Cliffs, NJ: Prentice-Hall, Inc., 1990, pp. 37–39.

22. Myers, G., *Composite/Structured Design*, New York: Van-Nostrand-Reinhold, 1978.

23. Curtis, B., S. B. Sheppard, and P. Milliman, "Third Time Charm: Stronger Prediction of Programmer Performance by Software Complexity Metrics," *Proceedings of the Fourth International Conference on Software Engineering*, (July 1979), pp. 356–360.

24. Rambo, R., P. Buckley, and E. Branyan, "Establishment and Validation of Software Metric Factors," *Proceedings of the International Society of Parametric Analysts Seventh Annual Conference*, (May 1985), pp. 406–417.

25. Drake, D., "A Pre-Release Measure of Software Reliability," *HP Software Productivity Conference Proceedings*, (April 1986), pp. 2–58 — 2–71.

26. Musa, J., A. Iannino, and K. Okumoto, *Software Reliability: Measurement, Prediction, Application*, New York: McGraw-Hill 1987.

27. Drake, D., "Reliability Theory Applied to Software Testing," *Hewlett-Packard Journal*, (April 1987), pp. 35–39.

28. Ehrlich, W., S. Lee, and R. Molisani, "Applying Reliability Measurement: A Case Study," *IEEE Software*, (March 1990), pp. 56–64.

29. Boehm, Barry W., *Software Engineering Economics*, Englewood Cliffs, NJ: Prentice-Hall, Inc., 1981.

30. Curtis, B, "Fifteen Years of Psychology in Software Engineering: Individual Differences and Cognitive Science," *IEEE Proceedings of the Eighth International Conference on Software Engineering*, London (August 1985), pp. 97–106.

31. Silverman, B., "Software Cost and Productivity Improvements: An Analogical View," *Computer*, (May 1985), pp. 86–95.

14

Justifying
Change

*Thesis: Evaluate all software process changes in terms of **measurable ROI**.*

We use different processes, methods, and tools because they help us to do our jobs more effectively. Some of them fit better than others depending on our current development environment and on the type of software we are producing. Software failure analysis helps us to identify opportunities for improvement. Measuring and validating improvements gives us confidence that they will work as well in the future.

This chapter extends the example introduced in Chapter 11 for justifying process change in terms of return on investment (ROI). There are five more justifications for using some common methods and tools. It also extends the justifications by adding "sanity checks."

A sanity check is a common scientific technique that evaluates an answer by comparing it to other readily believed numbers, and by then asking if the answer still seems reasonable. It doesn't guarantee that your answer is right, but it sometimes shows you when the answer is embarrassingly wrong. It is a good practice for you to adopt when you create your own justifications.

SOME BASIC CALCULATIONS FOR A TYPICAL PROJECT _____

We need to build a believable project basis, a common set of recognizable circumstances, to do a sanity check. Some of this was already done in the Chapter 11 example. We selected a 50 KNCSS project that would be done by six engineers. Let's use some of the Chapter 2 "rules of thumb" to extend our beliefs concerning this project. We saw average rates of generating code and average engineering times for different activities. We also used a HP average for prerelease defect density of 7 defects/KNCSS in the Chapter 11 example. Let's also assume that there are about 160 effective engineering hours per month, and that the six engineers are available and can effectively work in parallel for the whole project (an imprecise assumption, particularly as you scale up such numbers to much larger projects). There are some interesting calculations that we can now make.

Total project duration:

(50,000 NCSS * 1 calendar month/350 NCSS) + 6 eng. = 23.8 calendar months

50,000 NCSS * 160 eng. hours/350 NCSS = 22857 eng. hours

Calendar time for different phases (assuming no overlap of phases):

Spec./Req: .18 * 23.8 = 4.3 months;
Design: .19 * 23.8 = 4.5 months;
Code: .34 * 23.8 = 8.1 months;
Test: .29 * 23.8 = 6.9 months.

Total number of defects expected during test:

50 KNCSS * 7 Defects/KNCSS = 350 defects

These numbers are all believable. How are they affected by introducing different processes, methods, and tools? The answer to this question is the basis for our sanity checks. For each of our justifications, we will ask what the net changes were to project time and defects found. The results must be believable.

Sanity Check for a Defect Discovery Model

Let's first examine the Kohoutek defect-discovery model that we saw in Chapter 7. The model gave average times to find and fix defects for defects of different difficulties.

25 percent of defects are found and fixed in 2 hours/defect => 350 * .25 * 2 = 175 eng. hours
50 percent of defects are found and fixed in 5 hours/defect => 350 * .50 * 5 = 875 eng. hours
20 percent of defects are found and fixed in 10 hours/defect => 350 * .20 * 10 = 700 eng. hours
4 percent of defects are found and fixed in 20 hours/defect => 350 * .04 * 20 = 280 eng. hours
1 percent of defects are found and fixed in 50 hours/defect => 350 * .01 * 50 = 175 eng. hours

Total = 2205 eng. hours
Average = 6.3 eng. hours/defect

Total testing time spent finding and fixing defects:

2205 eng. hours * 1 eng. month/160 eng. hours = 13.8 eng. months

Percent of testing spent finding and fixing defects:

13.8 eng. months finding and fixing + (6.9 months in test * 6 eng.) = 33%

The results of our sanity check suggest that one third of testing time is spent on finding and fixing defects. The other two thirds is spent on writing and executing tests and on preparing the software for release and support. This feels about right. This short example does two things for us. First, it illustrates how the high-level project numbers can be usefully applied when doing sanity checks. Second, now that we have increased confidence in this model, we can use the resulting "average times for finding and fixing defects" when we perform later sanity checks.

Note that these results also suggest that there is an upper bound on how much we can expect to save in the test phase through just defect elimination. Compared with total project costs, 33 percent of our typical test costs is not the large, break-through savings that we often desire. On the other hand, we can hypothesize that similar savings are possible in other phases, as well.

If a large number of defects were eliminated, other savings would follow. We would undoubtedly change our processes so that we would eliminate some types of test. They would no longer be necessary, since we would have eliminated the need for them. No assumptions are made about such additional savings in our examples. Some of the examples do assume that the required time for test preparation is reduced, because better work products would be available for the test writers (for example, availability of structure charts for the first time). At the same time, it will often take some additional time to prepare such work products, at least for the first project on which they are used. In such cases, it is fair to assume that the time to generate them for later projects would be offset by their benefits (for example, improved communications, reduced complexity, and so forth).

The best techniques will ultimately save you substantially more time than you invest. They will help you to recognize patterns for solutions that you have seen before. In short, they will facilitate reuse of components, work products, or designs from previous products. Again, we have not included any assumptions about reuse in the examples here.

One final word about these justifications. All of them contain assumptions that may or may not be appropriate for your development environment. Be careful that you don't blindly take these assumptions and use them. These justifications will probably be too optimistic in some cases, and in others, too pessimistic. They are included here to help you to develop your own recommendations, not to save you the necessary thought process.

We'll start by repeating the design inspection justification from Chapter 11. Then we'll look at five others.

ANALYSIS OF SAVINGS FROM USE
OF DESIGN INSPECTIONS

Previously measured results (for various different organizations):

- Average rate of generating code = 350 NCSS/eng. mo. => 22857 eng. hours for a 50 KNCSS project.
- Average prerelease defect density = 7 defects/KNCSS. [1]
- Average number of design defects = 35 percent of total defects. [Chapter 12]
- Optimum number of inspectors during inspections = 4 to 5. [2]
- Ratio of preparation/inspection time for inspections > 1.75. [2]
- Average number of defects found/inspection hour = 2.5. [2]
- Average percentage of defects found by design inspections = 55 percent. [3]
- Optimum lines of text (LOT) per inspection hour = 400.
- Ratio of cost to find and fix defects during test to cost during design = 6.25. [4] Note that we also assume that ratio applies equally to find times and fix times.

Assumptions:

- Training takes 8 hours * 6 engineers, and costs $275 * 6 engineers.
- Start-up costs are 16 hours * 6 engineers.

Design defects expected for a 50 KNCSS project:

$$50 \text{ KNCSS} * \frac{7 \text{ defects}}{\text{KNCSS}} * \frac{35 \text{ design defects}}{100 \text{ defects}} = 123 \text{ design defects}$$

Time cost to find the design defects using inspections (assume 55 percent might be found):

$$\frac{123 \text{ design defects} * 0.55}{2.5 \text{ defects found/insp. hour}} * 4.5 \text{ eng.} * \frac{(1.75 \text{ prep} + 1 \text{ insp}) \text{ hours}}{1 \text{ insp hour}} = 335 \text{ eng. hours}$$

Time to find the same 55 percent (123 * 0.55 = 68) of the design defects during test:

$$335 \text{ design eng. hours} * \frac{6.25 \text{ find/fix hours in test}}{1 \text{ find/fix hour in design}} = 2094 \text{ eng. hours}$$

Net savings: 2094 eng. hours - 335 eng. hours = 1759 eng. hours to find defects

1759 eng. hours * [1 cal. mo./(6 eng. * 160 hours)] = 1.8 cal. months

Cost/Benefit Analysis (of Design Inspections)

ITEMS	COSTS	BENEFITS
Training	48 Engineering hours $1650	
Start-up costs	96 Engineering hours 0.5 Months	
Reduced defect finding time		1759 Engineering hours
Time to market		1.8 Calendar Months

Sanity Check

We first compare the number of defects eliminated to the total number expected.

Percent of all defects eliminated: (68/350) * 100 = 19.4%

The percentage seems neither too small nor too large. Any project manager should be happy with a technique that will eliminate close to 20 percent of their defects. Furthermore, it is easy to see its basis. It basically came from 55 percent (the percentage of defects found in inspections) of 35 percent (the percentage of total defects).

Second, we derive the amount of engineering time saved from the benefit column minus the cost column.

Percent of total eng. time saved: [(1759 - 48 - 96)/22857] * 100 = 7.1%
on subsequent projects: (1759/22857) * 100 = 7.7%

The percentages here are small, yet still worthwhile when we look at the cost/benefit analysis.

Finally, we compute the average hours per defect, and compare the answer to our defect discovery model.

Average hours/defect to find in test: 2094/68 = 30.8 hours/defect

This figure seems a little high, particularly since our calculations don't include fix times. An average of 30.8 hours/defect corresponds to the model's region of between 95 and 99 percent. We will revisit this number later in this chapter when we look at a justification for code inspections.

So we have tested our results in three different ways, and the results have stood up to the tests. As we said at the beginning, this doesn't guarantee that they are correct, but at least it adds to our confidence.

In addition to these checks, there are two more checks that we can make for this example. We can compute the expected number of pages of design documentation from some of the inspection results that were given in Table 13-2, and we can compute the number of inspections that we will do assuming each inspection is two hours.

Amount of inspected design documentation:

$$\frac{68\ \text{defects}}{2.5\ \text{defects/insp. hour}} * \frac{400\ \text{LOT/insp. hour}}{55\ \text{LOT/page}} = 198\ \text{pages of design documentation}$$

Number of inspections:

$$\frac{68\ \text{design defects}}{2.5\ \text{defects found/insp. hour}} * \frac{1\ \text{insp.}}{2\ \text{insp. hours}} = 13.6\ \text{inspections}$$

If we assume that all of the design inspections will be held in the last three-quarters of the design phase (which is 4.2 months long), then we must average slightly over one inspection per week. These numbers also sound realistic for a project of this size.

ANALYSIS OF SAVINGS FROM USE
OF STRUCTURED ANALYSIS _____

The core argument of this analysis is that the use of an SA tool produces diagrams and a data dictionary that provide insights to engineers. These insights help them to see problems that are not normally found until test. Remember the work-product analysis discussion in Chapter 8. It strongly argued that graphical work-product representations and metrics can help engineers discover problems much earlier than during test. Figure 13-3 also gave evidence that at least one HP organization experienced a reduction of 75 percent of certain defect types.

This justification makes no assumptions about the presence or absence of inspections. You may want to combine the costs and benefits of inspections into a single justification when you create your own.

Previously measured results (for various different organizations):

- Average rate of generating code = 350 NCSS/eng. mo. => 22857 eng. hours for a 50 KNCSS project.
- Average prerelease defect density = 7 defects/KNCSS. [1]
- Find and fix time in test for SA type defects averages more than "less difficult" defects = 15 hours/defect. [see first sanity check]
- Average time spent in requirements phase = 18 percent; test = 29 percent.

Assumptions:

- SA with data dictionary only reduces the number of interface, functionality, and data definition defects. These defect types are 20 percent of all defects. Without the tool, 10 percent are introduced in specifications, 10 percent in design. [Chapter 12]
- SA training = 16 hours * 6 engineers; start-up costs are included in increased requirements time.
- Tools for SA will cost approximately $1500 * 6 engineers plus $275 training * 6 engineers.
- Use of the tool helps to eliminate 75 percent of the target defects.
- All of these defects would normally be caught in test (justification improves if caught later).
- Time to create SA diagrams increases requirements phase by 10 percent.
- Availability of diagrams decreases test phase by 5 percent (not including defect reduction time).

SA-type defects expected for a 50 KNCSS project:

50 KNCSS * 7 defects/KNCSS * 10% = 35 spec. defects and 35 design defects

Increased engineering time in requirements phase that helps to find 75 percent of the SA-type defects:

$$50 \text{ KNCSS} * \frac{1 \text{ eng. mo.}}{0.350 \text{ KNCSS}} * \frac{160 \text{ eng. hrs.}}{\text{eng. mo.}} * 0.18 \text{ (\% spec. time)} * .1 \text{ (\% incr.)} = 411 \text{ more eng. hours}$$

Time to find and fix the same 75 percent (0.75 * 70 = 52) defects during test:

52 defects * 15 eng. hours/defect = 780 eng. hours

Net defect find and fix savings: 780 eng. hours - 411 eng. hours = 369 eng. hours
Decreased time in test phase: 22857 eng. hrs. * 0.29 (% test time) * 0.05 (% decr.) = 331 fewer eng. hours
Calendar savings: (369 eng. hours + 331 eng. hours) * [1 cal. mo./ (6 eng. * 160 hours)] = 0.7 cal. months

Cost/Benefit Analysis (of Structured Analysis)

ITEMS	COSTS	BENEFITS
Training	96 Engineering hours $1650	
Start-up costs	2 Calendar days	
Reduced defect finding time		369 Engineering hours
Reduced test-writing time		331 Engineering hours
	$9000	
Purchased software		
Time to market		0.7 Calendar Months

Sanity Check

We have the same three checks to perform for this justification as we did in the previous example.

Percent of all defects eliminated: (52/350) * 100 = 14.9%
Percent of total eng. time saved: [(369 + 331 -96)/22857] * 100 = 2.6%
 on subsequent projects: (700/22857) * 100 = 3.1%
Average hours/defect to find and fix in test: 15 hours/defect
Diagrams created: 411 eng. hours * 1 diagram/3 hours = 137 diagrams

Compared to our first example, we see a relatively small return for a large percentage of error elimination here. Everything else about this justification sounds right. Are there any possible explanations?

As noted in the introduction to this chapter, these justifications are very conservative regarding engineering times for new process, methods, and tools. In the long term, we probably shouldn't expect the creation of SA diagrams to increase the requirements phase, but rather to decrease it.

A second important consideration is that we haven't accounted for any postrelease savings. Remember that Table 5-2 showed that in at least one environment, requirements defects averaged 575 engineering hours to find and fix after product release. Even modest defect reductions here can produce a large postrelease savings.

A third difficult-to-quantify factor is that poor early analysis complicates design and can significantly increase both the design time and the number of design defects.

All of these additional potential savings will probably increase your return substantially over the conservative calculations here.

ANALYSIS OF SAVINGS FROM USE
OF STRUCTURED DESIGN _____

The primary premise of this analysis is like that of the SA justification. In this case, we can reason that SD diagrams and a data dictionary provide insights to engineers. These insights help them to see problems that are not normally found until test.

Figure 7-12 gave evidence that the structural complexity of at least one product correlated well with the postrelease defect density, although the distribution of defect types was not given. Having graphic representations that help to show this complexity can help engineers to improve designs. The divisional defect patterns shown in Figures 12-10 and 12-11 are good examples of cases where an SD tool could significantly help.

This justification makes no assumptions about the presence or absence of inspections. You may want to combine the costs and benefits of inspections into a single justification when you create your own.

Previously measured results (for various different organizations):

- Average generating code rate = 350 NCSS/eng. mo. => 22857 eng. hours for a 50 KNCSS project.
- Average prerelease defect density = 7 defects/KNCSS. [1]
- Find and fix time for SD type defects averages a little more than "less difficult" defects = 12 hours/defect. (See first sanity check.)
- Average time spent in design phase = 19 percent; test = 29 percent.

Assumptions:

- SD with data dict. only improves SW and HW interface, module design, process comm., and data definition defects. These defect types are 25 percent of all defects. [Chapter 12]
- SD training =16 hours * 6 engineers; start-up costs are included in increased design time.
- Tools for SD will cost approximately $1000 * 6 engineers plus $275 training * 6 engineers.
- Use of the tool helps to eliminate 75 percent of the target defects.
- All of these defects would normally be caught in test (justification improves if caught later).
- Time to create SD diagrams increases design phase by 5 percent.
- Availability of diagrams decreases test phase by 5 percent (not including defect reduction time).

SD-type defects expected for a 50 KNCSS project:

$$50 \text{ KNCSS} * \frac{7 \text{ defects}}{\text{KNCSS}} * \frac{25 \text{ SD-type defects}}{100 \text{ defects}} * 0.75 \text{ (\% elim.)} = 66 \text{ SD-type defects}$$

Increased engineering time in design phase that helps to find 75 percent of the SD-type defects:

$$50 \text{ KNCSS} * \frac{1 \text{ eng. mo.}}{0.350 \text{ KNCSS}} * \frac{160 \text{ eng. hrs.}}{\text{eng. mo.}} * 0.19 \text{ (\% design time)} * 0.05 \text{ (\% incr.)} = 217 \text{ more eng. hours}$$

Time to find and fix the same 66 defects in test:

66 defects * 12 eng. hours/defect in test = 792 eng. hours

Net Savings: 792 eng. hours - 217 eng. hours = 575 eng. hours to find defects
Decreased time in test phase: 22857 eng. hrs. * 0.29 (% test time) * 0.05 (% decr.) = 331 fewer eng. hours
Calendar savings: (575 eng. hours + 331 eng. hours) * [1 cal. mo./ (6 eng. * 160 hours)] = 0.9 cal. months

Cost/Benefit Analysis (of Structured Design)

ITEMS	COSTS	BENEFITS
Training	96 Engineering hours $1650	
Start-up costs	2 Calendar days	
Reduced defect finding time		575 Engineering hours
Reduced test-writing time		331 Engineering hours
Purchased software	$6000	
Time to market		0.9 Calendar Months

Sanity Check

Percent of all defects eliminated: (66/350) * 100 = 18.9%
Percent of total eng. time saved: [(575 + 331 -96)/22857] * 100 = 3.5%
on subsequent projects: (906/21333) * 100 = 4.0%
Average hours/defect to find and fix in test: 12 hours/defect
Diagrams created: 217 eng. hours * 1 diagram/2 hours = 109 diagrams

These calculations show a slightly higher return for a slightly higher percentage of eliminated defects than the justification for SA. The higher return is primarily a result of assuming a smaller increase of engineering time than for SA.

The additional comments made for SA, except for the design comments, probably apply equally to this justification. Another source of savings that was not assumed here is the identification of requirements defects while creating SD diagrams. Such defects would cost considerably more if they are not found until test or customer usage.

ANALYSIS OF SAVINGS FROM USE
OF COMPLEXITY ANALYSIS

Again, a primary thrust of this analysis is that a tool (that does complexity analysis and graphics, in this case) helps engineers to see problems that are not normally found until test. If these problems are found while an engineer is coding, the code can be modified and restructured before it gets too complex. This will help to reduce coding and unit test time, and should also reduce defects in system test.

Figures 8-2 and 8-3 showed how complexity differences can be clearly seen and a story in Chapter 5 described how cyclomatic complexity acted as a team-unifying catalyst. The divisional defect patterns shown in Figures 12-4 and 12-11 are good examples of cases where a complexity analysis tool could significantly help.

This justification makes no assumptions about the presence or absence of inspections. It would be strengthened by combining it with the costs and benefits of inspections into a single justification when you create your own.

Previously measured results (for various organizations):

- Average generating code rate = 350 NCSS/eng. mo. => 22857 eng. hours for a 50 KNCSS project.
- Average prerelease defect density = 7 defects/KNCSS. [1]
- Average number of design defects = 35 percent of total defects; coding defects = 45 percent of total defects. [Chapter 12]
- Ratio of cost to find and fix defects in test to cost during coding = 2.5. [4] Note that we also assume that ratio applies equally to find times and fix times.
- Find and fix time for less difficult defects = 10 hours/defect. [1]

Assumptions:

- Use of tool helps engineers to identify 25 percent of the design defects normally left before test.
- Use of tool helps engineers to identify 25 percent of the coding defects normally left before test.
- The toolset will cost $1200 * 6 engineers; start-up costs are 16 hours * 6 engineers.
- Training = 8 hours * 6 engineers, and costs $275 * 6 engineers.

Design and coding defects that are assumed to be found using tool on a 50 KNCSS project:

$$50 \text{ KNCSS} * \frac{7 \text{ defects}}{\text{KNCSS}} * \frac{35 \text{ design defects}}{100 \text{ total defects}} * 0.25 \text{ (\%)} = \begin{array}{c} 31 \text{ design defects} \\ \text{found and fixed} \end{array}$$

$$50 \text{ KNCSS} * \frac{7 \text{ defects}}{\text{KNCSS}} * \frac{45 \text{ coding defects}}{100 \text{ total defects}} * 0.25 \ (\%) = 39 \text{ coding defects found and fixed}$$

To find and fix the 70 additional defects during coding:

$$70 \text{ defects} * \frac{10 \text{ eng. hours}}{\text{defect}} * \frac{1 \text{ eng. hour during coding}}{2.5 \text{ eng. hours during test}} = 280 \text{ eng. hours}$$

To find and fix the same 70 defects during test: 70 defects * 10 eng. hours/ defect = 700 eng. hours

Net savings:
700 eng. hours - 280 eng. hours = 420 eng. hours
420 eng. hours * [1 cal. mo./(6 eng. * 160 hours)] = 0.4 cal. months

Cost/Benefit Analysis (of Complexity Analysis)

ITEMS	COSTS	BENEFITS
Training	48 Engineering hours $1650	
Start-up costs	48 Engineering hours	
Reduced defect find/fix time		420 Engineering hours 1 Calendar months
Purchased software	$7200	
Time to market		0.4 Calendar months

Sanity Check

Percent of all defects eliminated: 70/350 = 20%
Percent of total eng. time saved: [(420 - 48 - 48)/22857] * 100 = 1.4%
　　　　　　　on subsequent projects: (420/22857) * 100 = 1.8%
Average hours/defect to find and fix in test: 10 eng. hours/defect

The percentage of time saved here seems very low for the percentage of defects eliminated. The development time savings is not the primary benefit from such a tool, though. The primary benefit is the production of less-complex software. Such software will cost much less over the typical long life of software systems than more complex software.

Another factor to consider for this type of tool used in conjunction with others is that, eventually we can decrease the amount of time spent in testing and inspections.

ANALYSIS OF SAVINGS FROM A CERTIFICATION PROCESS
FOR A SINGLE PROJECT

Let's build a case for the value of a test-certification program such as the one described in Chapter 7. Remember that Figure 7-9 showed that the use of a certification program can reduce your postrelease defects by better than a factor of three.

We will take the specific case of a project that will involve 6 engineers, produce 50 KNCSS of code, and take about 2 years. We will assume that a normal high-quality suite of tests will be created. HP historical data shows that projects that don't use the certification process experience an average of around 7 defects/KNCSS before release of a product. Let's assume that this level of defect discovery resulted in a defect-removal efficiency of 95 percent and that certification will push that total up to 99 percent. The Kohoutek model suggests that the average time to find and fix these defects is 20 hours/defect.

Previously measured results (for various different organizations):

- Average rate of generating code = 350 NCSS/eng. mo. => 22857 eng. hours for a 50 KNCSS project.
- Average prerelease defect density = 7 defects/KNCSS. [1]
- Find and fix time for difficult defects = 20 hours/defect.[1]
- Ratio of cost to find and fix defects postrelease to cost during integration-level test = 3.75.[4,5]

Assumptions:

- Defect removal efficiency improves from 95 percent to 99 percent (related to find and fix assumption above).
- Certification training takes 8 hours * 6 engineers, and costs $275 * 6 engineers.
- Start-up costs are 16 hours * 6 engineers.
- Tools to support the process will cost $4000 (e.g., branch coverage, line counters, etc.)

Expected defects for a project of 50 KNCSS of code that is certified:

50 KNCSS * 7 defects/KNCSS * (.99 - .95) = 14 additional defects
found and fixed

Engineering hours and calendar time to find and fix additional defects:

14 defects * 20 eng. hours/defect = 280 eng. hours

$$\frac{280 \text{ eng. hours}}{6 \text{ eng.}} * \frac{1 \text{ week}}{40 \text{ hours}} = 1.17 \text{ additional calendar weeks}$$

To find and fix the same 14 additional defects after product release:

$$280 \text{ eng. hours during test} * \frac{3.75 \text{ eng. hours after release}}{1 \text{ eng. hour during test}} = 1050 \text{ eng. hours}$$

Net savings:

1050 eng. hours - 280 eng. hours = 770 eng. hours

770 eng. hours * [1 cal. mo./(6 eng. * 160 hours)] = 0.8 cal. months

Cost/Benefit Analysis (of Certification)

ITEMS	COSTS	BENEFITS
Class costs	48 Engineering hours $1650	
Start-up costs	96 Engineering hours	
Reduced defect finding time		770 Engineering hours 0.8 Cal. months postrelease
Purchased software	$4000	
Time to market	1.17 weeks	

Sanity Check

Percent of all defects eliminated: 14/350 = 4%

Percent of total eng. time saved: [(770 - 48 - 96)/22857] * 100 = 2.7%

on subsequent projects: (770/22857) * 100 = 3.4%

Average hours/defect to find and fix after release: 1050/14 = 75 hours/defect

The percentages here are small, yet still worthwhile when we look at the cost/benefit analysis. Seventy-five hours/defect is larger than the largest value for our model (50 hours/defect). This makes sense, though, since defects found after release definitely cost more than they do prerelease. If anything, this result feels like it may not be as large as we might experience on a real project.

ANALYSIS OF SAVINGS FROM USE
OF CODE INSPECTIONS (FIRST TRY)

Of all the justifications, this one was the most difficult. Inspections have been used for many years. Their value has been accepted for some time, now. I have managed groups that have found them very beneficial. I'm sure that many people's expectations for this justification are quite high. Yet, the analysis reveals some interesting conclusions about their value and about some of the past measurements that have been taken.

We will first do a justification for 100 percent code inspections.

Previously measured results (for various different organizations):

- Average rate of generating code = 350 NCSS/eng. mo. => 22857 eng. hours for a 50 KNCSS project.
- Average prerelease defect density = 7 defects/KNCSS. [1]
- Ratio of cost to find and fix defects in test to cost during coding = 2.5. [4] Note that we also assume that ratio applies equally to find times and fix times.
- Optimum number of inspectors during inspections = 4 to 5. [2]
- Ratio of preparation/inspection time for inspections > 1.75. [2]
- Optimum number of inspected LOC per hour = 250 [Table 13-2]
- Average percentage of defects found by code inspections = 60 percent. [3]

Assumptions:

- There are three comment lines for every ten NCSS.
- Training takes 8 hours * 6 engineers, and costs $275 * 6 engineers.
- Start-up costs are 16 hours * 6 engineers.

Total expected defects for a 50 KNCSS project (assuming we inspect all code):

$$50 \text{ KNCSS} * \frac{7 \text{ defects}}{\text{KNCSS}} = 350 \text{ defects}$$

Estimate the time to inspect all code:

$$50000 \text{ NCSS} * \frac{(10 + 3) \text{ LOC}}{10 \text{ NCSS}} * 4.5 \text{ eng.} * \frac{(1.75 \text{ prep} + 1 \text{ insp}) \text{ hours}}{1 \text{ insp hour}} * \frac{1 \text{ hour}}{250 \text{ LOC}} = \frac{3218}{\text{eng.}} \text{ hours}$$

Assume that inspections will find 60 percent of the defects (350 * 0.6 = 210); time to normally find them in test:

$$(3218 * 0.6) \text{ coding eng. hours} * \frac{2.5 \text{ find hours in test}}{1 \text{ find hour in coding}} = 4827 \text{ eng. hours}$$

Net Savings:

4827 eng. hours - 3218 eng. hours = 1609 eng. hours to find defects
1609 eng. hours * [1 cal. mo./(6 eng. * 160 hours)] = 1.7 cal. months

Before we bother to do the cost/benefit analysis, we will do a sanity check that reveals some interesting anomalies.

Sanity Check

Percent of all defects eliminated: $(210/350) * 100 = 60\%$
Percent of total eng. time saved: $[(1609 - 48 - 96)/22857] * 100 = 6.4\%$
on subsequent projects: $(1609/22857) * 100 = 7\%$
Average hours/defect to find in inspections: $3218/210 = 15.3$ hours/defect
Average hours/defect to find in test: $4827/210 = 23$ hours/defect

The percentages of defects eliminated and engineering time saved match our initial expectations for a high return for code inspections. The average hours per defect are way too high, though. The average of 15.3 hours is much higher than the JPL (1.5 hours in Figure 5-2) and one HP project (1.057 hours in Table 13-1) averages. The average of 23 hours is almost four times the average of our earlier defect discovery model. This says that there is definitely something wrong with some of our assumptions.

A recent study in one HP division sheds some light on the inspection averages. They did a series of inspections that took 208 eng. hours to inspect 4 KNCSS of code. They found 389 defects, for a defect density of 97 defects/KNCSS *before system test*. Remember that the average prerelease defect density that HP has reported during system test is 7 defects/KNCSS. Clearly, the inspections were finding many defects that are not normally found (or reported) in system test. This suggests that many of the defects found in inspections are caught in unit test. These represent another source of savings that was not included in our calculations.

In pursuing the high average hours/defect in test, we first ask, "Is the inspection time calculation believable?" It's based on an older study of 45 inspections. We can use the numbers from the above recent HP study to check this. When you scale this up to 50 KNCSS and adjust by the same factor of 1.3 LOC/NCSS, the result is 3380 eng. hours. This is remarkably close to 3218 eng. hours, so we must accept the inspection time calculation.

How about the time-to-find calculation? The only factor in that calculation that can be questioned is the ratio of 2.5 to 1 of time to find/fix in test versus coding. This factor was derived from the averages for finding and fixing defects from five large studies, and, in addition, it is also very believable. So where is the problem?

The problem is in the hidden assumption that the time to find defects by large-scale inspections is as short as the methods that were used in the five studies. We must conclude that there is a point of diminishing returns for inspections (indeed, we can generalize that such a point undoubtedly exists for all defect-finding techniques). This argues favorably for the approach used by many organizations of selecting the most risk-prone modules for inspections. (We will discuss some approaches after reassessing this example.)

Now we can try building our justification again while taking these new insights into account. *Three new assumptions are highlighted in italics.*

ANALYSIS OF SAVINGS FROM USE
OF CODE INSPECTIONS (SECOND TRY) _____

Previously measured results (for various different organizations):

- Average rate of generating code = 350 NCSS/eng. mo. => 22857 eng. hours for a 50 KNCSS project.
- Average prerelease defect density = 7 defects/KNCSS. [1]
- Optimum number of inspectors during inspections = 4 to 5. [2]
- Ratio of preparation/inspection time for inspections > 1.75. [2]
- Optimum number of inspected LOC per hour = 250 [Table 13-2]
- Average percentage of defects found by code inspections = 60 percent. [3]

Assumptions:

- *20 percent of the code contains 80 percent of the defects and we are able to choose the correct 20 percent to inspect.*
- *In addition to finding defects that aren't normally found until system test, we also find five times this number of defects and they normally cost 2 hours/defect in unit test.*
- *Because of the large percentage of defects here, the average time to find during test is 5 hours (slightly less than the average find/fix time given by earlier model).*
- There are three comment lines for every ten NCSS.
- Training takes 8 hours * 6 engineers, and costs $275 * 6 engineers.
- Start-up costs are 16 hours * 6 engineers.

Total expected defects for a 50 KNCSS project:

$$50 \text{ KNCSS} * \frac{7 \text{ defects}}{\text{KNCSS}} = 350 \text{ defects}$$

Estimate the time to inspect the correct 20 percent of the code (50 KNCSS * 0.2 = 10 KNCSS):

$$10000 \text{ NCSS} * \frac{(10 + 3) \text{ LOC}}{10 \text{ NCSS}} * 4.5 \text{ eng.} * \frac{(1.75 \text{ prep} + 1 \text{ insp}) \text{ hours}}{1 \text{ insp hour}} * \frac{1 \text{ hour}}{250 \text{ LOC}} = 644 \text{ eng. hours}$$

Time to find 60 percent of 80 percent (350 * 0.6 * 0.8 = 168) of the coding defects during test:

168 defects * 5 eng. hours/defect = 840 eng. hours

Time to find other defects that are normally found in unit test:

168 test defects * (5 unit test defects/1 test defect) * 2 eng. hours = 1680 eng. hours

Net Savings:
840 eng. hours + 1680 eng. hours - 644 eng. hours = 1876 eng. hours
1876 eng. hours * [1 cal. mo./(6 eng. * 160 hours)] = 2 cal. months

Cost/Benefit Analysis (of Code Inspections)

ITEMS	COSTS	BENEFITS
Training	48 Engineering hours	
	$1650	
Start-up costs	96 Engineering hours	
	0.5 Months	
Reduced defect finding time		1876 Engineering hours
Time to market		2 Calendar Months

Sanity Check

Percent of all test defects eliminated: (210/350) * 100 = 60%

Percent of total eng. time saved: [(1876 - 48 - 96)/22857] * 100 = 7.6%

on subsequent projects: (1876/22857) * 100 = 8.2%

Average hours/defect to find in inspections:644/(168+840) = 0.6 hours/defect

Average hours/defect to find in test: 840/168 = 5 hours/defect

This justification has fixed the problems that we saw with our first try. The average defect-finding rate for inspections is close to the average rate shown in Table 13-1. The percentage of engineering time saved is similar to the percentage that was calculated for design inspections. Because this analysis was based on only inspecting 20 percent of the code and it turned out so well, the point of diminishing returns for inspections may be even higher. One possible way of improving these returns even more is to use less rigorous (and therefore less costly) inspection methods on some of the less risky code. One HP division defined three inspection types: large-team inspection, small-team inspection, and bench review.

We could rework this example many times with different assumptions that change the results in various ways. The reason for doing this one twice was to emphasize the value of sanity checks, not to come up with the final word on inspections. I'm sure that some people will criticize this example as wrong because the payback is too small. Others will still argue that they shouldn't do any inspections. My bias is that I believe in inspections. I also believe in monitoring code inspection results so that you know when to quit inspecting and to use some other method of test.

One of our new assumptions deserves some additional thought. How do we choose the correct 20 percent of the code to inspect? There are several approaches. If we are inspecting existing or modified code, we can look at past defect patterns. If we did design inspections, we can look at defect patterns from those. We can look at code complexity measures, such as cyclomatic complexity. Perhaps most important of all, we can ask our team for their subjective assessment of which modules they think might be most defect prone.

This justification is conservative. It doesn't include one of the most important values of inspections — that of the shared knowledge among a team. Inspections help to increase the knowledge of your engineers. Inspections help engineers to see common mistakes before they make them and to see other people's solutions to problems. This increased knowledge will help your team later when they need to make changes and enhancements. Inspections also help build team ownership of problems, and they help to increase communication.

How do the changes in this second code inspection justification affect our earlier design inspection example? The flaw in our code example was in the hidden assumption that the cost to find defects by large-scale inspections is as short as the methods that were used in previous studies. It seems less likely that there is a similar flaw for design defects. They will take considerably more effort to find in test than in inspections. The average hours-to-find ratio for design defects turned out to be high, but now that we've seen additional savings hours for coding defects in unit test, it is easy to argue that there are corresponding savings in the design case. The conclusion is that the design inspection example still seems sound, even if it isn't stated in its most precisely correct form.

FINAL THOUGHTS

Justifications take a lot of energy to develop, but they are invaluable aids for changing your process. These justifications are examples. They were each developed using assumptions that reflected one specific hypothetical environment. Feel free to use them, but *adapt them to your environment*. State your assumptions clearly and collect accurate data that will measure your success or (heaven forbid) failure.

Finally, be careful to not let these example's percentages too strongly influence your decisions regarding what to change. Use the failure analysis techniques discussed in Chapters 11 and 12 to identify your greatest opportunities. Decide what changes will help you to improve the control and consistency of your process, and then adapt these justifications to help you to sell the changes.

BIBLIOGRAPHY

1. Grady, R. and D. Caswell, *Software Metrics: Establishing a Company-Wide Program*, Englewood Cliffs, NJ: Prentice-Hall, Inc., 1987, p. 112, 128.
2. Scott, B. and Decot, D., "Inspections at DSD — Automating Data Input and Data Analysis," *HP Software Productivity Conference Proceedings*, (April, 1985), pp. 1-79–1-89.
3. Jones, C., *Programming Productivity*. New York: McGraw-Hill Book Co., 1986, p. 179.
4. Boehm, B., *Software Engineering Economics*. Englewood Cliffs, NJ: Prentice-Hall, Inc., 1981, p. 40.
5. Moller, K., "Increasing of Software Quality by Objectives and Residual Fault Prognosis," *1er Seminaire E. O. Q. C. sur la Qualite des Logiciels*, Brussels (April 1988), pp. 478-488.

15

Measuring
the Health
of a Software
═══ Business ═══

Thesis: Help your boss's boss to better understand software process issues through tracking a balanced set of metrics.

Every week, the government announces the value of one or more economic indicators, like unemployment, new construction starts, capital equipment spending, or the rate of growth of the money supply. These numbers help the government and the business community to understand the economy and to predict future events. In HP divisions, we also have many indicators that we track in order to manage effectively, such as inventory, orders, backlog, and monthly shipments. In the face of rapid growth of software as a major component of business, we have been slow to develop a balanced set of such indicators for software. Instead, we typically make intuitive decisions that are not backed by quantitative data. As a result, we see frequent adjustments for strategic changes that are often accompanied by scheduling problems. We need to determine the health of our operations using measurable attributes that function like the economic leading indicators.

Most of this book is designed to help project managers to organize and successfully run individual projects. It is also desirable to know how such individual data might be combined with other project data for higher-level decision making. This chapter presents nine graphs of software metrics that provide a balanced business perspective of productivity, quality, and predictability. They are based on data that is either already collected today or could be collected with minimal additional effort. They address the effectiveness of new product development, maintenance, and responsiveness to customer needs; and managers have used most of them individually to measure progress in focused areas, such as scheduling or defect levels.

BUSINESS GOALS

When we talk about goals for a successful software business, these four are almost always included:

> Improve software quality,
>
> Improve schedule accuracy,
>
> Improve productivity,
>
> Maximize customer satisfaction.

The final objective of all four goals is customer satisfaction. It is useful to keep it as a separate goal here, though, because the other goals better lend themselves to activities that labs directly control. Factors that affect customer satisfaction also include activities by many other parts of a business. The customer satisfaction goal is identical to one of the three strategies introduced in Chapter 3. What about the others?

Even though it is just one of many possible approaches in pursuing the goal of improving software quality, the strategy to minimize defects discussed in Chapter 3 is one of the most important. The strategy to minimize engineering effort and schedule from Chapter 3 can serve the goal of improving productivity but won't necessarily help with improving schedule accuracy. The four goals in this chapter are ones that were used by one HP division to derive its own set of leading indicators.

In order to establish measurable baselines and then monitor progress, we must look at the natural set of questions that help us to recognize progress toward our goals. Some answers to these questions are measurement-oriented, while others are organizational issues. Examples of the former are:

Goal: Improve Software Quality

> Q1. What data do we have now to tell us our current software quality?
>> M. Prerelease: certification data, performance data, prerelease defects, system test reports
>> M. Postrelease: defect density, # of critical and serious defects, # and length of hotsites, survey data

Q2. How can we predict product quality based on early development processes?

M. Prerelease defects, certification data, prerelease customer sample testing, % of design/code inspected

Q3. What are the dimensions of software quality? Prioritized by release? By products?

M. QFD (Quality Function Deployment, an analytical method of comparing customer requirements against proposed product features)

From primitive metrics (like engineering months, defects, etc.) associated with the questions, we then develop one or more graphs that help to show whether we are achieving specific goals. Looking at the questions and metrics in the example above, we should expect that our graphs will neither explain how to fix undesirable trends nor perfectly predict the future, any more than individual economic indicators do. But they will be useful in monitoring overall progress.

NINE SOFTWARE BUSINESS MANAGEMENT GRAPHS _____

We used the goal/question/metric approach to derive this set of nine graphs. Graphs were selected to provide a broad range of answers to a balanced set of questions without creating excessive overhead in data collection and analysis costs. We felt that the paragraphs on interpretation would help to minimize confusion. References are given for each graph that provide more detailed discussions of their use.

Improve Software Quality

The primary indicator of software quality is defects. Defects are a well-established form of customer feedback, and by tracking them accurately during different phases of development, it is possible to predict later levels of quality. While we would prefer to have a graph that also reflects FURPS+ attributes (functionality, usability, reliability, performance, supportability) more directly, as well, we have not discovered a good way to do so. As a result, we must assume that all FURPS+ attribute problems are reflected as defects.

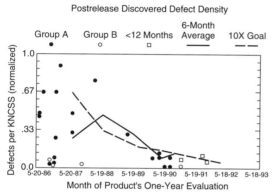

Figure 15-1

Goal: Improve software quality.
Questions that this graph helps to answer: What is our current software quality?
How this graph is interpreted: The graph shows postrelease defect density of products according to one of HP's 10X improvement measures. It is only an after-the-fact indicator of the quality level produced by our processes, and thus can only influence future products through cause-effect analysis. We must also remember to not emphasize this metric to the exclusion of the other FURPS+ attributes.
Figure reference: 6-9, 16-2.

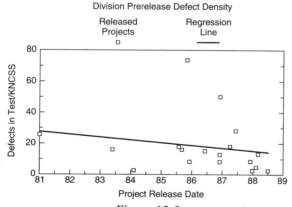

Figure 15-2

Goal: Improve software quality.
Questions that this graph helps to answer: How can we predict product quality based on early development processes?
How this graph is interpreted: This data can be used to predict the performance of graph 1. For an unchanging process, there is a roughly predictable ratio between pre- and postrelease defects. Keep in mind that an upward trend in this graph could show either better testing techniques or poorer pretest defect avoidance. A downward trend could reflect better pretest defect avoidance or poorer testing.
Reference: [1], pp. 138, 171.

Improve Schedule Accuracy

The primary measure of schedule accuracy is time and how well we estimate. In order to track our progress effectively, we need to formalize when estimates are made and how project estimates interrelate with program milestones.

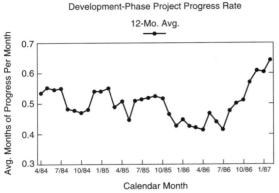

Goal: Improve schedule accuracy.
Questions that this graph helps to answer: How accurate are our estimates?
How this graph is interpreted: Each point represents the monthly project progress rate (ratio of completed and projected milestones to estimated milestones) averaged for the past 12 months. The ideal project progress rate is 1 if all milestones are being achieved per original schedules.
Figure reference: [2], 10-1.

Figure 15-3

Improve Productivity

Our primary cost is in engineering months and calendar months. Our output today is most effectively measured in NCSS or function points for new development and in defects fixed for maintenance. Productivity measurement is a particularly sensitive topic. It is best not to measure any finer level of detail than in these examples, and it is best to drive improvements from Figure 15-4.

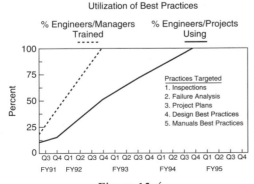

Goal: Improve productivity.
Questions that this graph helps to answer: What progress are we making toward adopting industry-proven best practices?
How this graph is interpreted: This graph shows goals for our investment in training and use of selected best practices. If the goals are met, it should be a leading indicator for later improvement in lab assessment results and improvements in productivity.
Chapter reference: 13.

Figure 15-4

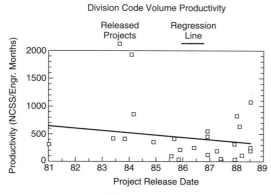

Figure 15-5

Goal: Improve productivity.
Questions that this graph helps to answer: How effective have process changes been?
How this graph is interpreted: Process improvements should result in improved quality and productivity. The trend of this graph should be up and to the right as processes are improved. Points considerably above the trend are of interest, because they might suggest new possibilities for improvement.
References: [1], pp. 138, 170.

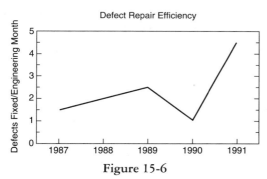

Figure 15-6

Goal: Improve productivity.
Questions that this graph helps to answer: How efficient are defect-fixing activities?
How this graph is interpreted: This graph shows the trend of efficiency in fixing defects. It helps to insure that we reduce the average effort to fix defects besides whatever staffing actions we might take to reduce the backlog.
(This graph does not show real data)
Figure reference: 4-5, 4-6.

Maximize Customer Satisfaction

The next three graphs show more direct aspects of customer satisfaction than the others. They deal with responsiveness to important customer problems and indirectly with how well we understand all our customer needs.

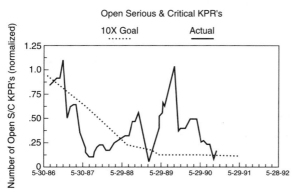

Figure 15-7

Goal: Maximize customer satisfaction.
Questions that this graph helps to answer: How many significant problems do our customers experience and are we reducing the backlog?
How this graph is interpreted: This graph shows the number of critical and serious defects (known problem reports) our customers have. It is another of HP's 10X improvement measures.
Figure reference: 6-8, 16-3.

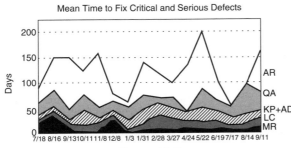

Figure 15-8

Goal: Maximize customer satisfaction.

Questions that this graph helps to answer: How long does it take to fix a problem?

How this graph is interpreted: The trend of the total area under the curve is related to how long customers have to wait before they see fixes. The largest area represents the best opportunity to shorten cycle time. MR = marketing review, LC = lab classification, KP = known problem, AD = awaiting data, QA = final quality assurance testing, AR = awaiting release.

Figure reference: 5-8, 5-9, Table 5-2; [1], pp. 120, 122.

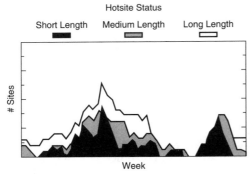

Figure 15-9

Goal: Maximize customer satisfaction.

Questions that this graph helps to answer: How long does it take to fix urgent customer problems?

How this graph is interpreted: This chart represents how efficient we are in resolving urgent customer problems. We should be prepared to show this chart to customers and use it to set their expectations for timely responses to problems.

Figure reference: 4-4, 7-10.

HOW THE MANAGEMENT GRAPHS PRESENT A BALANCED PICTURE

Now that we have nine views of the health of a software business, how usable are they? First, the data the graphs use must also be useful at different levels in the organization in order for it to be accurate. Second, people in the organization get extra motivation to work to achieve important business goals when they see their data tied to organizational graphs that represent progress toward the goals. If the data isn't useful and visibly used, then the motivation to report accurate data will be low and the effort will be wasted.

Figure 15-10 shows key metric usage by project managers and division/lab managers. They illustrate that the primitive metrics of engineering time, calendar time, size, and defects are the basis for a wide range

	Metric	Project Management	Division and Lab Management
Quality	Defects/KNCSS	Certification process ⟶	⟶ and company 10X goal
	Open critical & serious defects/month	Monitoring project completion	Company 10X goal
	QFD	Managing implementation priorities ⟶	↑
	Certification data	Ensuring correctness ⟶	↑
	Customer survey data		Feedback on customer satisfaction
Productivity	KNCSS/Eng. month		Monitoring development cost
	Defects fixed/Eng. Month		Monitoring development cost
	Organizational assessments	Best practice guidance	Monitoring development and support methods
Predictability	Project progress rate		Measuring estimation accuracy
	Calendar months/phase		On-time probability
	KNCSS/Eng. Month trends	Monitoring project completion	Evaluate effectiveness of methods
	Defects fixed/Eng. Month	Monitoring project completion	Evaluate effectiveness of methods
	Eng. Months/phase	Background for better estimates	

Figure 15-10 Usage of software metrics.

of project tracking and decision making. Some metrics are also included that were not part of our nine management graphs. The nine graphs provide a reasonably balanced view of quality, productivity, schedule accuracy, and customer satisfaction.

These graphs should be created monthly or quarterly and posted in a management conference room for regular reference and review. Even though it is natural to collect the underlying data for these graphs, don't underestimate the resources necessary to produce the graphs themselves. It takes special effort to set up the organizational mechanisms to do this. However, once you do, you will be able to monitor a balanced picture of your software business and measure the results of major program and business decision changes.

CONCLUSION

Once there was a Little League pitcher who won a trophy for the best earned-run (runs scored by the other team, not including those scored as a result of fielding errors) average during a season. Unfortunately, the season was still very discouraging, because his team didn't win any games. Winning teams also hit well, field well, and put together a combination of skills that result in overall effectiveness. We need to visualize a similar combination of skills and progress in order to manage our software business. No one or two of the management graphs provide the visibility necessary to understand all the elements required to consistently win in our software league.

Software managers have struggled for a long time to understand how to measure their businesses. The graphs proposed here represent some of the most effective methods used today to achieve such understanding. They provide a balanced view of productivity, quality, predictibility and overall customer satisfaction that is a prerequisite for leadership products.

BIBLIOGRAPHY

1. Grady, R. and D. Caswell, *Software Metrics: Establishing a Company-Wide Program*, Englewood Cliffs, NJ: Prentice-Hall, Inc., 1987, p. 161.
2. Levitt, D., "Process Measures to Improve R&D Scheduling Accuracy," *Hewlett-Packard Journal*, (April 1988), pp. 61-65.

16

The Evolution of HP's Software Metrics Program

This book has extended the principles first presented in *Software Metrics: Establishing a Company-Wide Program* by providing practical advice and examples for both project managers and for people responsible for process improvement. The many graphs, charts, and stories taken from many HP divisions have given some feeling for how HP's software metrics program has progressed. This chapter takes a broader perspective of our program's evolution, and the last chapter looks at software metrics and their future use throughout industry.

When we convened the first meeting of the group that became the HP Software Metrics Council, the idea we had was simple. We didn't envision a "Metrics Program." We already were responsible for an overall productivity and quality improvement program. We merely wanted some way of measuring the success of the new processes, methods, and tools that we knew we would have to introduce. The idea of software process and product measurement was good though, and it has played a key role in Hewlett-Packard.

It's useful to periodically stop and ask yourself how you think your organization is evolving. We discussed the recent popular idea of process maturity in Chapter 1. In the SEI five-stage process maturity model, the higher stages increasingly depend on the use of metrics. [1] So there is an implied relationship between a metrics program and achieving greater process maturity, which should lead to greater productivity and quality. I believe this, but I also believe that a metrics program itself goes through stages that are perhaps orthogonal to those of the maturity model. Figure 16-1 shows a hierarchy of metrics acceptance and practice that we have observed in our program.

In order for a program to be successful, it must be successful from the bottom up, one layer at a time. It didn't take us much time to proceed through the bottom three layers of the triangle. We have spent much more time in the fourth layer, and the fifth layer seems difficult to achieve.

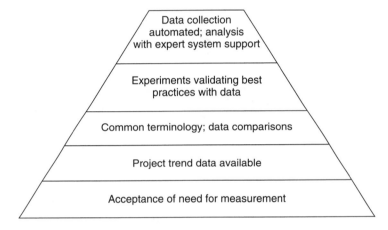

Figure 16-1 Hierarchy of metrics acceptance and practice.

WHAT DOES OUR MEASUREMENT PROGRAM LOOK LIKE TODAY?

HP's software metrics program is very much alive and well. What we're doing today takes a more mature view of metrics than we had when we started. We better understand what data provides the best information, how to best gather the data, and what kinds of questions we need to ask.

There is also an organizational infrastructure in place now that encourages consistent usage of metrics and sharing of results among the various divisions. Teams in our Corporate Engineering and Corporate Quality departments support company-wide tools (like our defect tracking system and the Software Metrics Data Base). They do an organizational assessment called a Software Quality and Productivity Analysis (SQPA) for divisions on request. After the assessment, recommendations are made on how to improve processes. They also support the collection and analysis of data related to company goals. For example, our company CEO, John Young, set two major, company-wide software "10X" improvement goals in 1986. [2] The first of these was to improve our product postrelease defect density by a factor of ten in five years. The second was to reduce the number of open critical and serious defects by a factor of ten in five years. Figures 16-2 and 16-3 are examples of graphs for one division that show its progress toward meeting the goals.

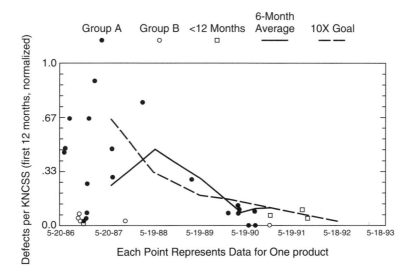

Figure 16-2 Postrelease discovered defect density.

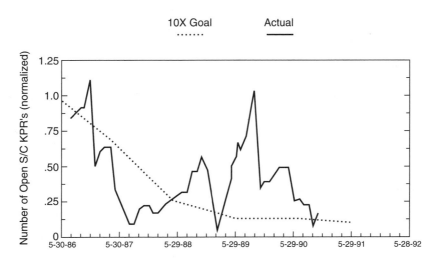

Figure 16-3 Open serious and critical KPR's.

These graphs are somewhat typical of the progress that HP as a whole has made since setting the goals. It appears that we will either meet the postrelease defect density goal on time, or we will meet it slightly behind schedule. On the other hand, the open critical and serious goal has proven to represent a more complex problem. In Figure 16-3 we can see several spikes. They characterize a software release process that causes large changes in the data. More significantly though, business decisions by individual divisions are driven by other goals besides the defect-reduction goal. Often the decision has been made to improve functionality or delivery rather than work on reducing the defect backlog.

Of course, the product delivery schedules are also complicated by the need to meet fixed release windows (for example, operating system releases). This complication extends to the starting point of the graph, as well. Within a short time after setting the goal, we had several major releases of software that produced a large, to-be-expected spike that we are now just beginning to work to reduce.

Below HP's corporate organization are the product groups. They have various lab-level metrics that have become part of the standard business-reporting process. Many of our process-improvement efforts are driven by group-level productivity and quality organizations. They try to identify problems that are common in the groups, and they work with division productivity and quality managers to leverage individual improvement programs.

Finally, there are quality and productivity managers in most divisions who support the individual R&D teams. Our quality managers are similar to those in other companies. The job of productivity manager was created in HP in 1984. It is designed to complement the usual quality focus by also measuring and improving the efficiency of R&D development processes. Both jobs are key to rapid technology transfer of best practices. Each has its own specific emphasis.

One last key component of our metrics program is a two-day Software Metrics class. This class was first designed in 1984. Since then, it has continuously evolved and been taken by a large number of project managers and engineers.

WHAT OBSTACLES DID WE HAVE TO OVERCOME?

Our first obstacle was to convince people that collecting data could lead to process improvements. When we first started HP's metrics program, we looked at published metrics articles. At that time, a large number came from university research studies that were very narrowly focused and often applied statistical analyses as part of a mathematics or computer science instructional method. That emphasis had unfortunately introduced a strong bias in perceptions of how metrics could be applied. It gave people the impression that useful metrics required time-consuming, sophisticated techniques that were outside of the normal decision-making processes of managers. It's interesting to speculate how differently we would approach metrics as a field if most early research had been done in business schools instead of mathematics and computer science programs.

Not wanting to propagate this perception, we didn't start our program with people who were experts in metrics. We started with a group of project managers who were expert in managing projects and asked them, "What do you think would help you manage your projects more effectively?" and "What data are practical to collect?" A foundation had to be put in place before we tried anything more sophisticated.

Once we gained agreement on a basic set of primitive metrics, we then had to convince our managers and engineers to use them. In *Software Metrics: Establishing a Company-Wide Program*, we included a chapter called "The Selling of Metrics" that discusses the steps that we took. [2] We recognized that we needed the support of three primary groups: top management, project managers, and engineers. Each of the groups had different needs and concerns.

This selling was a delicate process. When you sell something, you have to make some promises. You must be careful that these promises don't create expectations that are too high. The strategy that we followed was to focus on the primitive metrics and on the use of metrics data to help track progress and identify improvements, not predict them.

Another problem that we saw was that some groups attempted to change too rapidly. For example, they tried to collect a lot of data before they understood what they would do with it. Others collected more detail than was needed, because it happened to be available. An early warning signal of this type of problem is when data collection is set up in too rigid a manner right from the start. A good example of such a rigid collection process is the collection of effort data on timecards by an accounting department. Such systems usually do not lend themselves well to breakdown of data by development activity or by totals less than or greater than multiples of 40.

One of my greatest nightmares is that someone will walk up to me and say, "We're going to have our accounting department do all data collection." I simply don't think that the field of software metrics is mature enough for that level of "bean counting." And I don't think that any amount of raising awareness can improve the odds of making that approach successful. Most accounting departments aren't organized to be responsive enough for the needs of project managers, or flexible enough to deal with the evolving needs for data.

Another obstacle that we faced was pressure for breakthroughs. Americans are known to look for big breakthroughs. This has been both a blessing and a curse for us. When some groups implemented metrics, their managers expected miracles shortly to follow. While we have learned that metric data is very valuable for pointing out problem areas, the fixes to these problems are not guaranteed to be either simple or inexpensive.

As we implemented our metrics program, we sometimes saw people who would focus too much attention on one metric. This kind of oversimplification has led to poor decisions.

Yet another obstacle was that HP itself changed often to adjust to changing business conditions. Each new manager brought a new agenda to an organization. The danger that our program faced was that it took time to get metrics integrated enough into an organization so that they were not casually set aside in favor of new priorities.

What Did We Do Right?

Another way of looking at obstacles is to look at some of the key things that we did that worked out well. First, we started with a council of (mostly) first and second-level managers who were both respected and interested. This helped us to focus our attention on project-level metrics that would be of immediate value. It also helped to protect us against larger organizational changes, since projects tend to remain the same during such changes.

We started small with metric primitives and a focus on consistent usage by interested projects in a large number of divisions. This gave us the opportunity to make sure the basic metrics that we had chosen were the right ones before individual divisions made too large a commitment. It also allowed us to find and cultivate early successes.

We provided an environment for reinforcing success. This began with a two-day training class for all functional managers to increase their general knowledge of software. One of the six modules in the class was devoted to metrics. The class was particularly important, since a large percentage of our functional managers did not have software backgrounds. We gave them a better understanding of software development. We particularly gave them numerical examples and guidelines for how the use of metrics data would help them to understand their divisional progress better. By including this strong initial introduction, we set the stage for them not only accepting initial measurement attempts, but also for them actually to drive some of these attempts.

We initiated annual Software Engineering Productivity Conferences where the emphasis was on proven success stories. We seeded the first conference with talks that included metrics by finding people who had success stories and by convincing them to share them. Subsequent conferences followed this model without the necessity of looking for the stories any more. Selection committees welcome such talks, since they are practical, believable examples of changes that we want to encourage.

The job of productivity manager was created, and all divisions were strongly encouraged by top management to assign a person to the job. These people have been invaluable contact points and distribution channels for new processes, methods, and tools.

We designed a two-day Software Metrics class. It was targeted toward project managers, although we have found it valuable for engineers to attend, as well. Three-quarters of the people in a typical class today are engineers. The class includes a large number of practical examples, a series of exercises that reinforce key ideas, structured discussions of human-element issues, and a set of high-quality video tapes that include success stories by various project managers.

Finally, we provided good tool support. We created an excellent prerelease defect tracking system in addition to the one that we already had for postrelease defects. We provided counters for all the major languages used in HP, and we created the Software Metrics Database to keep track of project-level data.

Even these steps weren't optimal. For example, we were never able to gain enough high-level support to staff the tool efforts to meet the demand from the labs. Some of the council members weren't as active or motivated as we would have liked. The addition of productivity managers to some key divisions seemed to take forever. Despite some of these shortcomings, all the steps in this section helped to eliminate major obstacles that stood in our way.

WHAT ARE THE COSTS FOR SUCH A PROGRAM? _____

It is difficult to pin down the costs of a metrics program, because metrics are just one aspect of an overall improvement program. Also, many such costs are related to data collected for other reasons. For example, Table 16-1 gives estimated costs for engineers and project managers to collect primitive metric data at the start of HP's metrics program. [2] It assumed that the checked items were already collected for other purposes, so we can't claim that those costs are additional costs attributable to the metrics program.

Development Phase	Metric Primitive	What Mngrs. Collect Already	Tools	Estimated Additional Time/Week (Minutes)	
				Engineer	Manager
Investigation	Time –Calendar	✔		*	*
	–Progrmr		Time Matrix	1	5
	Defects		Defect Log	–	–
Design	Time –Calendar	✔		*	*
	–Progrmr		Time Matrix	1	5
	Defects		Defect Log	10	10
Coding	Time –Calendar	✔		*	*
	–Progrmr		Time Matrix	1	5
	NCSS		Code Count.	3	–
	Code Status	✔	Code Summ.	*	*
	Defects		Defect Log	3	5
Test	Time –Calendar	✔		*	*
	–Progrmr		Time Matrix	1	5
	Code Status	✔	Code Summ.	*	*
	Defects	✔	Defect Log	*	*
Postrelease	Time –Calendar	✔		*	*
	–Progrmr		Time Matrix	1	5
	Defects	✔	Defect Log	*	*
* It is assumed that these times are already spent as part of job!			Total	1 to 11	5 to 15

Table 16-1 Existing tools for software metrics collection.

The costs for measuring large programs are a little easier to identify than for smaller ones, because they are generally centralized. For example, a project manager with a team of six engineers who were responsible for metrics data, supported the efforts of several hundred engineers who were porting HP's operating systems to our Precision Architecture hardware. Even these numbers can be misleading, since these people weren't the only ones who spent time getting this data. They primarily spent their time setting data standards, validating data, analyzing it, and reporting it. So their time was supplemented by engineer and project manager times similar to those in Table 16-1.

We can look at the larger organizational costs involved with starting a metrics program. When we started HP's program, one person worked full-time on the research, definitions, aggregation of data, setting up the council meetings and providing follow-up, and general contacts with the divisions. This person did this for about a year. Their time gradually shifted partially to tool activities during the second year. In addition, I had an average of one more person dedicated to tool activities in direct support of the metrics program during the same period.

Just like the large program example, though, these small costs can be misleading. For example, I had one engineer and a project manager who teamed with three engineers from other divisions to create a prerelease defect tracking system. Were these costs directly associated with the metrics program? Similarly, several divisions also invested in tools that ultimately have added significant contributions to our metrics efforts.

These organizational costs have increased as many of the metrics have become included as standard practices. Today, there are about four engineers at the corporate level who work full time supporting the metrics program. I don't include those who continue to work and improve our defect tracking systems, who do the SQPA assessments, or who do customer surveys. Including these people probably increases the numbers to 15 or 20.

Each division in HP handles metrics in different ways. Some analyze and report data from within traditional quality assurance functions. Others have productivity managers who do it. Because we are tracking and reporting data in ways that we never did before, we can probably generalize and say that the overhead for this in each division is maybe one more person than before.

All these attempts to pin down the cost of metrics hide the real issue, though. That issue is that I don't believe that companies really have a choice. I believe that the cost of *not* implementing a software metrics program in the 1990s will be measured in terms of project and business failures. Those projects and companies who have made the investment in measuring their products and processes have a competitive advantage over those who don't. They have the advantage of more informed and timely decisions that will ultimately make them more successful.

WHAT ARE THE BENEFITS SO FAR?

It is just as hard to separate out benefits of a metrics program as it was to isolate the costs. The process of software development is very complex. The idea that you can do an experiment where you keep all the variables the same and measure just one is not realistic. So, the notion that you can collect data that is going to make substantial changes in your software productivity is overly simplistic.

There are some clear benefits, even though they are difficult to quantify. One indication of success is the use of metrics by our high-level managers. Many of them had a hardware background when we started our program, and they did not understand software well. They were not familiar with the terminology and the underlying processes. Metrics terminology has clearly been accepted at this point, and the sophistication of the graphs we now use in presenting data to these managers is quite high. I believe that the use of software metrics has helped them to learn to manage better.

Second, we have found that metrics help to speed technology transfer of best practices. This was somewhat more of a surprise to us, since we believed that we would be making measurements in order to determine what changes we needed to make. It turns out that we understood what changes we needed to make; the difficulty was in convincing people to make the changes. But if you can back up your claims with data, it simplifies the job of convincing people to make changes more quickly.

The composition of talks at our Software Engineering Productivity Conferences provides evidence that metrics data is being used to prove validity. Over 40 percent of the papers from the most recent conference specifically discussed metrics or used metrics to prove the validity of a technique. The approach of using data to discuss changes and improvements has clearly been embraced by our people.

The 10X improvement program focuses on improvements in some of our key metric values. While our total company progress for one of the key measures (open critical and serious defects) appears to have been too ambitious, we have made excellent progress toward the postrelease defect density goal. Even for the first goal, we have seen several benefits just in its pursuit. For example, it has helped to clarify our maintenance and release processes. It has also helped us to better understand our product mix of new versus old software.

A Couple of Concrete Results

We have talked in general terms about benefits. Now let's look at two specific examples. The first is an example of software failure analysis. This type of analysis has become quite widespread during the past several years in HP. Figure 16-4 shows a breakdown of the top eight causes of defects found during system and integration testing for one division that was discussed in Chapter 12. [3]

They decided to concentrate on the category of error checking, since it had more defects than any other. They introduced new standard procedures for doing error checking. They also checked for conformance to these standards during design, when their analysis had suggested that these defects were introduced. Figure 16-5 shows the progress that they made over three releases of their products. They effectively eliminated their largest source of defects.

Our second example comes from the team who supported the conversions of all our operating systems software from our old hardware architecture to HP's Precision Architecture. Part of their job was the support of a metrics-driven Certification Process. Customers were already using previous versions of the systems that were being certified. Since these systems were in use on our

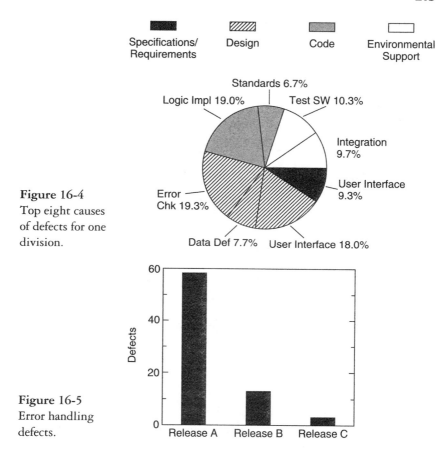

Figure 16-4
Top eight causes
of defects for one
division.

Figure 16-5
Error handling
defects.

older hardware configurations, there were high expectations for software quality on the new architecture. Figure 16-6 shows three curves of incoming defects (in the form of service requests) for the first year after release of one major HP software system that was certified. [4] We first saw this graph in Chapter 7. The number of defects in each case is normalized by the amount of code represented in thousands of non-comment source statements (KNCSS).

The top curve represents several products that either were not certified or were released without meeting the certification criteria. The bottom curve represents a dozen products that were certified. The middle line shows that the defect rate of even the worst certified product was considerably better than the products that did not meet the certification standards. Here the chief benefit was that the introduction of certification was quite successful. If millions of lines of software had not successfully met these levels of quality, an entire product line might have failed.

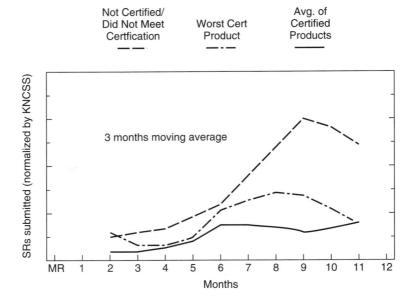

Figure 16-6 Postrelease incoming SRs submitted by customers.

CONCLUSION

For many people in HP today, it is hard to imagine managing software development and maintenance without metrics data to help guide decisions. We have not gotten to this point without costs associated with measurements and process improvements, but it is clear to us that the benefits have been worth it. Our evolution isn't over yet, but clearly metrics will be a part of our future.

BIBLIOGRAPHY

1. Humphrey, W., *Managing the Software Process*, Reading, MA: Addison-Wesley Co., Inc., 1989.
2. Grady, R. and D. Caswell, *Software Metrics: Establishing a Company-Wide Program*, Englewood Cliffs, NJ: Prentice-Hall, Inc., 1987, pp. 194, 218.
3. Nishimoto, Alvina, Private communications, (May 1991).
4. Lau, Danny, "The Success of the Spectrum Software Certification Program," *HP Software Productivity Conference Proceedings*, (August 1988), pp. 109–117.

17

One Perspective on the Future of Software Metrics

This final chapter starts with a short summary of the state of metric usage. It then explores my vision of the future. If I may use yet another analogy, a software project is like a train in a tunnel rushing toward a light. With knowledge of its speed and schedule, knowing that it is on the right track, we can be reasonably assured that it's daylight we see at the end of the tunnel. Without such quantifiable facts, it is just as likely that the light we see is another train (or disaster) rushing toward us on the same track.

This analogy emphasizes the importance of planning and measurement to project management. Software metrics provide measures to see progress, plus feedback that is necessary to adjust plans. From the start, software metrics have been closely aligned with visions of software engineering. Indeed, we will never have "engineering" without measurement integrated into our methods.

So my vision of the future is not of software metrics in isolation. It is a vision of software engineering where metrics data helps engineers "to measure and help manage software change and complexity." [1] It is a vision that fulfills one of the greatest promises of CASE - the automated delivery of metrics data to the project manager where metrics "act as an early warning system for complexity in the software under development and provide visible means for showing progress." [1]

THE BENEFITS OF SOFTWARE METRICS _____

There are many practical uses of software metrics. Four of the more significant ones that have been explored by both academics and industry are

1. project estimation and progress monitoring,
2. evaluation of work products,
3. process improvement through defect analysis,
4. experimental validation of best practices.

Project Estimation and Progress Monitoring

There has been a lot of work on estimation, with limited success. Today our industry knows that there are many aspects of software development that influence estimates, but we are not much better at guessing the degree of their influence than we are at making total estimates. [2,3] The recent emphasis on process improvement gives us some hope here, for much of our estimation inaccuracy is a result of long development cycle times and process variability.

Managers use metrics data far too little for progress monitoring, even though intuition and evidence both suggest that such use is highly practical. One reason that metrics aren't used is that project managers often don't have time. Another reason is that we seem to be held back by our fears of people's reactions to measurement.

Evaluation of Work Products

Analysis of code is the single largest area of metrics research. All software development ultimately results in a work product of code. Code is expressed in a standard language that can be processed automatically. Each language is well defined, and code is the complete form of the desired result, unlike any intermediate work product. Therefore, code has been a convenient research vehicle.

The increasing availability of CASE tools should lead to some much-needed research into work products other than code (like data flow diagrams, structure charts, data dictionaries, pseudocode, and so forth). For example, several past theoretical studies proposed design metrics based on the analysis of design documents or code. [4,5,6] Without consistent use of such metrics during actual design, they were of limited value. Today, we should be able to repeat these experiments rigorously using CASE design work products.

Process Improvement through Defect Analysis

I believe that this area is the most promising one for today's development processes. Defect analysis and the finding and removal of major sources of defects offer the greatest short-term potential for improvements. Unfortunately, many proposed changes will yield only a 5 or 10 percent improvement, and many managers still believe that changes of 50 percent or more can be quickly achieved. As a result, they won't invest in process changes with more modest improvements. Ironically, this prevents them from gaining 50 percent improvements through a series of smaller gains (investments in six such changes are justified in Chapters 11 and 14).

Experimental Validation of Best Practices

This use of software metrics has been the most successful of the four. People have validated some important engineering practices (for example, prototyping [7], reducing coupling, increasing cohesion [8], limiting complexity [9], inspections and testing techniques [10], reliability models [11]), and this should lead to quicker, widespread acceptance of these practices. Software is a rapidly changing field. It is critical for us to continue to use metrics data to examine the sometimes unrealistic claims that are made for new methods and tools.

WHERE ARE WE GOING? _____

I believe that metrics are a key part of a major transition to the use of software engineering practices. Several years ago, we defined the four-stage model for standards that is shown in Figure 17-1. [12] It is useful in understanding where we are going.

Experimental approach: a practice whose implementation shows promise of benefits that have not yet been widely proven.

Guideline: a desired practice whose implementation allows adaptation to local needs.

Recommended practice: a well-defined practice that has proven successful whose consistent usage is encouraged throughout the industry.

Standard: a well-defined practice whose consistent usage is required throughout industry.

Figure 17-1 Stages in the life of a standard.

The practical use of metrics passed into the guideline stage in the decade of the 1980s. During that transition, our industry moved from isolated metrics experiments by individuals to more widespread, but still inconsistent, use by teams of people. The decisions to use metrics were then made primarily by project managers.

We have already begun the next transition for the 1990s to the use of metrics as an industry-wide, recommended practice. This transition is a more difficult one, because decisions now must be made for entire organizations. This involves change on a much larger scale, and we face new training and support issues.

A Vision of the Future

What role will metrics play in software engineering by the year 2000? There are three parts to this vision. First, tools will automatically measure size and complexity for all the work products that engineers develop. Besides warnings and error messages, the tools will predict *potential* problem areas based on metric data thresholds. For example, they will flag excessive design complexity when the coupling between modules on a structure chart exceeds a predefined value.

Second, this data will be automatically gathered together into a database that is *convenient* for project managers to access and manipulate. Like the engineering tools, tools for project managers will also provide timely warnings, error messages, and software metrics data. Project management feedback will apply to entire projects.

Third, the project-level data will automatically be consolidated with other projects' data at an organizational level. At this level, current practices will be evaluated, and opportunities for process improvements will be visible.

WHAT SHOULD WE BE DOING TO GET THERE?

This vision is not radical. Much of the technology necessary to support the vision is available today. So who is responsible for the implementation?

- The *academic community* must adapt to the new transition. They influence the direction for new technology by establishing the mindsets of new engineers entering the job market. They have outstanding research opportunities to explore the wide variety of software work products other than code. There are also opportunities to work with industrial partners to understand and evaluate practical process changes. This is important to both communities. Metrics best practices must also be integrated into the courses taught in management curricula.

- We must make *CASE vendors* more aware of the importance of measurement to their future business. There exist very few CASE tools that allow programmed access to intermediate and final work products. This makes it hard for experimenters to try promising metric approaches. This must change if we are to be successful. One possible solution to this problem is for the metrics researchers to partner with vendors. Vendors could give researchers better access to the work products generated by their tools. The vendors, in turn, would benefit from seeing a prototype demonstration of features that customers will want.

- *Industrial producers of software* must resist holding out for large improvements. We have to set expectations for a series of smaller, incremental changes. The focus must be on tying proposed process improvements to the removal of specific types of defects from the development process. Results of those improvements must be validated with metrics data and reported.

- Finally, *government agencies* must find ways to encourage their contractors to collect some company-private metrics that can be used by the companies to make their own process improvements without fear of the data being used against them.

We have referenced the SEI process maturity model several times in the book. It is a model that will help software producers move toward continuous process improvement, and this is a key to our future. But most software projects are managed by individuals. What can you do to influence the academic community, CASE vendors, the government, or even your own organization?

A lot depends on what you believe you can do. When my son was six or seven years old, he used to go jogging with me. He would seldom finish a whole lap around the quarter-mile track. Then I happened to find an article in the newspaper that had a picture of a five-year old who had run a marathon (over twenty-six miles). The next time we went jogging, my son completed four laps and other times he did even more.

Don't wait for these larger organizations to define the limits of your potential. Use the techniques described here and ideas contained in models like the SEI model, and apply them to the project you control. Use them to set continuous process-improvement goals for your project team. You, like my son, may be surprised at what it is possible to accomplish.

BIBLIOGRAPHY

1. Grady, R. and D. Caswell, *Software Metrics: Establishing a Company-Wide Program*, Englewood Cliffs, NJ: Prentice-Hall, Inc., 1987, pp. 194, 218.
2. Kitchenham, B., "Software Cost Models," *ICL Technical Journal*, (May 1984) pp. 73–102.
3. Kusters, R., M. van Genuchten, and I. Heemstra, "Are Software Cost Estimation Models Accurate?" *Information and Software Technology*, (April 1990).
4. Troy, D., and S. Zweben, "Measuring the Quality of Structured Designs," *The Journal of Systems and Software 2*, (June 1981), pp. 113–120.
5. Yau, S., and J. Collofello, "Design Stability Measures for Software Maintenance," *IEEE Transactions on Software Engineering*, Vol. SE-11, no. 9 (Sept. 1985), pp. 849–856.
6. Yin, B. H., and J. W. Winchester, "The Establishment and Use of Measures to Evaluate the Quality of Software Designs," *Proceedings of the Software Quality and Assurance Workshop*, New York: Association for Computing Machinery, 1978, pp. 45–52.
7. Boehm, B. W., T. Gray, and T. Seewaldt, "Prototyping vs. Specifying: A Multi-Project Experiment," *IEEE Proceedings of the Seventh International Conference on Software Engineering*, (March 1984), pp. 473–484.
8. Card, D. with R. Glass, *Measuring Software Design Quality*, Englewood Cliffs, NJ: Prentice-Hall, Inc., 1990.
9. Rambo, R., P. Buckley, and E. Branyan, "Establishment and Validation of Software Metric Factors," *Proceedings of the International Society of Parametric Analysts Seventh Annual Conference*, (May 1985), pp. 406–417.
10. Lauterbach, L., and W. Randell, "Six Test Techniques Compared: The Test Process and Product," *Proceedings of the NSIA Fifth Anniversary National Joint Conference and Tutorial on Software Quality and Productivity*, National Security Industrial Association, Washington, D.C., 1989.
11. Ohba, Mitsuru, "Software Quality = Test Accuracy X Text Coverage," *0270-5257/82/0000/0287, IEEE* (1982), pp. 287–293.
12. Grady, R., "A Strategy for Development of HP Software Standards," (Nov. 18, 1986).

Appendix A

Defect Origins, Types, and Modes

A defect is any flaw in the specification, design, or implementation of a product. There are three categories of defect information: problem recognition, status, and analysis/action/disposition. Information in the first two categories facilitates accurate communications among parties during the life of a defect. Information for analysis of a problem, action to eliminate it, and final disposition is useful to discover fundamental process changes to prevent future defects. *The purpose of this model and these definitions is to provide standard terminology for defect nomenclature that different groups will use to report, analyze, and focus efforts to eliminate defects and their root causes.* The following defect list is not meant to be an exhaustive list. It provides consistent categories for the majority of commonly occurring defects.

An enhancement is not a defect. Restraint must be exercised when software changes are labeled "enhancements." The use of the term enhancement should be restricted to those cases where either the customer needs or the product scope have truly changed since the release of the product, thereby creating new requirements which could not have been anticipated in the original development effort. For example, the performance of a software product was competitive on release, but it needed to be improved two years later to remain competitive. Such a change is an enhancement. If the performance was not competitive at the original time of release, then any subsequent change to improve performance is considered a defect fix.

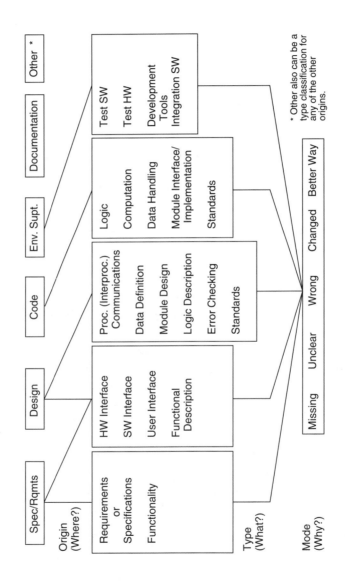

Enhancement:

A change which could not possibly have been detected, or, if detected, would not have been corrected.

The figure above shows defect origins, types, and modes. In the following definitions, "incorrect" is used to mean any one of the five modes. For example, a defect might be a design defect where part of the user interface described in the internal specification is missing. Another defect might be a coding defect where some logic is wrong.

Specifications/Requirements Defect:

A mistake in the definition of the customer/target needs for a system or system component. Such mistakes can be in functional requirements, performance requirements, interface requirements, design requirements, test requirements, development standards, and so on.

REQUIREMENTS OR SPECIFICATIONS: The specifications do not adequately describe the needs of target users. Includes the effects of product strategy redirection and cases where functionality is increased to add market value.

FUNCTIONALITY: Incorrect, or incompatible product features.

HARDWARE, SOFTWARE, AND USER INTERFACE: Incorrect specification of how the product will interact with its environment and/or users.

FUNCTIONAL DESCRIPTION: Incorrect description of what the product does. Generally discovered during requirements or design inspection.

Design Defect:

A mistake in the design of a system or system component. Such mistakes can be in algorithms, control logic, data structures, database access, input/output formats, interface descriptions, and so on.

HARDWARE, SOFTWARE, AND USER INTERFACE: Problems with incorrect design of how the product will interact with its environment and/or users. For example, incorrect use of libraries, design does not implement requirements, device capabilities overlooked or unused, or design does not meet usability goals.

FUNCTIONAL DESCRIPTION: Design does not effectively convey what the intended module/product should do. Generally a defect found during design inspection or during implementation (coding).

PROCESS OR INTER-PROCESS COMMUNICATIONS: Incorrect interfaces and communications between processes within the product.

DATA DEFINITION: Incorrect design of the data structures to be used in the module/product.

MODULE DESIGN: Problems with the control (logic) flow and execution within processes.

LOGIC DESCRIPTION: Design is incorrect in conveying the intended algorithm or logic flow. Generally a defect found during design inspection or implementation.

ERROR CHECKING: Incorrect error condition checking.

STANDARDS: Design does not adhere to locally accepted design standards.

Code Defect:

A mistake in the implementation of a computer program. Such mistakes can be in product or test code, JCL, build files, and so on.

LOGIC: Forgotten cases or steps, duplicate logic, extreme conditions neglected, unnecessary function, or misinterpretation errors.

COMPUTATION PROBLEMS: Equation insufficient or incorrect, precision loss, or sign convention fault.

DATA HANDLING PROBLEMS: Initialized data incorrectly, accessed or stored data incorrectly, scaling or units of data incorrect, dimensioned data incorrectly, or scope of data incorrect.

MODULE INTERFACE/IMPLEMENTATION: Problems related to the calling of, parameter definition of, and termination of subprocesses. For instance, incorrect number of, or order of, subroutine arguments, ambiguous termination value for a function, or data types incorrect.

STANDARDS: Code does not adhere to locally accepted coding standard.

Documentation Defect:

A mistake in any non-code product material delivered to a customer. Such mistakes can be in user manuals, installation instructions, data sheets, product demos, and so on. Mistakes in requirements specification documents, design documents, or code listings are assumed to be specifications defects, design defects, and coding defects, respectively.

Environmental Support Defect:

Defects that arise as a result of the system development and/or testing environment. Such mistakes can be in the build/configuration process, the development/integration tools, the testing environment, and so on.

TEST SOFTWARE: Problems in software used to test the product software's capabilities. For example, another application program, the operating system, or simulation software.

TEST HARDWARE: Problems with the hardware used to run the test software, NOT the hardware on which the product software runs.

DEVELOPMENT TOOLS: Problems which are a result of development tools not behaving according to specification or in a predictable manner.

INTEGRATION SOFTWARE: Problems that result from integration software/tools or processes.

Other:

This classification should be used sparingly, and when it is used, the defect should be very carefully and extensively described in associated documentation. [Note: All "others" should be reviewed to refine the Failure Analysis process.]

Modes:

The first definition of "work product" is not a defect mode, but it is used as part of several of the subsequent mode definitions.

WORK PRODUCT: An intermediate or final output of software development that describes the design, operation, manufacture, or test of some portion of a deliverable or salable product. It is not the final product. The final product is the result of the work products.

MISSING: Information was left out of a work product.

UNCLEAR: Information was misleading, ambiguous, or hard to understand.

WRONG: The information in the work product was clearly not correct.

CHANGED: Changes in a work product caused changes to other work products.

BETTER WAY: There was a better way to do a work product, usually for efficiency, performance, readability, maintainability, and supportability.

Appendix B

Example of Process Background Information

The background information for the case studies in Chapter 12 wasn't complete enough to answer some of the questions we had. This appendix gives a model for collecting such information. *This example does not contain real data.* The data and analysis are included to clarify what might be recorded. In HP's case, some of this data is normally collected on a project by project basis (effort, size, defects, and calendar time data; the data collection forms are shown in *Software Metrics: Establishing a Company-Wide Program*, Chapter 5). Collection and documentation of the remaining data requires a higher level of commitment and resources for continuous process improvement.

PROCESS AND PRODUCT DESCRIPTIONS _____

Development type (underline one): <u>Applications</u>, Systems, Firmware,
   Other (specify) _____.
Language(s): Cobol
Types of products (include any particularly unusual requirements):
   Financial packages.

Development methods:

Method/Tool	Percentage of Team Trained	How Extensively Applied?	Applied by This Team Before?	Team Perception of Value
Prototypes	0	4 iterations with customers	Yes	High
QFD	25	100 by 50 matrix	No	Low
Structure charts & data dictionary	100	100% high-level design	Yes	Necessary
Design inspections	75	100% high-level 35% low-level	Yes	High
Complexity tool	25	100% code	No	High
Code inspections	75	20% high-risk modules	Yes	Mixed
Branch coverage	100	All modules, 85% goal	Yes	High
Goel-Okumoto reliability model	15	Throughout test	No	High

PROCESS MEASUREMENTS

Productivity before changes: 400 NCSS/eng. mo. (20 percent avg. reuse)
Productivity after changes: 450 NCSS/eng. mo. (25 percent avg. reuse)
Defect density before changes: 9.5 defects/KNCSS (system test)
Defect density after changes: 7.2 defects/KNCSS (system test)

Percentages of the eight most frequent defect source types:

Type	Past Percentage	Targeted for Reduction?	New Percentage	What Will You Target Next?
Requirements	19	**	13	**
Design, user interface	17		20	**
Design, SW interface	12		13	
Data dictionary	8		10	
Logic description	8		12	
Logic	26	**	17	**
Module interface	5		9	
Data handling	5			
Integration SW			6	

How were these defects found and reported? (underline all that apply; you must use same finding methods for both past and new):
Requirements inspection, <u>Design inspection</u>, <u>Code inspection</u>, <u>System test</u>, Maintenance, Other (specify) _____.

How much engineering effort was spent on each new process? QFD, 130 eng. hours; complexity tool, 60 eng. hours; Goel-Okumoto reliability model, 40 eng. hours.

How much engineering effort do you expect it would take you on your next project for each new process, assuming the next project is identical to the last? QFD, 40 eng. hours; complexity tool, 40 eng. hours; Goel-Okumoto reliability model, 30 eng. hours.

Compute your final return on investment: Assume that there were 150 defects after our hypothetical process changes.
QFD: 9 requirements defects * 30 test hours/defect = 270 hours - 130 hours cost = 140 hours saved
Complexity tool: 14 code defects * 10 test hours/defect = 140 hours - 60 hours cost = 80 hours saved
Reliability model: 4 defects * 75 postrelease hours/defect = 300 hours - 40 hours cost = 260 hours saved

PROCESS RECOMMENDATIONS

Summarize how process changes were implemented (Extend your analysis to defect types that still occurred which you expected to be eliminated. Was there a flaw in the process change or in your implementation of it? Can you expect better results next time? Are there any differences in the product you are producing or maintaining that influenced your results?)

(This should typically be a half-page to two pages of narrative. Since the data in this appendix was not real, no artificial analysis will be given.)

FINAL NOTE

The example here centered on defect reduction. Note that the eight most frequent defect source types could easily be replaced by the eight largest engineering costs or largest schedule components, if they were the analysis focus instead of defects. I prefer to focus on defects, because I believe that defects dramatically affect engineering costs and schedules, and that we must initially focus on their reduction before any significant progress can be made.

Appendix C

Metrics Definitions and Glossary

This appendix contains a summary of brief definitions for most of the key metrics discussed in this book. In some cases, where the definitions are particularly compressed, there are references elsewhere.

Note that the definitions for defect origins, types, and modes given in Appendix B are not repeated here.

Alert status: a customer site is placed on alert status when a critical or serious defect is found. The status remains until a workaround is found or the status changes to hot.

Applications software: software that operates on top of and uses systems software. Applications software also generally solves a generic class of problems for a narrow set of customers and needs.

Bang: "a quantitative indicator of usable function from the user's point of view." [refer to Tom DeMarco's *Controlling Software Projects*] There are two methods for computing Bang. Computation of Bang for function-strong systems involves counting the tokens entering and leaving the function multiplied by the weight of the function. For data-strong systems it involves counting the objects in the database weighted by the number of relationships of which the object is a member.

Branch: any executable statement that results in a choice of which statement to execute next.

Breadth: a measure of the external and internal functionality of a product. These typically can include entry points, commands, parameters, options, features, syntax, messages, screens, menus, dialog boxes, icons, buttons, scales, and so forth.

Break/fix ratio: the count of defects introduced versus the count of defects fixed.

Calendar month: time elapsed between specific project checkpoints. The total calendar time must equal the sum of the calendar times for individual activities. A project that started in January and ended in March of the same year took three calendar months independent of the actual effort expended.

Cohesion: the degree to which the tasks performed by a module are functionally related.

Control token: a data element used to determine the control flow of a function.

Coupling: a measure of the interdependence among modules in a program.

CPE: Current Product Engineering (maintenance and enhancements).

Cyclomatic complexity: a metric based on a graph-theoretic measure that is derived from the number of potential paths through source code. (see original article by Tom McCabe)

Data token: a data element that is used as data instead of for control.

Defect: any flaw in the specification, design, or implementation of a product.

Defect (critical): the customer is unable to use the product, resulting in a critical impact on their operation. This problem requires an immediate solution.

Defect (serious): the customer is able to use the product, but is severely restricted. A temporary solution should be supplied.

Defect (medium): the customer can use the product with limitations that are not critical to overall operations.

Defect (low): the customer can circumvent the problem and use the product with only slight inconvenience.

Defect (unclassified): a defect which has been reported but has not yet been analyzed to determine severity or difficulty to fix.

Defect density: defects/KNCSS

Defect removal efficiency: the ratio of defects found before release to the sum of those found both before and after release of a product.

Design phase: start of the Internal Specification (IS) through start of coding for final product.

Design weight: "Design weight is a simple sum of the module weights over the set of all modules in the design." [refer to Tom DeMarco's *Controlling Software Projects*] Each module weight is a function of the token count associated with the module and the expected number of decision counts that are predicted based on the structure of data.

Engineering months: the sum of calendar payroll months attributed to each project engineer, including people doing testing, adjusted to exclude extended vacations and extended leaves. This does not include time project managers spend on management tasks.

Enhancement: a change which could not possibly have been detected, or, if detected, would not have been corrected.

Fanin: the number of calls to a given module.

Fanout: the number of calls from a given module.

Firmware: software generally designed to execute from ROM (Read Only Memory) or RAM (Random Access Memory) under control of a microprocessor.

Flesch-Kincaid readability: a documentation readability metric primarily based on the average length of words and the average sentence length in a document.

FURPS+: functionality, usability, reliability, performance, supportability (see Figure 4-1).

Halstead metrics: these are a family of code metrics introduced by Halstead in 1977 that include various mathematical combinations of operators and operands. Different HP divisions have experimented with these metrics. The conclusions have generally been that they are interesting, but not particularly useful since the code has already been written and people are resistent to change solely on the basis of numbers.

Hot status: a customer site is esclated to hot status after it has been on alert status for a fixed period of time without a workaround being found.

Implementation phase: start of coding for final product through start of system (formal, public) testing.

Information-flow metric: length * (fanin * fanout)^2 (refer to articles by Henry and Kafura)

Investigation/external specification phase: start of investigation through approval of the external specification (ES) document.

KNCSS: thousands of non-comment source statements (also see NCSS)

KPR: Known Problem Report

LOC: Lines Of Code

Maintenance phase: starts after release of the product and continues until its obsolescence.

McCabe metric: (see cyclomatic complexity)

MTBF: Mean Time Between Failure.

MTTC: Mean Time To Classify (service requests).

MTTR: Mean Time To Repair (service requests).

NCSS: non-comment source statements that include compiler directives, data declarations, and executable code. Each physical line of code is counted once. Each include file is counted once. Print statements are non-comment source statements.

Patch: a modification to an individual source program or object program to quickly fix a customer problem.

(Phase) activity: an activity relates engineering hours to actions performed rather than to the formal project phase currently in progress. Thus, engineering hours spent performing design during the implementation phase should be counted as design hours.

Primitive (metric): a metric that is directly measurable or countable.

Reused software: software incorporated into a product that was used intact from a different product or another part of the same product.

SR (Service Request): a documented request, frequently coming from a customer, for changes caused by a defect or needed enhancement.

Stability: the degree of change experienced by a program or group of programs.

Strength (module): (see cohesion)

Systems software: software generally designed to execute from the memory of minicomputers. It functions as the framework for developing and executing other software.

Test phase: start of system testing through product release.

Testing time: time spent on all activities relating to system (formal, public) testing. This includes writing test plans, writing test code, system and integration testing, and finding and removing defects found during test activities.

Appendix D

Software Metrics Reference Bibliography

This bibliography extends the one that Debbie Caswell and I published in *Software Metrics: Establishing a Company-Wide Program*. Like the one in that book, it consists of two parts. The first section gives a limited list of references for specific topics, and the second section contains a complete list of up-to-date references related specifically to metrics.

The selected topics differ from those in the first book. This difference reflects some changes in interest and emphasis from when we wrote the book. The original comments in the book are still valid, so only those that are important to these new groupings are repeated. All of the selected articles have practical information that will help organizations make decisions regarding the application and use of metrics.

FUNCTIONALITY

1. DeMarco, T., *Controlling Software Projects*, New York: Yourdon Press, 1982.
   DeMarco's delightfully readable book offers motivation for why software data collection and analysis is essential to the success of any software producer. One of the points we like the most about the book is that it advocates measures specific to each of the major stages of development, and not just overall measures. Unfortunately, these are not backed up with a lot of data or graphs, so it is difficult to pick any set as a starter set with the belief that you are starting at the highest leveraged point. The book does have metrics for functionality (bang) and design (design weight) that look useful.
2. Cohen, L., "Quality Function Deployment: An Application Perspective from Digital Equipment Corporation," *National Productivity Review*, (Summer 1988), pp. 197–208.
   This is an excellent presentation of how QFD can be applied to software. QFD basically guides you to capture the "voice of the customer" and to methodically analyze your proposed

product against customer needs, as well as against the competition. QFD may or may not prove to provide major metric principles for specifications/requirements activities in the future, but it looks promising. The article gives a brief, but very good, example of how QFD is applied.

3. Albrecht, A. and J. Gaffney, "Software Function, Source Lines of Code, and Development Effort Prediction: A Software Science Validation," *IEEE Transactions on Software Engineering*, Vol. SE-9, no. 6 (Nov. 1983), pp. 639–648.

   We have not used function points (that I know of) at HP, and this article helped convince us initially not to. It does a good job of explaining what they are, relating them to some of Halstead's metrics, and showing that they can be used effectively to estimate software size and effort. There are two reasons we steered clear of function points initially. First, their calculation and measurement violated our ease-of-use criteria, because the whole process seemed complicated to teach and use. Second, we had reservations over whether they would apply equally well outside the EDP or applications areas due to the way they were defined and the projects to which they had been applied. While our focus included these areas, we were reluctant to advocate measurements that didn't meet our ease of use and wide applicability criteria.

4. Knafl, G. J., and J. Sacks, "Software Development Effort Prediction Based on Function Points," *Proceedings of the Computer Software and Applications Conference*, (1986), pp. 319–325.

   This article presents a statistical analysis of published function point data and concludes that function points cannot be effectively used for predicting project schedules.

5. Drummond, S., "Measuring Applications Development Performance," *Datamation*, Vol. 31, (1985), pp.102–108.

   This article describes the successful use of function points by Hallmark Cards, Inc. to compare a series of projects.

6. Boehm, B. W., T. Gray, and T Seewaldt, "Prototyping vs. Specifying: A Multi-Project Experiment," *IEEE Proceedings of the Seventh International Conference on Software Engineering*, (March 1984), pp. 473–484.

   This article describes an experiment in duplicate development of a software product by seven student teams. Four used a specifications-driven approach, while three others used a prototyping approach. The results of the experiment were that each approach demonstrated certain measured advantages over the other approach.

DESIGN

7. Card, D. with R. Glass, *Measuring Software Design Quality*, Englewood Cliffs, NJ: Prentice-Hall, Inc., 1990.

   This is a nice little book with quite a few interesting results. Some of the most significant ones include measures on optimum module size, coupling, and cohesion. The most important chapter presents his measure of design complexity, which includes structural, data, and procedural components. The structural component is a variation of the Henry-Kafura information-flow metric. The data component involves the number of variables and the fanout. The procedural component is basically a predictor of cyclomatic complexity. A very exciting graph (although it has fewer data points than one would like) shows a high correlation between defect density and design complexity.

8. (refer to DeMarco, *Controlling Software Projects*)

9. Yau, S., and J. Collofello, "Design Stability Measures for Software Maintenance," *IEEE Transactions on Software Engineering*, Vol. SE-11, no. 9 (Sept. 1985), pp. 849–856.

   This article defines some design metrics that were created to specifically control stability. The metrics are related to both the DeMarco and Card approaches. Some simple examples are illustrated, and some degree of validation is offered through classroom examples.

10. Troy, D., and S. Zweben, "Measuring the Quality of Structured Designs," *The Journal of Systems and Software* (June 1981), pp. 113–120.
    A study involving 21 metrics taken from software design documents was performed on a single project. These metrics measured coupling, cohesion, complexity, modularity, and size. Within the limited context of the study, the coupling metrics seemed most important and the complexity metrics second.
11. Shepperd, M., and D. Ince, "Metrics, Outlier Analysis and the Software Design Process," *Information and Software Technology*, Vol. 31, no. 2 (March 1989), pp.91–98.
    This short article uses the Henry and Kafura information flow metric to illustrate how metrics can help focus a designer's attention on potential design problems in order to produce a better software design. Despite the authors' skepticism with the metric, they still conclude that the metric is useful and the illustrations are very persuasive.
12. Yin, B. H., and J. W. Winchester, "The Establishment and Use of Measures to Evaluate the Quality of Software Designs," *Proceedings of the Software Quality and Assurance Workshop*, New York: Association for Computing Machinery, 1978, pp. 45–52.
    This article is one of the older articles that suggests design metrics, but it at least validated its metrics against two real projects at Hughes. Again, the metrics are related to the ones in the other articles referenced here.

CODING

13. Curtis, B., S. Sheppard, and P. Milliman, "Third Time Charm: Stronger Prediction of Programmer Performance by Software Complexity Metrics," *IEEE Proceedings of the Fourth International Conference on Software Engineering*, (1979), pp. 356–360.
    This article discusses the usefulness of LOC, Halstead's E, and McCabe's cyclomatic complexity in predicting defect-prone software modules.
14. Rambo, R., P. Buckley, and E. Branyan, "Establishment and Validation of Software Metric Factors," *Proceedings of the International Society of Parametric Analysts Seventh Annual Conference*, (May 1985), pp. 406–417.
    This article from General Electric contains some interesting results of how they are trying to use complexity measurement to reduce defects. One conclusion presented lists eight possible threshold values which statistically showed a relationship to fewer than a nominal error rate. Another conclusion was that the maximum number of decision statements is 14 to optimize reliability. This conclusion was specifically related to the use of McCabe metrics. Finally, it goes on to list five specific variables which contributed to error updates in their study.
15. Ward, J., "Software Defect Prevention Using McCabe's Complexity Metric," *Hewlett-Packard Journal*, (April 1989), pp. 66–69.
    This article describes the use of the McCabe metric at HP in conjunction with a commercially available tool that not only provides the metric values but also a graphical representation of the analyzed code. HP engineers responded well to the visual image of complexity, and this has helped project managers to control complexity better and produce more maintainable products.
16. Shen, V., S. Thebaut, and L. Paulsen, "Identifying Error-Prone Software — An Empirical Study," *IEEE Transactions on Software Engineering*, Vol. SE-11, no. 4 (April 1985), pp. 317–323.
    This article discusses statistical analysis of five IBM projects to explore the use of several metrics in predicting software defects. It concludes that metrics related to the amount of data and to the structural complexity of programs appear useful in identifying error-prone modules at an early stage. It also sheds some interesting light on errors in new versus modified or translated code.

TESTING

17. Freedman, D., and G. Weinberg, *Handbook of Walkthroughs, Inspections, and Technical Reviews*, Boston: Little, Brown, and Co., 1982.
    This book is the best single reference on inspections that I have found. It is written in a question and answer style. At first, this seems like it wouldn't be as useful if you were starting an inspections effort from scratch, but the book is very readable and my final conclusion is that I don't think that the format detracts from the book's usefulness.

18. Davey, S., R. D. Classick, D. Lau, J. Loos, and B. Noble, *Spectrum Program Metrics and Certification Handbook*, HP Software Metrics Technology, Software Development Technology Lab, Information Software Division. Version 2.0 (Oct. 12, 1990)
    This document (only available with the HP Metrics Class) describes a practical product certification process that has been successfully applied in HP. Its purpose is to set uniform testing and quality requirements, to identify quantitative measurements that demonstrate progress toward objectives, and to provide a mechanism for reporting progress and identifying issues. It establishes three stages of testing and sets goals for breadth, depth, reliability, and defect density.

19. Lauterbach, L., and W. Randell, "Six Test Techniques Compared: The Test Process and Product," *Proceedings of the NSIA Fifth Anniversary National Joint Conference and Tutorial on Software Quality and Productivity*, National Security Industrial Association, Washington, D.C., 1989.
    This article was difficult reading, but it is short and has fascinating data comparing the effectiveness of six different test techniques. They include three dynamic (branch, random, and functional) and three static (code review, error analysis, and structured analysis) types of tests. The study examined two completed systems. Each of the techniques were applied to the two systems, and their effectiveness was measured. Among other things, the tests uncovered over 20 defects that were unknown when the tests began.

20. Herington, D., P. Nichols, and R. Lipp, "Software Verification Using Branch Analysis," *Hewlett-Packard Journal*, (June 1987), pp. 13–22.
    This article does an excellent job of putting branch coverage into its proper perspective as part of an overall quality assurance program. There are not as many metric results as might be desired, but it also has a good discussion of management issues.

21. Musa, J., A. Iannino, and K. Okumoto, *Software Reliability: Measurement, Prediction, Application*, New York: McGraw-Hill 1987.
    The field of software reliability modeling has matured in the last five years. This book describes the various reliability model theories well and gives some practical advice for how to use one particular model.

22. Kruger, G. A., "Project Management Using Software Reliability Growth Models," *Hewlett-Packard Journal*, (June 1988), pp. 30–35.
    This is an excellent description of the application of a software reliability growth model (the Goel-Okumoto model) to a large industrial application to help manage the testing process.

23. Ohba, Mitsuru, "Software Quality = Test Accuracy X Text Coverage," *0270-5257/82/0000/0287, IEEE* (1982), pp. 287–293.
    This article describes the application of a reliability growth model to a relatively small program. It uses the exciting concept of validating the model's performance by using defects found earlier in the process to seed the software during testing. The degree of finding these known defects was used to determine the completeness of testing. The model performed well, and the number of seeded defects remaining on completion accurately predicted the number of postrelease defects found, as well.

MAINTENANCE

24. Kafura, D., "The Use of Software Complexity Metrics in Software Maintenance," *IEEE Transactions on Software Engineering*, Vol. SE-13, no. 3 (March 1987), pp. 335–343.
    This is a well-written article that examines the applicability of seven metrics for guidance of maintenance activities. It examines the results of activities involved in three versions of a medium-size database system with positive indications that the metrics are very useful in helping to identify problems and to guide decisions.
25. Vessey, I., and R. Weber, "Some Factors Affecting Program Repair Maintenance: An Empirical Study," *Communications of the ACM*, Vol. 26, no. 2 (Feb. 1983), pp. 128–134.
    This is a very thought-provoking article. It describes the results of two studies of a large number of Cobol programs. Its conclusions regarding the effects of a number of factors on repair maintenance were much weaker than expected. These factors included complexity, structure, modularity, programmer ability, frequency of maintenance, and number of production runs.
26. Davis, J. S., "Investigation of Predictors of Failures and Debugging Effort for Large MIS," *Information and Software Technology*, Vol. 31, no.4 (May, 1989), pp. 170–174.
    This is an excellent little article that summarizes a study of the maintenance of over 500,000 lines of Cobol. It found that none of the usual code metrics were good predictors of effort, but that they were good predictors of the number of defects. Number of changes to the source and the frequency of use of the software were also good predictors of defects.

FAILURE ANALYSIS

27. Endres, A., "An Analysis of Errors and Their Causes in System Programs," *IEEE Transactions on Software Engineering*, Vol. SE-1, no. 2 (June 1975), pp. 140–149.
    This classic article contains an excellent breakdown of defect types. It also presents thorough data which supports the importance of studying the development process through analysis of defects, their categorization, and their causes.
28. Basili, V., and R. Selby, "Four Applications of a Software Data Collection and Analysis Methodology," *Collected Software Engineering Papers: Volume III*, Goddard Space Flight Center, Greenbelt, MD, (Nov. 1985), pp. 3-23 – 3-37.
    This article has an interesting analysis of 215 errors from a large applications program for satellite planning. It also explores some different testing techniques (code reading, functional testing, and structural testing) and gives their relative effectiveness.
29. Ostrand, T., and E. Weyuker, "Collecting and Categorizing Software Error Data in an Industrial Environment," *Journal of Systems Software*, Vol. 4, (1983), pp.289–300.
    Although the focus of this article is only on defects found in coding, the methodology seems sound and the results give some interesting insights into what types of tests can find some faults.

DATA COLLECTION

30. Basili, V., and D. M. Weiss, "A Methodology for Collecting Valid Software Engineering Data," *IEEE Transactions on Software Engineering*, Vol. SE-10, no. 6 (Nov. 1984), pp. 728–738.
    This article does an excellent job of covering all of the basics of good procedures for data collection. It also describes the goal/question/metric paradigm, which we have found to be very useful in identifying good, appropriate metrics.

DOCUMENTATION _____

31. Losa, J., J. Aagard, and J. Kincaid, "Readability Grade Levels of Selected Navy Technical School Curricula," Naval Training Analysis and Evaluation Group, Orlando, FL, *Report No. TAEG-TM-83-2*, (Feb. 1983).

    This short article examines the relationship between a documentation readability metric (the Flesch-Kincaid metric) and the percentage of attrition for a set of courses taught at U.S. Navy technical schools. The correlation was high enough to suggest that this type of metric is a very useful indicator for technical documentation.

32. Basili, V., and D. Weiss, "Evaluation of a Software Requirements Document by Analysis of Change Data," *Proceedings of the Fifth International Conference on Software Engineering* (March 1981), pp. 253–262.

    This article discusses an in-depth study of changes to a specifications document. It presents the metrics used and a useful breakdown of the data into graphic form.

PROJECT TRACKING _____

33. Air Force Systems Command, "Software Quality Indicators," *AFSC Pamphlet 800-14* (January 20, 1987).

    This document suffers from its government format which leads to excessive length, repetition, and lack of interest-catching flow. Nevertheless, it contains some excellent ideas and a few interesting statistics. We have suggested a similar set of balanced management metrics for use inside of HP, particularly at an overall organizational level.

ESTIMATION _____

34. Boehm, B., *Software Engineering Economics*. Englewood Cliffs, NJ: Prentice-Hall, Inc., 1981.

    Barry Boehm's COCOMO is one of the best and most popular estimating models in the software business. He actually presents several models in his book, each of which requires more inputs and gives more accurate results than the previous one. Quite a few entities at HP use the COCOMO model.

35. Kusters, R., M. van Genuchten, and I. Heemstra, "Are Software Cost Estimation Models Accurate?" *Information and Software Technology*, Vol. 32, no. 3 (April 1990), pp. 187–190.

    This article describes an experiment using two commercial estimation models by a group of project managers at Philips. They estimated the duration of a project that had already been completed. Several interesting conclusions resulted: their gut estimates were better than the models; the model estimates differed by a factor of two; and all the estimates were considerably higher than the actual project had been. Nevertheless, the vast majority of participants concluded that they would use one of the models again, primarily because the models drew their attention to issues that might otherwise have been overlooked.

36. Abdel-Hamid, T., and S. Madnick, *Software Project Dynamics: An Integrated Approach*, Englewood Cliffs, NJ: Prentice-Hall, 1991.

    This is a useful new book in the difficult area of software estimation. Abdel-Hamid and Madnick use a modeling approach that draws on experiences from many organizations to represent some of the most notorious project downfalls. This is a good book for first-time project managers to read.

PEOLE FACTORS

37. Grady, R., and D. Caswell, *Software Metrics: Establishing a Company-Wide Program*, Englewood Cliffs, NJ: Prentice-Hall, 1987.
    Chapter 7 particularly discusses some of the complex human factors that arise when using software metrics. It uses actual HP and non-HP experiences to illustrate both successes and failures. It describes the process that engineers experience when data collection is initiated, and discusses the normal responses and reactions to expect.

38. Curtis, B., "Fifteen Years of Psychology in Software Engineering: Individual Differences and Cognitive Science," *IEEE Proceedings of the Eighth International Conference on Software Engineering*, London (August 1985), pp. 97–106.
    This outstanding article is full of good ideas. It discusses individual differences among programmers in terms of tests that have been tried, factors affecting performance, and motivating factors. It explores the concept of programmers learning information chunks or production rules and how better programmers seem more able to "encode" this information into their memories. It discusses problem-solving approaches and how these can interact with tools.

39. Weinberg, G., and E. Schulman, "Goals and Performance in Computer Programming," *Human Factors* Vol. 16, no. 1 (1974), pp. 70–77.
    This article describes an experiment conducted with six different programming teams given different objectives for the same program. It provides great insight into the dilemma all software managers face when presented with the challenge of which factors matter the most, and how programming teams respond to specifications for the job.

40. DeMarco, T., and T. Lister, *Peopleware*. New York, NY: Dorset House, 1987.
    This is another great book from DeMarco, this time joined by Tim Lister. It covers a lot of ground concerning the people part of the productivity equation in an anecdotal way. They describe a number of results from their so-called "Coding War Games." These involved having paired engineers from 92 different companies code the same routine in their normal work environments. The results were then compared and some conclusions drawn about the effects of different environments. Some of the other topics that will stick with you include the "furniture police," "uninterrupted time," and "teamicide."

41. Wiedenbeck, S., "Novice/Expert Differences in Programming Skills," *International Journal of Man-Machine Studies 23*, (1985), pp. 383–390.
    This article describes some experiments run with experienced programmers versus novices to validate the concept that there are three levels of knowledge and skill: cognitive, associative, and autonomous. They showed two different experiments that demonstrated that expert programmers did tasks more quickly with fewer errors. In other words, experts operated in the autonomous mode.

42. Silverman, B., "Software Cost and Productivity Improvements: An Analogical View," *Computer*, (May 1985), pp. 86–95.
    This article has some particularly disturbing (and in some ways encouraging) results about how software people approach the solution of problems. He argues that people predominantly take an analogical approach in the design of solutions, and that when they have direct experience with the problem at hand, this is very effective. When they don't have direct experience, they still draw from what experience they do have, and this can lead to poor solutions. The article suggests that the general solution of the reuse problem will help significantly.

PROCESS IMPROVEMENT

43. Humphrey, W., *Managing the Software Process*, Reading, Mass.: Addison-Wesley, 1989.
    This book set the standard in the exciting, growing area of software process improvement. It not only describes the SEI software process maturity model and much of the thinking behind the model, it also motivates and gives practical suggestions for improving processes.
44. Bollinger, T., and C. McGowan, "A Critical Look at Software Capability Evaluations," *IEEE Software*, (July 1991), pp. 25–41.
    This article gives a terrific evaluation of the SEI software process maturity model and some of the strengths and weaknesses of the approach used.

MISCELLANEOUS

45. Vosburgh, J., et al., "Productivity Factors and Programming Environments," *IEEE Seventh International Conference on Software Engineering* (March 1984), pp. 143–152.
    This article presents the results of in-depth measurements of 44 projects at ITT since 1980. It contains some interesting results concerning hardware constraints, customer participation, and specifications. It shows an impressive correlation of productivity against modern programming practices, and an interesting breakdown of programming environments into categories of real-time, nonreal-time, and business applications.

COMPLETE ALPHABETIC LISTING

Articles described earlier are marked with "**" in front of the authors' names.

1. Abdel-Hamid, T., and S. E. Madnick, "The Dynamics of Software Project Scheduling," *Communications of the ACM* (May 1983), Vol. 26, no. 5, pp. 340–346.
2. **Abdel-Hamid, T., and S. Madnick,** *Software Project Dynamics: An Integrated Approach*, Englewood Cliffs, NJ: Prentice-Hall, 1991.
3. Abe, Joichi, K. Sakamura, and H. Aiso, "An Analysis of Software Product Failure," *Proceedings of the Fourth International Conference on Software Engineering*, Munich, (Sept. 1979).
4. ACM Sigmetrics, "Performance Evaluation Review," Vol. 11, no. 3, (Fall 1982), pp. 49–67.
5. Adams, E., "Optimizing Preventive Service of Software Products," *IBM Journal of Research and Development*, (Jan. 1984), pp. 2–14
6. **Air Force Systems Command,** "Software Quality Indicators," *AFSC Pamphlet 800-14* (January 20, 1987).
7. Air Force Systems Command, "Software Risk Management," *AFSC Pamphlet 800-45* (June 1987).
8. Akiyama, F., "An Example of Software System Debugging," *Proceedings of the 1971 IFIP Congress* Amsterdam: North-Holland, 1971, pp. 353–359.
9. Albrecht, A. J., "AD/M Productivity Measurement and Estimate Validation — Draft," *IBM Corporate Information Systems and Administration AD/M Improvement Program*, (May, 1984).
10. Albrecht, A., "Measuring Information Processing," *Conference Presentations of the ASQC International Conference on Applications of Software Measurement*, San Diego, CA, (Nov 1990), pp. 29–45.

11. ****Albrecht, A., and J. Gaffney,** "Software Function, Source Lines of Code, and Development Effort Prediction: A Software Science Validation," *IEEE Transactions on Software Engineering*, Vol. SE-9, no. 6, (Nov. 1983), pp. 639–647.

12. Albrecht, A. J., "Measuring Application Development Productivity," *Proceedings of the Joint SHARE/GUIDE/IBM Application Development Symposium*, (Oct. 1979), pp. 83–92.

13. Allen, T., "Communications in the Research and Development Laboratory," *Technology Review*, (Oct./Nov. 1967).

14. Allen, T., and A. R. Fusfeld, "Design for Communication in the Research and Development Lab," *Technology Review*, (May 1976), pp. 65–71.

15. Altmayer, L., and J. DeGood, "A Distributed Software Development Case Study," *HP Software Productivity Conference Proceedings*, (April 1986), pp. 1-54 – 1-62.

16. An, K. H., D. A. Gustafson, and A.C. Melton, "A Model for Software Maintenance," *CH2442-2/87/0000/0057, IEEE*, (1987), pp. 57–62.

17. Aron, J. D., "Estimating Resources for Large Programming Systems," *Software Engineering: Concepts and Techniques, Proceedings of the NATO Conferences*, (Ed. by P. Naur, B. Randell, and J. Buxton), New York:Petrocelli/Charter, 1976, pp. 206–217.

18. Arthur, L. J., *Measuring Programmer Productivity and Software Quality*. New York: Wiley and Sons, (1985)

19. Bailey, J., and V. Basili, "A Meta-Model for Software Development Resource Expenditures," *5th International Conference on Software Engineering*, (March 1981), pp. 107–116.

20. Baker, F. T., "Chief Programmer Team Management of Production Programming," *IBM Systems Journal*, no. 1 (1972), pp. 56–73.

21. Balza, J., "Improving the Methods of Software Project Estimation at CNO," *HP Software Productivity Conference Proceedings*, (April 1986), pp. 1-2 – 1-18.

22. Basili, V., "Changes and Errors as Measures of Software Development." *EH0167-7/80/0000-0062, IEEE*, (July 1980) pp. 62–64.

23. Basili, V., "Quantitative Evaluation of Software Methodology," *Technical Report TR-1519*, Department of Computer Science, University of Maryland, College Park, Md., (July 1985).

24. Basili, V., "Software Development: A Paradigm for the Future," *IEEE 0730-3157/89/0000/0471*, (1989), pp. 471–485.

25. Basili, V., D. Hutchens, "An Empirical Study of a Syntactic Complexity Family," *IEEE Transactions on Software Engineering*, Vol. SE-9, no. 6, (Nov. 1983), pp.664–672.

26. Basili, V., and B. Perricone, "Software Errors and Complexity: An Empirical Investigation," *Communications of the ACM*, Vol. 27, no.1, (Jan. 1984), pp. 42–52.

27. Basili, V., and R. Reiter, "An Investigation of Human Factors in Software Development," *Computer*, (Dec. 1979), pp. 21–38.

28. Basili, V., and R. Reiter, "Evaluating Automatable Measures of Software Development," *Proceedings, Workshop on Quantitative Software Models*, (Oct. 1979), pp. 107–116.

29. Basili, V., and H. D. Rombach, "Tailoring the Software Process to Project Goals and Environments," *IEEE Ninth International Conference on Software Engineering*, Monterey, CA, (April 1987), pp. 345–357.

30. Basili, V., and R. Selby, "Calculation and Use of an Environment's Characteristic Software Metric Set," *CH2139-4/85/0000/0386 IEEE*, (1985), pp. 386–391.

31. Basili, V., and R. Selby, "Comparing the Effectiveness of Software Testing Strategies," *IEEE Transactions on Software Engineering*, Vol. SE-13, no. 12, (1987), pp. 1278–1296.

32. **Basili, V., and R. Selby**, "Four Applications of a Software Data Collection and Analysis Methodology," *Collected Software Engineering Papers: Volume III*, Goddard Space Flight Center, Greenbelt, MD, (Nov. 1985), pp. 3-23–3-37.

33. Basili, V., and R. Selby, "Metric Analysis and Data Validation Across Fortran Projects," *IEEE Transactions on Software Engineering*, Vol. SE-9, no. 6, (Nov. 1983), pp. 652–663.

34. Basili, V., R. Selby, and D. Hutchens, "Experimentation in Software Engineering," *IEEE Transactions on Software Engineering*, Vol. SE-12, no. 7, (July 1986), pp. 733–743.

35. **Basili, V., and D. Weiss**, "Evaluation of a Software Requirements Document by Analysis of Change Data," *Proceedings of the Fifth International Conference on Software Engineering*, (March 1981), pp. 314–323.

36. **Basili, V., and D. Weiss**, "A Methodology for Collecting Valid Software Engineering Data," *IEEE Transactions on Software Engineering*, Vol. SE-10, no. 6, (Nov. 1984), pp. 728–738.

37. Bassett, P., "Design Principles for Software Manufacturing Tools," *Proceedings ACM '84 Annual Conference: The Fifth Generation Challenge*, (Oct. 1984), pp. 85–93.

38. Beane, J., N. Giddings, and Jon Silverman, "Quantifying Software Designs," *Proceedings of the Seventh International Conference on Software Engineering*, (March 1984), pp. 314–322.

39. Behrens, C., "Measuring the Productivity of Computer Systems Development Activities with Function Points," *IEEE Transacations on Software Engineering*, Vol. SE-9, no. 6, (Nov. 1983) pp. 648–652.

40. Belady, L., and C. Evangelisti, "System Partitioning and Its Measure," *Journal of Systems and Software*, 2 (1981), pp. 23–39.

41. Belady, L., and M. Lehman, "The Characteristics of Large Systems," *Research Directions in Software Technology*, (Ed by P. Wegner) Cambridge, MA: MIT Press, 1979, pp. 106–142.

42. Belford, P., and R. Berg, "Central Flow Control Software Development: A Case Study of the Effectiveness of Software Engineering Techniques," *IEEE Proceedings of the Fourth International Conference on Software Engineering*, Munich (Sept. 1979), IEEE CH 1479-5/79/0000-0378, pp. 85–93.

43. Berry, R., and B. Meekings, "A Style Analysis of C Programs," *Communications of the ACM*, Vol. 28, no. 1, (Jan. 1985), pp. 80–88.

44. Blair, S., "A Defect Tracking System for the UNIX Environment," *HP Journal*, Vol. 37, no. 3, (March 1986), pp. 15-18.

45. Blakely, F., and Mark Boles, "A Case Study of Code Inspections," *HP Software Engineering Productivity Conference Proceedings*, (Aug. 1990), pp. 403–413.

46. Boehm, B., "An Experiment in Small-Scale Application Software Engineering," *IEEE Transactions on Software Engineering*, Vol. SE-7, no. 5, (Sept. 1981), pp. 482–493.

47. Boehm, B., "Improving Software Productivity," *Computer*, (Sept. 1987), pp 43–57.

48. Boehm, B., "Industrial Software Metrics Top 10 List," *IEEE Software*, (Sept 1987), pp. 84–85.

49. **Boehm, B.**, *Software Engineering Economics*, Englewood Cliffs, NJ:Prentice-Hall, Inc., 1981.

50. Boehm, B., "Software Engineering Economics," *IEEE Transactions on Software Engineering*, Vol. SE-10, no. 1, (Jan. 1984), pp. 4–21.

51. Boehm, B., "Verifying and Validating Software Requirements and Design Specifications," *IEEE Computer*, Vol. 17, no. 1, (Jan. 1984), pp. 75–88.

52. Boehm, B., J. Brown, H. Kaspar, M. Lipow, G. MacLeod, and M. Merritt, "Characteristics of Software Quality," *TRW Series of Software Technology*, Vol. 1. Amsterdam: TRW and North-Holland Publishing Company, (1978).

53. Boehm, B., J. Brown, and M. Lipow, "Quantitative Evaluation of Software Quality," *IEEE 2nd International Conference on Software Engineering*, San Francisco, CA, (Oct. 1976), pp. 592–605.

54. Boehm, B., J. Elwell, A. Pyster, E. Stuckle, and R. Williams, "The TRW Software Productivity System," *Proceedings 6th International Conference on Software Engineering*, (Sept. 1982), pp. 148–156.

55. **Boehm, B., T. Gray, and T Seewaldt**, "Prototyping vs. Specifying: A Multi-Project Experiment," *IEEE Proceedings of the Seventh International Conference on Software Engineering*, (March 1984), pp. 473–484.

56. Boehm, B., and P. Papaccio, "Understanding and Controlling Software Costs," *IEEE Transactions on Software Engineering*, Vol. 14, no. 10, (Oct 1988).

57. Boehm, B., M. Penedo, R. Stuckle, R. Williams, and A. Pyster, "A Software Development Environment for Improving Productivity," *Computer*, (June 1984), pp. 30–42.

58. Boehm, B., and R. Ross, "Theory-W Software Project Management: A Case Study," *0270-5257/88/0000/0030, IEEE*, (1988), pp. 30–40.

59. **Bollinger, T., and C. McGowan**, "A Critical Look at Software Capability Evaluations," *IEEE Software*, (July 1991), pp. 25–41.

60. Bouldin, B. M., "What Are You Measuring? Why Are You Measuring It?" *Software Magazine*, (August 1989), pp. 30–39.

61. Brettschneider, R., "Is Your Software Ready for Release?" *IEEE Software*, pp. 100–108.

62. Bridges, W., "How to Manage Organizational Transition," *Training*, (1985).

63. Bridges, William, "Managing Organizational Transitions," Presentation at Pajaro Dunes, CA (Feb. 1985).

64. Britcher, B., and J. Craig, "Upgrading Aging Software Systems Using Modern Software Engineering Practices," *IEEE Conference on Software Maintenance*, (Nov. 1985), pp. 162–170.

65. Brooks, F., *The Mythical Man-Month*, Reading, MA: Addison-Wesley, 1975.

66. Brooks, F., "The Mythical Man-Month," *Datamation*, (Dec. 1974), pp. 304–311.

67. Brooks, F., "No Silver Bullets—Essence and Accidents of Software Engineering," *Computer*, (April 1987) pp. 10–18.

68. Brooks, W. Douglas, "Software Technology Payoff: Some Statistical Evidence," *Structured Programming, The Journal of Systems and Software 2*, (1981), pp. 3–9.

69. Bugarin, J., "CNO Process Measures," (March 1984).

70. Bush, M., and N. Fenton, "Software Measurement: A Conceptual Framework," *Journal of Systems and Software 12*, (1990), pp. 223–231.

71. Campbell, R., S. Conte, and M. Rathi, "Early Prediction of Software Size and Effort," *Software Engineering Research Center, Department of Computer Sciences, Purdue University*, (March 1988), pp. 1–16.

72. Cantwell, F., "Factors Affecting the Productivity of Engineers," Texas Wesleyan College, Fort Worth, TX.

73. Card, D., "Measuring Software Design," *Proceedings of the NSIA Third Annual Joint Conference on SW Quality and Productivity*, (March 1987), pp. 83–100.

74. Card, D., "Software Product Assurance: Measurement and Control," *Information and Software Technology*, Vol. 30, no. 6, (July/August 1988), pp. 322–330.

75. Card, D., "A Software Technology Evaluation Program," *Information and Software Technology*, Vol. 29, no. 6, (Aug. 1987), pp. 291–300.

76. Card, D., and W. Agresti, "Measuring Software Design Complexity," *Journal of Systems and Software*, Vol. 8, no. 3, (June 1988), pp. 185–197.

77. Card, D., V. Church, and W. Agresti, "An Empirical Study of Software Design Practices," *IEEE Transactions on Software Engineering*, Vol. SE-12, no. 2, (Feb. 1986), pp. 264–271.

78. Card, D., T. Clark, and R. Berg, "Improving Software Quality and Productivity," *Information and Software Technology*, Vol. 29, no. 5, (June 1987), pp. 235–241.

79. Card, D. N., D. V. Cotnoir, and C. E. Goorevich, "Managing Software Maintenance Cost and Quality," *Proceedings of the Conference on Software Maintenance*, The Computer Society of the IEEE, (Sept. 1987), pp. 145–152.

80. **Card, D. with R. Glass**, *Measuring Software Design Quality*, Englewood Cliffs, NJ: Prentice-Hall, Inc., 1990.

81. Card, D., G. Page, and F. McGarry, "Criteria for Software Modularization," *Collected Software Engineering Papers: Volume III*, Goddard Space Flight Center, Greenbelt, MD, (Nov. 1985), pp. 4-16–4-21.

82. Card, D., F. McGarry, and G. Page, "Evaluating Software Engineering Technologies," *IEEE Transactions on Software Engineering*, Vol. SE-13, no. 7, (July 1987), pp. 845–851.

83. Carper, I., S. Harvey, and J. Wethesbe, "Computer Capacity Planning: Strategy and Methodologies," *Data Base*, (Summer 1983), pp. 3–11.

84. Chen, E., "Program Complexity and Programmer Productivity," *IEEE Transactions on Software Engineering*, Vol. SE-4, no. 3, (May 1978), pp. 187–194.

85. Chew, W., "No-Nonsense Guide to Measuring Productivity," *Harvard Business Review*, (Jan. 1988), pp. 110–118.

86. Christensen, K., G. Fitsos, and C. Smith, "A Perspective on Software Science," *IBM Systems Journal*, Vol. 20, no. 4, (1981), pp. 372–387.

87. Chumbley, S., "Applying TQC to the Traditional Software Lifecycle," (May 1984).

88. Classick, R. D., "A Primer on the Use of Code Stability Data in Controlling Software Development Projects," *HP Software Engineering Productivity Conference Proceedings*, (May 1987), pp. 3-17–3-35.

89. Coggins, M., L. Berger, P. Carter, "Apogee: Software Engineering in an MIS Project," *HP Software Engineering Productivity Conference Proceedings*, (Aug. 1988), pp. 473–491.

90. **Cohen, L.**, "Quality Function Deployment: An Application Perspective from Digital Equipment Corporation," *National Productivity Review*, (Summer 1988), pp. 197–208.

91. Collofello, J., and S. Woodfield, "Evaluating the Effectiveness of Realiability-Assurance Techniques," *The Journal of Systems and Software*, no. 9, (1989), pp. 191–195.

92. Compton, B., and C. Withrow, "Prediction and Control of ADA Software Defects," *Journal of Systems and Software 12*, (1990), pp. 199–207.

93. Conte, S., H. Dunsmore, and V. Shen, "Software Effort Estimation and Productivity," *Advances in Computers*, (Ed. by M. C. Yovits), Vol. 24. Academic Press, Inc., 1985, pp. 1–60.

94. Conte, S., H. Dunsmore, and V. Shen, *Software Engineering Metrics and Models*, Menlo Park, CA: Benjamin/Cummings Publishing Co., Inc., 1986.

95. Cook, M., "Software Metrics: An Introduction and Annotated Bibliography," *ACM Sigsoft, Software Engineering Notes*, Vol. 7, no. 2, (April 1982), pp. 41–60.

96. Cote, V., P. Bourque, S. Oligny, and N. Rivard, "Software Metrics: An Overview of Recent Results," *The Journal of Systems and Software 8*, (1988), pp. 121–131.

97. Coulter, N., "Software Science and Cognitive Psychology," *IEEE Transactions on Software Engineering*, Vol. SE-9, no. 2, (March 1983), pp. 166–171.

98. Currit, P., M. Dyer, and H. Mills, "Certifying the Reliability of Software," *IEEE Transactions on Software Engineering*, Vol. SE-12, no. 1, (Jan. 1986), pp. 3–11.

99. **Curtis, B.**, "Fifteen Years of Psychology in Software Engineering: Individual Differences and Cognitive Science," *IEEE Proceedings of the Eighth International Conference on Software Engineering*, London (August 1985), pp. 97–106.

100. Curtis, B., H. Krasner, and N. Iscoe, "A Field Study of the Software Design Process for Large Systems," *Communications of the ACM*, Vol. 31, no. 11, (Nov. 1988), pp. 1268–1287.

101. Curtis, B., S. Sheppard, E. Kruesi-Bailey, J. Bailey, and D. A. Boehm-Davis, "Experimental Evaluation of Software Documentation Formats," *The Journal of Systems and Software 9*, (1989), pp. 167–207.

102. Curtis, B., S. Sheppard, P. Milliman, M. Borst, and T. Love, "Measuring the Psychological Complexity of Software Maintenance Tasks with the Halstead and McCabe Metrics," *IEEE Transactions on Software Engineering*, Vol. SE-5, no. 2, (March 1979), pp. 96–104.

103. **Curtis, B., S. B. Sheppard, and P. Milliman**, "Third Time Charm: Stronger Prediction of Programmer Performance by Software Complexity Metrics," *Proceedings of the Fourth International Conference on Software Engineering*, (July 1979), pp. 356–360.

104. Daly, Edmund B., "Management of Software Development," *IEEE Transactions on Software Engineering*, (May 1977), pp. 229–242.

105. D'Angelo, V., A. Shenoy, and W. Utz, "Pathmet – A Design-Based Software Performance Evaluation Tool," (1987).

106. Datapro Research Corporation, "Estimating Application Software Life-Cycle Development Costs," Jan. 1980.

107. **Davey, S., R. D. Classick, D. Lau, J. Loos, and B. Noble**, *Spectrum Program Metrics and Certification Handbook*, HP Software Metrics Technology, Software Development Technology Lab, Information Software Division. Version 2.0 (Oct. 12, 1990)

108. **Davis, J.**, "Investigation of Predictors of Failures and Debugging Effort for Large MIS", *Information and Software Technology*, Vol. 31, no.4, (May, 1989), pp. 170–174.

109. Day, R., "A History of Software Maintenance for a Complex U.S. Army Battlefield Automated System," *IEEE Conference on Software Maintenance*, (Nov. 1985), pp. 181–187.

110. Dea, R. W., "Bang Metrics: An Ongoing Experiment at HP," *HP Software Engineering Productivity Conference Proceedings*, (May 1987), pp. 3-44–3-49.

111. Deardorff, E., "Better Project Estimates — The Easy Way," *HP Software Engineering Productivity Conference Proceedings*, (May 1987), pp. 4-32–4-38.

112. Deardorff, E., "Projection of Project Cost and Project Duration at Waltham," *HP Software Productivity Conference Proceedings*, (April 1986), pp. 1-70 – 1-85.

113. Decot, D., and B. Scott, "Inspections at DSD — Automating Data Input and Data Analysis," *HP Software Engineering Productivity Conference Proceedings*, (Aug. 1985), pp. 1-79 – 1-89.

114. DeMarco, Tom, "An Algorithm for Sizing Software Products," *SigMetrics Performance Evaluation Review*, Vol. 12, no. 2, (Spring/Summer 1984) pp. 13 – 22.

115. **DeMarco, Tom**, *Controlling Software Projects*, New York: Yourdon Press, 1982.

116. DeMarco, T., "Software Productivity: The Covert Agenda," *Information and Software Technology*, Vol. 32, no. 3, (April 1990), pp. 225 – 227.

117. **DeMarco, T., and T. Lister**, *Peopleware*. New York, NY: Dorset House, 1987.

118. DeMarco, T., and T. Lister, "Programmer Performance and the Effects of the Workplace," *IEEE Proceedings of the Eighth International Conference on Software Engineering*, London (Aug. 1985), pp. 268 – 272.

119. DeMarco, T., and T. Lister, "Software Development: State of the Art Vs. State of the Practice," *ACM 0270-5257/89/0500/0271*, (1989), pp. 271–275.

120. DiPersio, T., D. Isbister, and B. Shneiderman, "An Experiment Using Memorization/Reconstruction as a Measure of Programmer Ability," *International Journal of Man-Machine Studies*, no. 13, (1980), pp. 339–354.

121. Dniestrowski, A., J. Guillaume, and R. Mortier, "Software Engineering in Avionics Applications," *IEEE Proceedings of the Third International Conference on Software Engineering*, Atlanta (May 1978), pp. 124-131.

122. Doerflinger, C., and V. Basili, "Monitoring Software Development through Dynamic Variables," *IEEE Transactions on Software Engineering*, Vol. SE-11, no. 9, (Sept. 1985), pp. 978 – 985.

123. Drake, D., "A Pre-Release Measure of Software Reliability," *HP Software Productivity Conference Proceedings*, (April 1986), pp. 2-58 – 2-71.

124. Drake, D., "Reliability Theory Applied to Software Testing," *Hewlett-Packard Journal*, (April 1987), pp. 35 – 39.

125. Dreger, J., *Function Point Analysis*, Englewood Cliffs, N. J.: Prentice-Hall, Inc., 1989.

126. **Drummond, S.**, "Measuring Applications Development Performance," *Datamation*, Vol. 31, (1985), pp.102–108.

127. Duncan, A., "Software Development Productivity Tools and Metrics," *IEEE Proceedings of the Tenth International Conference on Software Engineering*, (April 1988), pp. 41– 48.

128. Dunham, J., "Experiments in Software Reliability: Life-Critical Applications," *IEEE Transactions on Software Engineering*, (Jan. 1986).

129. Dunham, J., "V & V in the Next Decade," *IEEE Software*, (May 1989), pp. 47–53.

130. Dunsmore, H., and J. Gannon, "Experimental Investigation of Programming Complexity," *16th ACM Technical Symposium on System Software: Operational Reliability and Performance Assurance*, (1977), pp. 117–125.

131. Dunsmore, H., and A. Wang, "A Step Toward Early Software Size Estimation for Use in Productivity Models," *1985 National Conference on Software Quality and Productivity*, (March 6-8 1985), pp. 1– 9.

132. Dyer, M., "An Approach to Software Reliability Measurement," *Information and Software Technology*, Vol. 29, no. 8, (Oct. 1987), pp. 415 – 420.

133. Ehrlich, W., S. Lee, and R. Molisani, "Applying Reliability Measurement: A Case Study," *IEEE Software*, (March 1990), pp. 56 – 64.

134. Emerson, T., "A Discriminant Metric for Module Cohesion," *IEEE Proceedings of the Seventh International Conference on Software Engineering*, (March 1984), pp. 294–303.

135. **Endres, A.**, "An Analysis of Errors and Their Causes in System Programs," *IEEE Transactions on Software Engineering*, Vol. SE-1, no. 2, (June 1975), pp.140–149.

136. Evanczuk, S., "New Tools Boost Software Productivity," *Electronics Week*, (Sept. 10, 1984), pp. 67–74.

137. Ezzell, S., "Software Failure Analysis at IND," *HP Software Engineering Productivity Conference Proceedings*, (Aug. 1990), pp. 539–548.

138. Fagan, M., "Advances in Software Inspections," *IEEE Transactions on Software Engineering*, Vol. SE-12, no. 7, (July 1986), pp. 744–751.

139. Fagan, M., "Design and Code Inspections and Process Control in the Development of Programs," *TR21.572* IBM System Development Division, Kingston, N.Y., (Dec. 1974).

140. Fagan, M., "Design and Code Inspections to Reduce Errors in Program Development," *IBM Systems Journal*, Vol. 15, no. 3, (1976), pp. 182–210.

141. Fagan, M., "Inspecting Software Design and Code," *Datamation*, Vol. 23, no. 10, (Oct. 1977), pp. 133–144.

142. Felix, G., and J. Riggs, "Productivity Measurement by Objectives," *National Productivity Review*, (Autumn 1983), pp. 386–393.

143. Fenick, S., "Implementing Management Metrics: An Army Program," *IEEE Software*, (March 1990), pp. 65–72.

144. Feuer, A., and E. Fowlkes, "Relating Computer Program Maintainability Software Measures," *AFIPS National Computer Conference Expo Conference Proceedings*, Vol. 48 (June 4-7 1979), pp. 1003–1012.

145. Fischer, B., "Scheduling of Software Engineering Projects," *HP Software Engineering Productivity Conference Proceedings*, (Aug. 1988), pp. 87–96.

146. Fischer, B., and J. Jost, "A Comparison of Structured and Unstructured Methodologies in an Embedded Microprocessor Project," *HP Software Engineering Productivity Conference Proceedings*, (Aug. 1988), pp. 271–281.

147. Flaherty, M., "Programming Process Productivity Measurement System for System/370," *IBM Systems Journal*, Vol. 24, no. 2, (1985), pp. 168–175.

148. Fuget, C., "Using Quality Metrics to Improve Life Cycle Productivity," *HP Software Productivity Conference Proceedings*, (April 1986), pp. 1-86–1-93.

149. Fujino, K., "Software Development for Computers and Communication at NEC," *Computer*, (Nov. 1984), pp. 57–61.

150. Fuller, F., "How to Construct and Use a Productivity Loss Index," *National Productivity Review*, (Spring 1988), pp. 99–113.

151. Gaffney, John E., "Estimating the Number of Faults in Code," *IEEE Transactions on Software Engineering*, Vol. SE-10, no. 4, (July 1984), pp. 459–465.

152. Gaffney, J., "The Impact on Software Development Costs of Using HOL's," *IEEE Transactions on Software Engineering*, Vol. SE-12, no. 3, (Mar. 1986), pp. 496–499.

153. Gaffney, J., "A Quantitative Analysis of the Impact of Modern Software Engineering Techniques on Software Quality and Development Productivity," *Eleventh Annual Software Engineering Workshop, NASA Goddard Flight Center*, (Dec. 1986).

154. Gibson, V., and J. Senn, "System Structure and Software Maintenance Performance," *Communications of the ACM*, Vol. 32, no. 3, (Mar. 1989), pp. 347–358.

155. Gilb, T., "Evolutionary Delivery Versus the 'Waterfall Model," *Software Engineering Notes (ACM SIGSOft)*, (July 1985).

156. Gilb, T, *Principles of Software Engineering Management*, Reading, MA: Addison-Wesley, 1988.

157. Glass, R., "Persistent Software Errors," *IEEE Transactions on Software Engineering*, Vol. SE-7, no. 2, (March 1981), pp. 162–168.

158. Glass, R., "Software Metrics: Of Lightning Rods and Built-up Tension," *Journal of Systems and Software 10*, (1989), pp. 157–158.

159. Goel, A., and K. Okumoto, "A Time-Dependent Error Detection Rate Model for Software Reliability and Other Performance Measures," *IEEE Transactions on Reliability*, Vol. R-28, (1979), pp. 206–211.

160. Gordon, R., "Measuring Improvements in Program Clarity," *IEEE Transactions on Software Engineering*, Vol. SE-5, no. 2, (Mar. 1979) pp. 79–90.

161. Grady, R., "Dissecting Software Failures," *Hewlett-Packard Journal*, (April 1989), pp. 57–63.

162. Grady, R., "Measuring and Managing the Software Maintenance Process," *IEEE Software*, (Sept., 1987), pp. 35–45.

163. Grady, R., "One Perspective on the Future of Software Metrics," *The International Conference on Applications of Software Measurement, Conference Papers*, (Nov 1990), pp. 166–169.

164. Grady, R., "Practical Rules of Thumb for Software Managers," *HP Software Engineering Productivity Conference Proceedings*, (Aug. 1990), pp. 647–651.

165. ****Grady, R., and D. Caswell**, *Software Metrics: Establishing a Company-Wide Program*, Englewood Cliffs, NJ: Prentice-Hall, 1987.

166. Grady, R., "The Role of Software Metrics in Managing Quality and Testing," (Jan. 30, 1990).

167. Grady, R., "Work-Product Analysis: The Philosopher's Stone of Software?" *IEEE Software*, (March 1990), pp. 26–34.

168. Grady, R., and E. Brigham, "A Survey of HP Software Development," *HP Software Productivity Conference Proceedings*, (April 1986), pp. 1-126–1-141.

169. Gremillion, L., "Determinants of Program Repair Maintenance Requirements," *Communications of the ACM*, Vol. 27, no. 8, (Aug. 1984), pp. 826–832.

170. Gustafson, D., A. Melton, and C. Hsieh, "An Analysis of Software Changes During Maintenance and Enhancement," *IEEE Conference on Software Maintenance*, (Nov. 1985), pp. 92–95.

171. Hamamura, A., "Measuring Programming Quality," *HP Software Engineering Productivity Conference Proceedings*, (May 1987), pp. 4-100–4-115.

172. Hamilton, G., "Improving Software Development Using Quality Control," *HP Software Productivity Conference Proceedings*, (April 1985), pp. 1-96–1-102.

173. Hamilton, P., and J. Musa, "Measuring Reliability of Computation Center Software," *Third International Conference on Software Engineering*, (May 1978), pp. 29–36.

174. Harrison, W., and C. Cook, "Reduced Form for Sharing Software Complexity Data," *Pacific Northwest Software Quality Conference Proceedings*, Portland, OR, (Sept. 1985), pp. 79–88.

175. Harrison, W., K. Magel, R. Kluczny, and A. DeKock, "Applying Software Complexity Metrics to Program Maintenance," *Computer*, (Sept. 1982), pp. 65–79.

176. Hatch, M., "The Organization as a Physical Environment of Work: Physical Structure Determinants of Task Attention and Interaction," Ph. D. Dissertation, Stanford University, (May 1985).

177. Henry, S., "A Research Tool for Measuring Software Quality," *Proceedings of the NSIA Third Annual Joint Conference on SW Quality and Productivity*, (March 1987), pp. 83–100.

178. Henry, S., and D. Kafura, "The Evaluation of Software Systems' Structure Using Quantitative Software Metrics," *Software-Practice and Experience*, Vol. 14 (6), (June 1984), pp. 561–573.

179. Henry, S., and D. Kafura, "Software Structure Metrics Based on Information Flow," *IEEE Transactions on Software Engineering*, Vol. SE-7, no. 5, (Sept. 1981), pp. 510–518.

180. Henry, S., and C. Selig, "Predicting Source Code Complexity at the Design Stage," *IEEE Software*, (March 1990), pp. 36–44.

181. **Herington, D., P. Nichols, and R. Lipp**, "Software Verification Using Branch Analysis," *Hewlett-Packard Journal*, (June 1987), pp. 13–22.

182. Hilgendorf, D., and J. Nissen, "A Code Inspections Success Story," *HP Software Engineering Productivity Conference Proceedings*, (Aug. 1990), pp. 415–426.

183. Hill, G., "Controlling the Maintainability of PL/I and PL/I-Like Software," *IEEE Conference on Software Maintenance*, (Nov. 1985), pp. 106–110.

184. Hoffman, G., "Early Introduction of Software Metrics," *IEEE CH2759-9/89/0000-0559*, (Sept 1989), pp. 559–563.

185. Holcomb, R., "An Amalgamated Model of Software Usability," *IEEE 0730-3157/89/0000/0559*, (1989), pp. 559–566.

186. House, C., "The Return Picture: Measuring R&D and Marketing Excellence," (1988).

187. Huff, K., J. Sroka, and D. Struble, "Quantitative Models for Managing Software Development Processes," *Software Engineering Journal*, (Jan. 1986), pp. 17–23

188. **Humphrey, W.**, *Managing the Software Process*, Reading, MA: Addison-Wesley, 1989.

189. Humphery W., D. Kitson, T. Kasse, "The State of Software Engineering Practice: A Preliminary Report", *0270-5257/89/0500/0277, ACM*, (1989), pp. 277–288.

190. Hutchens, D., and V. Basili, "System Structure Analysis: Clustering with Data Bindings," *IEEE Transactions on Software Engineering*, Vol. SE-11, no. 8, (Aug. 1985), pp. 749–757.

191. *IEEE Standard Glossary of Software Engineering Terminology*, IEEE Std 729–1983, New York (1983).

192. Ince, D., and M. Shepperd, "System Design Metrics: A Review and Perspective," *Proceedings of the 2nd IEE/BCS Conference on Software Engineering*, 88 IEE, London, UK (1988), pp. 23–27.

193. Inglis, J., "Standard Software Quality Metrics," *AT&T Technical Journal*, Vol. 65, no. 2, (March/April 1986), pp. 113–118.

194. Ishikawa, K., *Guide to Quality Control*, Tokyo: Asian ProductivitycOrganization, 1976.

195. Jeffery, D., "Time-Sensitive Cost Models in the Commercial MIS Environment," *IEEE Transactions on Software Engineering*, Vol. SE-13, no. 7, (July 1987), pp. 852–859.

196. Jensen, Randall W., "Projected Productivity Impact of Near-Term ADA Use in Software System Development," *Proceedings of the International Society of Parametric Analysts Seventh Annual Conference*, (May 1985), pp. 42–55.

197. Jensen, Randall W., "A Macro-Level Software Development Cost Estimation Methodology," *CH1625-3/80/0000/0320, IEEE*, (March 1980), pp. 320–325.

198. Jones, C., "A Process-Integrated Approach to Defect Prevention," *IBM Systems Journal*, Vol. 24, no. 2, (1985), pp. 150–167.

199. Jones, T. C., *Applied Software Measurement*, New York: McGraw-Hill Book Co., 1991.

200. Jones, T. C., "The Cost and Value of CASE," Software Productivity Research, Inc., Cambridge, MA, (1988).

201. Jones, T. C., "Measuring Programming Quality and Productivity," *IBM Systems Journal*, Vol. 17, no. 1, (1978), pp. 39–63.

202. Jones, T. C., "Measuring Software Productivity With Function Points," *Computerworld*, (Nov. 19, 1984), pp. 33–37.

203. Jones, T. C., *Programming Productivity*. New York: McGraw-Hill Book Co., 1986.

204. Jones, T. C., *Programming Productivity: Issues for the Eighties*, IEEE Computer Society Press (1981), pp. 5–8.

205. Jones, T. C., "U.S. Industry Averages for Software Productivity and Quality," Software Productivity Research, Inc., Cambridge, MA, Version 2.0 (Aug. l988).

206. Jorgensen, A. H., "A Methodology for Measuring the Readability and Modifiability of Computer Programs," *BIT*, Vol. 20, (1980), pp. 394–405.

207. Jost, J., and L. Schroath, "The Error-Prone Module Paradox," *HP Software Engineering Productivity Conference Proceedings*, (Aug. 1990), pp. 461–474.

208. Juran, J., F. Gryna, and R. Bingham Jr., Quality Control Handbook,, 3rd ed. New York: McGraw Hill, 1974.

209. **Kafura, D.**, "The Use of Software Complexity Metrics in Software Maintenance," *IEEE Transactions on Software Engineering*, Vol. SE-13, no. 3, (March 1987), pp. 335–343.

210. Kearney, J., R. Sedlmeyer, W. Thompson, M. Gray, and A. Adler, "Software Complexity Measurement," *Communications of the ACM*, Vol. 29, no. 29, (Nov. l986), pp. 1044–1050.

211. Kelly, J., and J. Sherif, "An Analysis of Defect Densities Found During Software Inspections," *Proceedings of the Fifteenth Annual Software Engineering Workshop*, Goddard Space Flight Center, (Nov 1990), pp. 1–34.

212. Kelly, P., "Cyclomatic Complexity as a Factor During the Design Phase," *HP Software Engineering Productivity Conference Proceedings*, (Aug. 1990), pp. 557–566.

213. Kenyon, D., "Implementing a Software Metrics Program," *HP Software Productivity Conference Proceedings*, (April 1985), pp. 1-103–1-117.

214. Kim, K., "A Look at Japan's Development of Software Engineering Technology," *IEEE Computer*, (May 1983), pp. 26–37.

215. Kishida, K., M. Teramoto, K. Torii, and Y. Urano, "Quality-Assurance Technology in Japan," *IEEE Software*, (Sept. 1987), pp. 11–18.

216. Kitchenham, B., and S. Linkman, "Design Metrics in Practice," *Information and Software Technology*, Vol. 32, no. 4, (May 1990), pp. 304–310.

217. Kitchenham, B., and J. McDermid, "Software Metrics and Integrated Project Support Environments," *Software Engineering Journal*, (January l986) pp. 58–64.

218. Kitchenham, B., and N. Taylor, "Software Cost Models," *ICL Technical Journal*, Vol. 4, no. 1, (1984), pp. 73–102.

219. **Knafl, G. J., and J. Sacks**, "Software Development Effort Prediction Based on Function Points," *Proceedings of the Computer Software and Applications Conference*, (l986), pp. 319–325.

220. Kohoutek, Henry J., "A Practical Approach to Software Reliability Management," *Proceedings of the 29th EOQC Conference, Quality and Development*, Vol. 2, (June 1985), pp. 211–220.

221. Kolkhorst, B., "IBM FSD Software Quality and Productivity Improvement," *Fifth International Conference on Testing Computer Software*, Washington, DC, (June 1988).

222. Kruger, G., "Better Project Management through Software Reliability Growth Models," *HP Software Engineering Productivity Conference Proceedings*, (May 1987), pp. 4-132–4-141.

223. **Kruger, G.**, "Project Management Using Software Reliability Growth Models," *Hewlett-Packard Journal*, (June 1988), pp. 30–35.

224. Kruger, G., "Validating and Expanding the Application of Software Reliability Models," *HP Software Engineering Productivity Conference Proceedings*, (Aug. 1988), pp. 79-86.

225. Kunkler, J., "A Cooperative Industry Study, Software Development/ Maintenance Productivity," Xerox Corporation, (March 1985).

226. **Kusters, R., M. van Genuchten, and I. Heemstra**, "Are Software Cost Estimation Models Accurate?" *Information and Software Technology*, (April 1990).

227. Lambert, G., "A Comparative Study of System Response Time on Program Developer Productivity," *IBM Systems Journal*, Vol. 23, no. 1, (1984), pp. 36–43.

228. Lau, D., "The Success of the Spectrum Software Certification Program," *HP Software Engineering Productivity Conference Proceedings*, (August 1988), pp. 109–117.

229. **Lauterbach, L., and W. Randell**, "Six Test Techniques Compared: The Test Process and Product," *Proceedings of the NSIA Fifth Anniversary National Joint Conference and Tutorial on Software Quality and Productivity*, National Security Industrial Association, Washington, DC, 1989.

230. Lawrence, M., "Programming Methodology, Organizational Environment, and Programming Productivity," *The Journal of Systems and Software*, (Sept. 1981), pp. 257–269.

231. Lawrence, P., "How to Deal with Resistance to Change," *Harvard Business Review*, (Jan/Feb 1969), pp. 4–12, 166–176.

232. Leath, C., and K. Cho, "A Software Defect Analysis," *HP Software Engineering Productivity Conference Proceedings,* (May 1987), pp. 4-147–4-161.

233. Levendel, Y., "Reliability Analysis of Large Software Systems: Defect Data Modeling," *IEEE Transactions on Software Engineering*, Vol. 16, no. 2, (Feb 1990), pp. 141–152.

234. Levitt, D., "Process Measures to Improve R&D Scheduling Accuracy," *HP Journal*, (April 1988), pp. 61–65.

235. Li, H. F., "An Empirical Study of Software Metrics," *IEEE Transactions on Software Engineering*, Vol. SE-13, no. 6, (June 1987), pp. 697–708.

236. Lientz, B., "Issues in Software Maintenance," *ACM Computing Surveys*, Vol. 15, no. 3, (Sept. 1983), pp. 271–278.

237. Lientz, B., and E. Swanson, "Software Maintenance: A User/ Management Tug-Of-War," *Data Management*, (April 1979), pp. 26–30.

238. Lientz, B., and E. Swanson, *Software Maintenance Management.*, Reading, MA: Addison-Wesley, 1980.

239. Lind, R., and K. Vairavan, "An Experimental Investigation of Software Metrics and Their Relationship to Software Development Effort," *IEEE Transactions on Software Engineering*, Vol. 15, no. 5, (May 1989), pp. 649–653.

240. Lipow, M., "Number of Faults per Line of Code," *IEEE Transactions on Software Engineering*, Vol. SE-8, no. 4, (July 1982), pp. 437–439.

241. Littlewood, B., "How to Measure Software Reliability, and How Not To . . . ," *Proceedings of the Third International Conference on Software Engineering*, (May 1978), pp. 37–45.

242. Littlewood, B., "Validation of a Software Reliability Model," *IEEE Second Software Life Cycle Management Workshop*, (Aug. 1978), pp. 146–152.

243. Loh, M., and R. Nelson, "Reaping CASE Harvests," *Datamation*, (July 1, 1989), pp. 31–34.

244. Lohse, J., and S. Zweben, "Experimental Evaluation of Software Design Principles: An Investigation into the Effect of Module Coupling on System Modifiability," *Journal of Systems and Software*, 4 (1984), pp. 301–308.

245. **Losa, J., J. Aagard, and J. Kincaid**, "Readability Grade Levels of Selected Navy Technical School Curricula," Naval Training Analysis and Evaluation Group, Orlando, FL, *Report No. TAEG-TM-83-2*, (Feb. 1983).

246. Lowell, N., "An Interview with Nathan Lowell," *Software Quality World*, Vol. 2, no. 2, (1990), pp. 1, 5–7.

247. Lundberg, D., "A Method of Predicting the Software Release Date Based Upon Source Code Changes," *HP Software Productivity Conference*, (April 1984), pp. 1-67–1-73.

248. Mathur, S., "Experiences in Using QFD Methodology on the Iris Project," *HP Software Engineering Productivity Conference Proceedings*, (Aug. 1990), pp. 383–392.

249. Mays, R., C. Jones, G. Holloway, and D. Studinski, "Experiences with Defect Prevention," *IBM Systems Journal*, Vol. 29, no. 1, (Jan 1990), pp. 4–32.

250. McCabe, T., "A Complexity Measure," *IEEE Transactions on Software Engineering*, (Dec. 1976), pp. 308–320.

251. McCabe, T., and C. Butler, "Design Complexity Measurement and Testing," *Communications of the ACM*, Vol. 32, no. 12, (Dec 1989), pp. 1415–1425.

252. McCall, J. A., P. K. Richards, and G. F. Walters, *Factors in Software Quality* (Tech. Rep. 77CIS 02), Sunnyvale, Calif., General Electric, Command and Information Systems 1977.

253. McGarry, F., and W. Agresti, Measuring Ada for Software Development in the Software Engineering Laboratory," *Journal of Systems and Software* 9, (1989), pp. 149–159.

254. Merlini, M., "Is Big Blue Big Brother," *Datamation*, (March 1984), pp. 52–61.

255. Military Standard, "Defense System Software Development," U.S. Government Printing Office, DOD-STD-2167 (Feb. 1986).

256. Miller, G. A., "The Magical Number Seven, Plus or Minus Two: Some Limits on Our Capacity for Processing Information," *The Psychological Review*, Vol. 63, no. 2, (March 1956), pp. 81–97.

257. Mills, H., M. Dyer, and R. Linger, "Cleanroom Software Engineering," *IEEE Software*, (Sept. 1987), pp. 19–25.

258. MITRE, "Software Reporting Metrics," ESD-TR-85-145 (Nov. 1985).

259. Mizuno, Y., "Software Quality Improvement," *IEEE Computer*, (March 1983), pp. 66–72.

260. Mohanty, S., "Entropy Metrics for Software Design Evaluation," *Journal of Systems and Software 2*, (1981), pp. 39–46.

261. Moller, K., "Fault Rate as a Function of the Modification Rate, Module Length, and Programming Language — An Empirical Investigation," Siemens AG, Corporate Research and Technology, (1989).

262. Moller, K., "Increasing of Software Quality by Objectives and Residual Fault Prognosis," *First E.O.Q.C. Seminar on Software Quality*, Brussels, Belgium, (April 1988), pp. 478–488.

263. Monray, J., R. Merckling, and R. Villafana, "Best Practices Expanded from Pilot Projects to the Whole Lab," *HP Software Productivity Conference Proceedings*, (August 1988), pp. 207–219.

264. Monray, J., "How Two Engineers Made the Difference," *HP Software Productivity Conference Proceedings*, (April 1986), pp. 1-19–1-28.

265. Munson, J., "Software Maintainability: A Practical Concern for Life-Cycle Costs," *Computer*, Vol. 14, no. 11, (Nov. 1981), pp. 103–109.

266. Munson, J., and T. Khoshgoftaar, "Applications of a Relative Complexity Metric for Software Project Management," *Journal of Systems and Software 12*, (1990), pp. 283–291.

267. Munson, J., and R. Yeh, "Report by the IEEE Software Engineering Productivity Workshop," (March 8-9, 1981), San Diego, CA, CH1702-0/81, pp. 329–359.

268. Musa, J., "The Measurement and Management of Software Reliability," *Proceedings of the IEEE*, Vol. 68, no. 9, (Sept. 1980), pp. 1131–1143.

269. Musa, J., "Measuring Reliability of Computation Center Software," *IEEE Proceedings of the Third International Conference on Software Engineering*, (May 1978), pp. 29–36.

270. Musa, John D., "Software Reliability Measurement," *The Journal of Systems and Software*, Vol. 1 (1980), pp. 223–241.

271. **Musa, J., A. Iannino, and K. Okumoto**, *Software Reliability: Measurement, Prediction, Application*, New York: McGraw-Hill 1987.

272. Myers, G., "A Controlled Experiment in Program Testing and Code Walkthrough/Inspection," *CACM*, 21(9), (1978), pp. 760–768.

273. Myers, W., "An Assessment of the Competitiveness of the United States Software Industry," *Computer*, (March 1985), pp. 81–92.

274. Nakagawa, Y., and S. Hanata, "An Error Complexity Model for Software Reliability Measurement," *ACM 00270-5257/89/0500/0230*, (1989), pp. 230–236.

275. Nakajo, T., "A Case History Analysis of Software Error Cause-Effect Relationships," *IEEE Transactions on Software Engineering*, Vol. 17, no. 8, (Aug. 1991), pp. 830–838.

276. Nakajo, T., "Mechanisms of Software Defect Occurrence and Effective Design Methods of Eliminating Them," (Sept. 1989).

277. Nakajo, T., and H. Kume, "A New Method of Analyzing Software Defects: Structured Defect Analysis," University of Tokyo, (1990).

278. Nakajo, T., K. Sasabuchi, and T. Akiyama, "A Structured Approach to Software Defect Analysis," *Hewlett-Packard Journal*, (April 1989) pp. 50–56.

279. Nichols, P, D. Herington, and R. Lipp, "A Software Testing Methodology Using Branch Analysis," *HP Software Productivity Conference Proceedings*, (April 1986), pp. 2-72–2-82.

280. Nielson, L., "Using NCSS as a Tool to Estimate Effort and Schedule," *HP Software Productivity Conference Proceedings*, (April 1986), pp. 1-94–1-105.

281. Nishimoto, A., "Evolution of an Inspection and Metrics Program at MPD," *HP Software Engineering Productivity Conference Proceedings*, (Aug. 1990), pp. 527–537.

282. Norcio, A. F., and L.J. Chmura, "Designing Complex Software," *The Journal of Systems and Software 8*, (1988) pp. 165–184.

283. Norman, R. J., and J. F. Nunamaker, "CASE Productivity Perceptions of Software Engineering Professionals," *Communications of the ACM*, Vol. 32, no. 9, (September 1989) pp. 1102–1108.

284. Ohba, M., S. Yamada, K. Takeda, and S. Osaki, "S-Shaped Software Reliability Growth Curve: How Good Is It?" *Proceedings of the Compsac International Software and Applications Conference*, (Nov. 1982), pp. 38–44.

285. Ohba, Mitsuru, "Software Reliability Analysis Models," *IBM J. Res. Develop.*, Vol. 28, no. 4, (July 1984), pp. 428–443.

286. **Ohba, Mitsuru**, "Software Quality = Test Accuracy X Text Coverage," *0270-5257/82/0000/0287, IEEE* (1982), pp. 287–293.

287. Oman, P., C. Cook, and N. Murthi, "Effects of Programming Experience in Debugging Semantic Errors," *Journal of Systems and Software 9*, (1989), pp. 197–207.

288. Osborne, K., "An Experiment in Programming Methodologies," *HP Software Productivity Conference Proceedings*, (April 1984), pp. 1-18–1-23.

289. **Ostrand, T., and E. Weyuker**, "Collecting and Categorizing Software Error Data in an Industrial Environment," *Journal of Systems Software*, Vol. 4, (1983), pp. 289–300.

290. Page-Jones, M., "Attempts to Increase Productivity," Wayland Systems Institute.

291. Paige, Michael, "A Metric for Software Test Planning," *Proceedings of the Fourth International Conference on Computer Software and Application*, Chicago, Ill.: Oct. 27–31, 1980, pp. 499–504.

292. Peercy, D., "A Software Maintainability Evaluation Methodology," *IEEE Transactions on Software Engineering*, Vol. SE-7, no. 4, (July 1981), pp. 343–351.

293. Perry, D., and W. Evangelist, "An Empirical Study of Software Interface Faults," AT&T Bell Laboratories.

294. Petschenik, Nathan H., "Practical Priorities in System Testing," *IEEE Software*, (Sept. 1985), pp. 18–23.

295. Pettijohn, C., "Achieving Quality in the Development Process," *AT&T Technical Journal*, Vol. 65, no. 2, (March/April 1986), pp. 85–93.

296. Pfleeger, S., and C. McGowan, "Software Metrics in the Process Maturity Framework," *Journal of Systems and Software 12*, (1990), pp. 255–261.

297. Porter, A., and R. Selby, "Empirically-Guided Software Development Using Metric-Based Classification Trees," *IEEE Software*, (March 1990), pp. 46–54.

298. Potier, D., J. Albin, R. Ferreol, and A. Bilodeau, "Experiments with Computer Software Complexity and Reliability," *Proceedings of the IEEE Sixth International Conference on Software Engineering*, (Sept. 1982), pp. 94–101.

299. Putnam, L. H., "SLIM, A Quantitative Tool for Software Cost and Schedule Estimation (A Demonstration of a Software Management Tool)," *Proceedings of the NBS/IEEE/ACM Software Tool Fair*, (March 1981), pp. 49-57.

300. Putnam, L. I., "A General Empirical Solution to the Macro Software Sizing and Estimating Problem," *IEEE Transactions on Software Engineering*, Vol. SE-4, no. 4, (July 1978), pp. 345–361.

301. Putnam, L. H., and A. Fitzsimmons, "Estimating Software Costs," *Datamation*, (Sept. 1979), pp. 312–315.

302. Ramamoorthy, A., W. Tsai, and Y. Usuda, "Software Engineering: Problems and Perspectives," *Computer*, (Oct. 1984), pp. 191–207.

303. Ramamoorthy, C. V., W. Tsai, T. Yamaura, and A. Bhide, "Metrics Guided Methodology," *0730-3157/85/0000/0111, IEEE*, (1985) pp. 111–120.

304. **Rambo, R., P. Buckley, and E. Branyan,** "Establishment and Validation of Software Metric Factors," *Proceedings of the International Society of Parametric Analysts Seventh Annual Conference,* (May 1985), pp. 406–417.

305. Rambo, R., D. Usavage, and E. Branyan, "A Software Metrics Research Initiative: Data Collection, Tools, and Methods," *Proceedings of the NSIA Third Annual Joint Conference on SW Quality and Productivity,* (March 1987), pp. 83–100.

306. Ramsey, H., M. Atwood, and J. Van Doren, "Flowcharts Versus Program Design Languages: An Experimental Comparison," *Communications of the ACM,* Vol. 26, no. 6, (June 1983), pp. 445–449.

307. Ramsey, J., and V. R. Basili, "Analyzing the Test Process Using Structural Coverage," *CH2139-4/85/0000/0306, IEEE,* (1985), pp. 306–312.

308. Rapp, B., "Reliability Growth Modeling," *HP Software Engineering Productivity Conference Proceedings,* (Aug. 1990), pp. 493–504.

309. Rees, Michael J., "Automatic Assessment Aids for Pascal Programs," *SIGPLAN Notices,* Vol. 17, no. 10, (Oct. 1982), pp. 33–42.

310. Reynolds, R., "The Partial Metrics System: Modeling the Stepwise Refinement Process Using Partial Metrics," *Communications of the ACM,* Vol. 30, no. 11, (Nov. 1987), pp. 956–963.

311. Roberts, E. B., "Generating Effective Corporate Innovation," *Technology Review,* (Nov. 1977), p. 29.

312. Robinson, P., and P. Bartlett, "CPB's Use of Structured Methods for Real-Time Peripheral Firmware," *HP Software Productivity Conference Proceedings,* (August 1988), pp. 285–295.

313. Rombach, H., "Design Measurement: Some Lessons Learned," *IEEE Software,* (March 1990), pp. 17–25.

314. Rombach, H. D., "Design Metrics for Maintenance," *Proceedings of the 9th Annual Software Engineering Workshop,* NASA, Goddard Space Flight Center, Greenbelt, MD, (Nov. 1984), pp. 100–135.

315. Rombach, H. D., "Quantitative Assessment of Maintenance: An Industrial Case Study," *Proceeding of the IEEE Conference on SW Maintenance, Austin, TX.,* (Sept. 1987) pp. 134–144.

316. Rombach, H. D., "Impact of Software Structure on Maintenance," *IEEE Conference on Software Maintenance,* (Nov. 1985), pp. 152–160.

317. Rombach, D., and B. Ulery, "Establishing a Measurement-Based Maintenance Environment Program: Lessons Learned in the SEL," *Proceedings of the IEEE Conference on Software Maintenance,* Miami Beach, FL, (Oct 1989), pp. 50–57.

318. Rombach, H. D., and B. T. Ulery, "Improving Software Maintenance Through Measurement," *Proceedings of the IEEE,* Vol. 77, no. 4, (April 1989), pp. 581–595.

319. Rubey, R. J., J. A. Dana, and P. W. Biche, "Quantitative Aspects of Software Validation," *IEEE Transactions on Software Engineering,* Vol. SE-1, no. 2, (June 1975), pp. 150–155.

320. Rubin, H., "How to Configure Your Measurement Dashboard," *Conference Papers of the ASQC International Conference on Applications of Software Measurement,* San Diego, CA, (Nov 1990), pp. 125–132.

321. Rubin, H., "Macro-Estimation of Software Development Parameters: The Estimacs System," *CH1919-0/83/0000/0109, IEEE,* (1983), pp. 109-113.

322. Rubin, H., "Metrics with Muscle or Metrics with Meaning?" *System Development,* (Oct 1989), pp. 1–4.

323. Russell, M., "International Survey of Software Measurement Education and Training," *Journal of Systems and Software 12*, (1990), pp. 233–241.

324. Sakai, B., and S. Davey, "Spectrum Metrics Collection Program," *HP Software Productivity Conference Proceedings*, (April 1986), pp. 1-113–1-125.

325. Schaefer, H., "Metrics for Optimal Maintenance Management," *IEEE Conference on Software Maintenance*, (Nov. 1985), pp. 114–119.

326. Schneidewind, N., "The State of Software Maintenance," *IEEE Transactions on Software Engineering*, Vol. SE-13, no. 3, (March 1987), pp. 303–310.

327. Schneidewind, N. F., and H. M. Hoffman,, "An Experiment in Software Error Data Collection and Analysis," *IEEE Transactions on Software Engineering*, Vol. SE-5, no. 3, (May 1979), pp. 276–286.

328. Schroath, L., "Root Cause Analysis: Lessons Learned," *HP Software Engineering Productivity Conference Proceedings*, (Aug. 1990), pp. 475–484.

329. Scott, B., and D. Decot, "Inspections at DSD — Automating Data Input and Data Analysis," *HP Software Productivity Conference Proceedings*, (April 1985), pp. 1-79–1-89.

330. Selby, R., V. Basili, and F. Baker, "Cleanroom Software Development: An Empirical Evaluation," *IEEE Transactions on Software Engineering*, Vol. SE-13, no. 9, (Sept. 1987), pp. 1027–1036.

331. Sgarlatti, A., "Measuring Quality Trends Using Complilation Metrics," *ASQC Quality Congress Transactions*, San Francisco, (1990), pp. 983–987.

332. Shaikh, K., and F. T. Fuller, "Does Success Have a Secret," HP Direct Marketing Division (Dec. 1987).

333. ****Shen, V. Y., T. Yu, S. M. Thebaut, and L. R. Paulsen**, "Identifying Error-Prone-Software — An Empirical Study," *IEEE Transactions on Software Engineering*, Vol. SE-11, no. 4, (April 1985), pp. 317–323.

334. Shen, V. Y., "The Relationship Between Student Grades and Software Science Parameters," *CH1515-6/79/0000-0783, IEEE*, (June 1979), pp. 783–785.

335. Shepperd, M., "A Critique of Cyclomatic Complexity as a Software Metric," *Software Engineering Journal*, (March 1988), pp. 30–36.

336. ****Shepperd, M., and D. Ince**, "Metrics, Outlier Analysis and the Software Design Process," *Information and Software Technology*, Vol. 31, no. 2, (March 1989), pp. 91–98.

337. Shirey, G., "Code Inspections: Doing the Right Thing the Right Way," *HP Software Engineering Productivity Conference Proceedings*, (Aug. 1988), pp. 129–140.

338. Shneiderman, B., "Control Flow and Data Structure Documentation," *Communications of the ACM 25*, (1982), pp. 55–63.

339. Shooman, M., "Types, Distribution, and Test and Correction Times for Programming Errors," *IEEE Proceedings of the 1975 Conference on Reliable Software*, Los Angeles, CA, (April 1975), pp. 347–357.

340. Sieloff, C., "Software TQC: Improving the Software Development Process Through Statistical Quality Control," *HP Software Productivity Conference Proceedings*, (April 1984), pp. 2-49–2-62.

341. ****Silverman, B.**, "Software Cost and Productivity Improvements: An Analogical View," *Computer*, (May 1985), pp. 86–95.

342. Silverstein, A., "Some QA Metrics Support Tools," *HP Software Productivity Conference Proceedings*, (April 1986), pp. 1-106–1-112.

343. Sink, D. S., "Strategic Planning for Successful Design, Development, and Implementation of Productivity Management Programs," *IEEE 1984 Fall Industrial Engineering Conference Proceedings*, (Fall 1984), pp. 391–397.

344. Stanford, C., "Managing Software Projects through a Metrics-Driven Lifecycle," *HP Software Engineering Productivity Conference Proceedings*, (May 1987), pp. 4-232–4-241.

345. Stanley, M., "Software Cost Estimating," *Royal Signals and Radar Establishment Memorandum no. 3472*, U.S. Department of Commerce National Technical Information Service (May 1982).

346. Stetter, F., "Comments on 'Number of Faults per Line of Code," *IEEE Transactions on Software Engineering*, Vol. SE-12, no. 12, (Dec. 1986), p. 1145.

347. Stott, D., "Improving the Quality of Critical Decisions," *ASQC Quality Congress Transactions*, San Francisco, (1990), pp. 518–523.

348. Sudman, S., and N. Bradburn, *Asking Questions: A Practical Guide to Questionnaire Design*, San Francisco, Ca.: Jossey-Bass, 1985.

349. Sunazuka, T., M. Azuma, and N. Yamagishi, "Software Quality Assessment Technology," *IEEE, Proceedings of the Eighth International Conference on Software Engineering*, London, (August 1985), pp. 142–148, IEEE CH21394/85/0000/0142.

350. Sunohara, T., A. Takano, K. Uehara, and T. Ohkawa, "Program Complexity Measure for Software Development Management," *IEEE CH1627-9/81/0000/0100*, (Sept. 1981), pp. 100–106.

351. Symons, C., "Function Point Analysis: Difficulties and Improvements," *IEEE Transactions on Software Engineering*, Vol. 14, no. 1, (Jan. 1988), pp. 2–11.

352. Tada, M., and F. Tsuruda, "Strategic Approach to Improve Quality in Analysis and Design Phases," *HP Software Engineering Productivity Conference Proceedings*, (Aug. 1988), pp. 259–267.

353. Tai, K., "A Program Complexity Metric Based on Data Flow Information in Control Graphs," *IEEE Proceedings of the Seventh International Conference on Software Engineering*, (March 1984), pp. 239–248.

354. Tajima, D., and T. Matsubara, "The Computer Software Industry in Japan," *Computer*, Vol. 14, no. 5, (May 1981), pp. 89–96.

355. Tajima, D., and T. Matsubara, "Inside the Japanese Software Industry," *Computer*, (March 1984), pp. 34–43.

356. Tanik, Murat M., "A Comparison of Program Complexity Prediction Models," *ACM SIGSOFT, Software Engineering Notes*, Vol. 5, no. 4, (Oct.1980), pp. 10–16.

357. Tausworthe, R., "Software Specifications Document, DSN Software Cost Model," Jet Propulsion Laboratory, JPL Publication 81-7, Pasadena, CA, (1981).

358. Thadhani, A. J., "Factors Affecting Programmer Productivity During Application Development," *IBM Systems Journal*, Vol. 23, no. 1, (1984), pp. 19–35.

359. Thayer, T., M. Lipow, and E. Nelson, *Software Reliability: A Study of Large Project Reality*, Amsterdam: North-Holland, Inc., 1978.

360. Thayer, R., A. Pyster, and R. Wood, "Validating Solutions to Major Problems in Software Engineering Project Management," *IEEE Computer*, (Aug. 1982), pp. 65–77.

361. Tillson, T., and J. Walicki, "Testing HP SoftBench: A Distributed CASE Environment: Lessons Learned," *HP Software Engineering Productivity Conference Proceedings*, (Aug. 1990), pp. 441–460.

362. **Troy, D., and S. Zweben**, "Measuring the Quality of Structured Designs," *The Journal of Systems and Software 2*, (June 1981), pp. 113–120.

363. Tuttle, T., and S. Sink, "Taking the Threat Out of Productivity Measurement," *National Productivity Review*, (Winter 1984-85), pp. 24–32.

364. U.S. Social Security Administration, "Productivity Measurement in Software Engineering," (Participants include Brown, B. , H. Herlich, M. Emerson, C. Williamson, M. Greco, W. Sherman), *U. S. Department of Commerce National Technical Information Service*, (June 1983), pp. 1–57.

365. Verner, G. T., B. Jackson, and R. G. Hayward, "Technology Dependence in Function Point Analysis: A Case Study and Critical Review," *ACM0270 -5257/ 89/0500/0375*, (1989), pp. 375–382.

366. **Vessey, I., and R. Weber**, "Some Factors Affecting Program Repair Maintenance: An Empirical Study," *Communications of the ACM*, Vol. 26, no. 2, (Feb. 1983), pp. 128–134.

367. Vomocil, Dave, "Locating Suspect Software and Documentation by Monitoring Basic Information About Changes to Source Files," *Pacific Northwest Software Quality Conference Proceedings*, (Sept. 1985), pp. 264–275.

368. Vosburgh, J., "Quantitative Software Management," *Proceedings of the National Conference on Software Productivity*, (April 1987), pp. 113–124.

369. **Vosburgh, J., B. Curtis, R. Wolverton, B. Albert, H. Malec, S. Hoben, and Y. Liu**, "Productivity Factors and Programming Environments," *0270- 5257/84/0000/0143, IEEE*, (1984), pp. 143–152.

370. Wagoner, W. L., "The Final Report on a Software Reliability Measurement Study," Prepared for: *Space and Missile Systems Organization*, (Aug. l973), p. 8.

371. Walker, W., "Practical Management of the Software Test Phase," *HP Software Productivity Conference Proceedings*, (April 1986), pp. 2-92–2-106.

372. Walsh, Thomas J., "A Software Reliability Study Using a Complexity Measure," *Proceedings of the 1979 National Computer Conference*, New Jersey: AFIPS Press (1979), pp. 761–768.

373. Walston, C. E., and C. P. Felix, "A Method of Programming Measurement and Estimation," *IBM Systems Journal*, no. 1, (1977), pp. 54–73.

374. Walters, Gene F., "Software Quality Metrics for Life-Cycle Cost-Reduction," *IEEE Transactions on Reliability*, Vol. R-28, no. 3, (Aug. 1979), pp. 212–219.

375. Ward, J., "Calculating the Real Cost of Software Defects," *HP Software Engineering Productivity Conference Proceedings*, (Aug. 1990), pp. 485– 492.

376. **Ward, J.**, "Software Defect Prevention using McCabe's Complexity Metric," **Hewlett-Packard Journal**, (April 1989), pp. 66–69.

377. Ward, J., "Using Quality Metrics for Critical Application Software," *HP Software Productivity Conference Proceedings*, (April 1985), pp. 1-39–1-51.

378. Weinberg, G., *Psychology of Computer Programming*. New York: Van Nostrand Reinhold Co., 1971.

379. Weinberg, G., "The Psychology of Improved Programming Performance," *Datamation*, (Nov. 1972), pp. 82–85.

380. **Weinberg, G., and E. Schulman**, "Goals and Performance in Computer Programming," *Human Factors,* Vol.16, no. 1, (1974), pp. 70–77.

381. **Weiss, D., and V. Basili**, "Evaluating Software Development by Analysis of Changes: Some Data from the Software Engineering Laboratory," *IEEE Transactions on Software Engineering*, Vol. SE-11, no. 2, (Feb. 1985), pp. 157–168.

382. Whitworth, M., and P. Szulewski, "The Measurement of Control and Data Flow Complexity in Software Designs," *CH1607-1/80/0000-0735, IEEE*, (Jan. 1980), pp. 735–743.

383. **Wiedenbeck, S.**, "Novice/Expert Differences in Programming Skills," *International Journal of Man-Machine Studies 23*, (1985), pp. 383–390.

384. Witkin, L., "The Renoir Project at PSD: Reflections on Our Experiences," *HP Software Engineering Productivity Conference 384*.

385. Wolverton, R., "SDE: The ITT Software Development Environment," *Proceedings of the National Conference on Software Productivity*, (April 1987), pp. 535–582.

386. Yamada, S., and S. Osaki, "S-Shaped Software Reliability Growth Models with Four Types of Software Error Data," *Int. J. Systems Sci.*, Vol. 14, no. 6, pp. 683–692.

387. Yamada, S., M. Ohba, and S. Osaki, "S-Shaped Reliability Growth Modeling for Software Error Detection," *IEEE Transactions on Reliability*, Vol. R-32, no. 5, (Dec. 1983), pp. 475–484.

388. Yamada, S., M. Ohba, and S. Osaki, "S-Shaped Reliability Growth Models and Their Applications," *IEEE Transactions on Reliability*, Vol. R-33, no. 4, (Oct. 1984), pp. 289–292.

389. **Yau, S., and J. Collofello**, "Design Stability Measures for Software Maintenance," IEEE Transactions on Software Engineering, Vol. SE-11, no. 9, (Sept. 1985), pp. 849–856.

390. Yau, S., and J. Collofello, "Some Stability Measures for Software Maintenance," *IEEE Transactions on Software Engineering*, Vol. 6, no. 6, (Nov. 1980), pp. 545–552.

391. **Yin, B. H., and J. W. Winchester**, "The Establishment and Use of Measures to Evaluate the Quality of Software Designs," *Proceedings of the Software Quality and Assurance Workshop*, New York: Association for Computing Machinery, 1978, pp. 45–52.

392. Young, M., and R. Taylor, "Rethinking the Taxonomy of Fault Detection Techniques," *ACM 0270-5257/89/0500/0053*, (1989), pp. 53–62.

393. Yourdon, E., "What Ever Happened to Structured Analysis?" *Datamation*, (June 1, 1986), pp. 133–138.

394. Yu, T., B. Nejmeh, H. Dunsmore, and V. Shen, "SMDC: An Interactive Software Metrics Data Collection and Analysis System," *Journal of Systems and Software 8*, (1988), pp. 39–46.

395. Yuen, Chong Hok, "An Empirical Approach to the Study of Errors in Large Software Under Maintenance," *CH2219-4/85/0000/0096, IEEE*, (April 1985), pp. 96–105.

396. Zultner, R., "Software Quality [Function] Deployment: Applying QFD to Software," *13th Rocky Mountain Quality Conference*, (1989).

Index